⊶ Acknowledgments ⊷

Many thanks to the extraordinary efforts made by research associates Larry Ramin, Dennis Lorio, and photo editor John Stanchak; to the talented group at Affinity Communications Corp., led by Peter Engel and Howard Cohl; and to Leah Jewett, director of the United States Civil War Center.

Editor's Note on the Photographs: Many photographers served the Union; because supplies were scarce on the Confederate side, there were far fewer photographers. Thus, the range of choice of photographs of Confederate soldiers in situations beyond the battlefield is much narrower than that of Union soldiers. By drawing on the variety of Union images, we strive to give impressions of the beyond-the-battlefield experiences of soldiers on both sides. (These photos were not selected by the United States Civil War Center.)

Beyond the

THE ORDINARY LIFE AND EXTRAORDINARY

Battlefield

TIMES OF THE CIVIL WAR SOLDIER

Edited by

DAVID MADDEN

Founding Director,
United States Civil War Center

THE UNITED STATES CIVIL WAR CENTER

A Touchstone Book
Published by Simon & Schuster

NEW YORK   LONDON   TORONTO   SYDNEY   SINGAPORE

TOUCHSTONE
Rockefeller Center
1230 Avenue of the Americas
New York, NY 10020

Designed by Irving Perkins Associates

Manufactured in the United States of America

1   3   5   7   9   10   8   6   4   2

Library of Congress Cataloging-in-Publication Data
Beyond the battlefield : the ordinary life and extraordinary times of the
Civil War Soldier/ edited by David Madden.
p. cm.
Includes bibliographical references and index.
1. United States, Army—History—Civil War, 1861–1865.
2. United States—History—Civil War, 1861–1865—Social aspects.
3. United States, Army—Military life—History—19th century.
4. Confederate States of America, Army—Military life.
5. Soldiers—United States—Social conditions—19th century.
6. Soldiers—Confederate States of America—Social conditions.
I. Madden, David.

E607 B49 2000

973.7'83—dc21   99-089055

ISBN 0-684-85633-6

Contents

INTRODUCTION

On the Path to War

The American Civil War, occurring between 1861 and 1865, forever altered the landscape of this country. The battle between the United States of America and the Confederate States of America did nothing less than redefine the political and cultural identity of the nation and the lives of all Americans who have lived since. The promising American "child" of the eighteenth-century revolution suffered a passage to twentieth-century adulthood that came too close to extinguishing not only its potential greatness but its very existence.

The war was fought by hundreds of thousands of people for a multitude of reasons—some noble, others base—while some simply joined the army for the adventure they expected to find. To this day, almost 140 years later, the question of what the root causes of the Civil War were can still instigate heated discussion. Perhaps the only origin of the war that can be universally agreed upon is that it was fought by men who fought to defend their vision of what America should be.

The war's most fundamental effect upon America occurred at a human level because it irrevocably changed the lives of millions of people—and none more so than the hundreds of thousands of men who went to fight. The nation changed because the men who fought the war were transformed by their experiences. Additionally, their perspective on what it meant to be an American and their basic awareness of the land itself also evolved. War changes people for many reasons. The ferocity and horror of combat has perhaps the greatest effect. But other aspects of going off to war also influence people. This was especially so in an era when transportation and communication were rudimentary. In the mid–nineteenth century, most Americans lived a sheltered life that was restricted in scope.

For the great majority of men who fought in the Civil War, going off to the battlefield was their first experience of being any great distance from home. Be-

General Robert E. Lee and General Ulysses S. Grant, the men who controlled the soldiers' time

fore the first shots were fired at Fort Sumter in the spring of 1861, the United States of America was an agricultural entity. Among the working population of 7.7 million, 4.9 million were farmers.[1] Farmers had little time or inclination to see the world, and their presence was required in the fields year round. By the time peace was agreed upon at Appomattox four years after that first battle, these men of the soil had been introduced, often with terrible results, to the modern industrial era.

For those who were not farmers and inhabited the cities and towns of the nation, options for travel were also limited. Although railroads were coming into their own and boat travel was advanced, the fundamental mode of travel was still on horseback. Trips of more than a few miles were a major effort and took a good deal of time. Though America was considered a country on the move, other than settlers and pioneers, most people stayed at home. Americans of the 1860s grew up in stable communities and grew old among familiar faces.

Further adding to the comparative isolation of life in the 1860s was the absence of a communications infrastructure, other than the mail, and the limited reach of the media. Letters transmitted news that was days old, and while peo-

On the eve of the Civil War, some famous Southern communities were more busy making money than political opinion. This is Savannah, Georgia, a hub of international shipping in the 1860s.

ple could read newspapers and magazines with up-to-date stories transmitted by wire, photography was in its infancy and pictures from distant places were rare.

What, then, was the nature of the newly established country that young men would soon willingly march off to defend and die for? As the routine of their prewar lives came to an end in the late 1850s, what would a snapshot of "American life" have looked like? How big were their homes? How difficult were their jobs? What were their meals like? What songs did they sing? What games did they play? What common experiences did they share that defined them as the sons and daughters of the American family?

To a great extent there was no collective "American identity" or background that unified these people scattered across the vast continent. Their lives were as different as can be imagined, and their only link to one another was a federal government that was an infinitely more abstract concept than it is today. In truth, a farmer living in Thetford, Vermont, really had no idea what life was like for a fisherman in Beaufort, South Carolina. They were, as it is often said, "brothers," but in actuality they were members of a dysfunctional family in which so-called intimates were, in truth, strangers.

New York City before the first shots of the Civil War were fired. Even then it was home to more Americans than any other city.

The Civil War would change all that.

Visitors to the United States in the years leading up to the Civil War wrote of a land of many identities, geographies, dialects, and attitudes. Already the North was a region of growing urban areas and fledgling industrial might. French citizen Salomon de Rothschild, who toured America between 1859 and 1861, found New York City a busy, dirty, vibrant place where hordes of wild pigs roamed the streets in lieu of organized garbage collectors.[2] Rothschild also found a new kind of financially oriented aristocracy ruling the social world, busy theaters, a vast "Central Park" under construction west of Fifth Avenue, and political rallies that reflected both the growing passions that would lead to Civil War and the practical manipulations required to incite people to demonstrate:

> Here I am back in New York, which, though it is filled with visitors, is sad and resembles Paris in August (minus Paris). . . . New York is completely caught up in the excitement of the presidential campaign. Immense banners advertising the different parties are hung over all the streets; every day, or every evening, there is some kind of demonstration. . . . On Wednesday a monster mass meeting was held at Joneswood in honor of Douglas [Democratic presidential candidate Stephen Douglas, who was running against Republican standard-bearer Abraham Lincoln]. Twenty or thirty thousand Democrats were assembled. Since it was cold, there was some fear of lack of enthusiasm, so it was decided to hold a feast for the crowd. A whole steer was roasted, as well as a sheep, a calf, and a pig, so that every taste could be satisfied. Five hundred barrels of beer were readied to wash down this immense pile of food. Yet the method of preparing the food was most primitive—a deep hole scooped out of the ground and two stakes supporting a huge spit. . . . The next day, Thursday was the Republicans' turn. Beginning at eight in the morning, traffic was blocked by a great demonstration. From all parts of the city, bands headed toward Cooper Institute, where the "meeting" was held. When the speeches were finished, the audience formed squads, each carrying a torch and most of them dressed in red. They went through the most densely populated sections of the city in perfect order, but with the most infernal shouting. I cannot tell you what an impression this scene, worthy of Dante, made on me.[3]

Emotions in the South were also building toward fever pitch. At the same time, however, a visitor could still discover another side of life, as Doctor Thomas Low Nichols did while visiting New Orleans:

> In the winter of 1859 I again visited New Orleans. . . . The Southern metropolis had increased in extent, trade, and population, but in all its essential features it was still the same. The St. Charles Hotel had been burnt, and rebuilt without its dome. Sherry cobblers and mint juleps were still drunk in the magnificent bar-room of the St. Louis, a circular domed room not quite as large as the reading room in the British museum. The French side of the city was as quiet and elegant as of old, and the American side as bustling and noisy. . . . New Orleans was full. Hotels, boarding

houses, lodgings were crowded. The population was 170,000 by census. The floating population of planters, merchants, and visitors from the North and West raised it to nearly 300,000. The theaters, French and English, concerts, balls, exhibitions of all kinds were crowded. . . . There was at this period a charm in the life and society of New Orleans difficult to understand and impossible to describe. "No place like New Orleans" was the verdict of all who had lived there long enough to know what it was; and this in spite of the river that threatens to drown you, and the swamp filled with mosquitoes and alligators; in spite of the yellow fever every three years, and months of every year with the thermometer above ninety degrees . . . the people are eminently social, generous, genial, and impulsive. The climate during eight months of the year is also indescribably delicious. Roses bloom, bananas ripen, and golden oranges cover the trees in January. . . . A bar-room in New Orleans will hold a thousand people. Men drink a great deal—they say the climate makes it necessary—but they also drink magnificently. In such a bar-room there is set out every day, free to all comers, a lunch composed of soups, fish, roast joints, fowls and salads, with bread and cheese . . . liquors without measure, food gratis, every man treating all his acquaintances, flush times, high wages, high profits, and high prices.[4]

Life in the countryside was, inevitably, less intense. At the start of the twenty-first century, most Americans live in suburbs, which, if greener than cities, still offer all the conveniences of urban living. Prior to the Civil War, most Americans lived in rural areas and had a demanding but quieter life. In contrast to the dynamic lifestyle of New Orleans, Dr. Nichols also recorded life in rural New Hampshire:

The township in which I was born had about 1000 inhabitants. There was a pretty village, with a Congregational meeting house, post office, tavern, two or three shops called stores, each with its assortment of draperies, ironmongery, groceries, wines, liquors, tobacco, crockery, glass—almost everything in fact. There were also two or three lawyers, and a blacksmith, hatter, shoemaker, wheelwright, cabinet maker, tailor. A small village, two or three miles back among the hills, supplied its own neighborhood. Grist mills which ground our corn, and saw mills which supplied our timber, were upon a mill brook. . . . There were no landlords in this country.

Almost every man owned the land he cultivated . . . any man could buy the best Government land in the new States for $1.25 an acre, and from that extreme price down to fifteen cents and acre, at which millions of acres might have been bought a few years ago.[5]

The southern countryside was similar in its beauty, even if the specifics were very different. It shared with the North a seemingly limitless potential for profitable farming. Barbara Leigh Smith Bodichon traveled on the river steamer *Baltic* in December 1857:

> We are on the MISSISSIPPI now, it is a magnificent river and the everlasting woods on either side are very striking. . . . The mistletoe here grows in the trees in immense quantities. I could not think what plant it could be. The mist often lies on the water in a very beautiful and curious manner. . . . We have seen six or seven families in their houses floating down on rafts. It is one of the most curious sights I ever saw in my life. They have an immensely long rudder, no oars, no sails. They just live quietly with their animals doing their household work every day, and at last finding themselves at their destination without any trouble but that of keeping away from banks and snags. . . . The banks of the river do really look as if their riches were inexhaustible.[6]

Visitors to the South often noted the engine of the region's economy—slave labor—and recorded their meetings with African Americans. In a number of Southern states the slave population outnumbered the white population, and the slaves' memories provide, accordingly, a perspective on what life was like in the antebellum era. Squire Irvin, a slave who lived in Tennessee, recalled:

> I was born on a plantation near Nashville in 1849. We all lived in the quarters in log cabins. There was a big central eating house for the grown people and one for the children. The old folks did the cooking I don't know what the grown folks had to eat but us children had a big skillet of mush cooked over an open fire. When it was cool milk was poured over it, and we were each given a spoon and allowed to eat all we wanted out of the skillet. We ate this at night and in the mornings. In the middle of the day we had greens and pot licker with cornbread. Nearly every day someone would go hunting or fishing, and we would have rabbit, coon, and possum meat or the nicest fish you ever seen. On sunday we had white bread. We liked that light bread better than anything . . . in the hot weather the children all went in their shirt tails. But the grown ups

wore homespun pants and shirts . . . the big white house what my white folks lived in was sure beautiful. It was at least two stories high and maybe more. The yard was filled with flowers and the grass looked like a soft green carpet. I don't know how many acres there was in that place. It was so big it looked like the whole world to me.[7]

Susan Jones, another slave, remembered a less nostalgic past:

All de slaves wuz fed jest what de white folks et and it wuz plenty good. Marsta Charlie Alexander wuz a pore man & he married Miss Jane Byrd, who owned all de slaves and land and she wouldn't let him treat us mean but when she died he raised cain. He beat up all de slaves and most any time you could hear niggers praying and hollering down at de neighbors house. He whipped jest cause he could. Why he's take dem in droves down to de city and sell em jest cause he didn't like em. He'd put em in de cattle pen til he sold dem. . . . After Miss. died we had an overseer and he sho wuz pore white trash and a meaner man never lived . . . and de niggers warnt no more than dogs on our place.[8]

After a time visitors to the South could no longer avoid the burgeoning political movements. English traveler William Howard Russell enjoyed lavish banquets offered by South Carolinian hosts, including champagne, claret, and French pâtés served with bracing doses of secessionism:

Secession is the fashion here. Young ladies sing for it; old ladies pray for it; young men are dying to fight for it; old men are ready to demonstrate for it. The founder of the school was St. Calhoun [former U.S. vice president and senator from South Carolina John Caldwell Calhoun]. Here his pupils carry out their teaching in thunder and fire. States' Rights are displayed after its legitimate teaching, and the Palmetto flag and the red bars of the Confederacy are its exposition. The utter contempt and loathing for the venerated Stars and Stripes, the abhorrence of the very words United States, the intense hatred of the Yankee on the part of these people, cannot be conceived by anyone who has not seen them.[9]

Attitudes were no less strongly held in the North, where New Yorker George Templeton Strong watched with concern as the split within the nation grew wider:

No material change in the state of the Union. It's a sick nation, and I fear it must be worse before it's better. The growing vigorous North must sooner or later assert its right to equality with the stagnant, semi barbarous South, and that assertion must bring on a struggle and convulsion. It must come.[10]

The hatreds expressed by people in both the North and South, and their desire for war, did not represent everybody's feelings. The calmer members of the American family worried that their passionate brothers would begin a fight that would end in mutual destruction. A great many Northern and Southern citizens regretted the approach of the maelstrom even if their political views covered a wide range of opinion. J. D. Imboden wrote a letter to his friend John McCue in December 1860, appealing for a solution to the problem that would spare the nation bloodshed:

I read your letter with interest. We are not really so far apart as you suppose. I understand that you are a "Union man"—so am I. You would resist Republicanism—so would I. We neither think Va. ought to secede, or rather revolt *just* now. You think S. Carolina ought to go out now, I think not—and here is the only point of difference between us, so far as I can see . . . to break up the Government for the mere loss of an election is not regarded by thousands as justifiable. It is regarded as a mere pretext on the part of disunionists per se to precipitate a revolution. You can't make the great mass of people—especially the non slaveholder's understand the political philosophy of our government, and the nice principles on which the Secessionists are now attempting to act . . . the non slave holder will fight for his section as long as the slave holder if you can convince him that *his* political rights are really threatened as a *citizen*. . . . I am afraid the die is cast and that no power on earth can avert the impending ruin of anarchy & bloodshed.[11]

In the North, similarly concerned people wished for an option other than war. The Reverend Abraham Essick noted in his diary, during the spring of 1861, that fighting would soon spread across the continent and be devastating:

Winter has gone and spring has come again . . . how pleasant it is to walk farther in green meadows or on the sunny side of the flower decked hills! . . . But alas, the din of war, and clash of arms are distracting our once happy land. The sectional strife, arising chiefly from the unfortu-

nate contest about slavery has culminated and the result is a civil war between the North and South. . . . Active preparations for war are going on
through the whole land.[12]

The sights, sounds, and smells of the world that were familiar to Americans
in 1860 would never be the same again. Indeed, our lives today are different
from what they might have been—because of what the soldiers of the Civil
War experienced together over the following four years. The food they ate, the
games they played, the songs they sang, the nights spent in the rain without
shelter, their loneliness, sicknesses, and triumphs, all influenced the development of these men—who would, in the following decades, mold the nation
and lay the foundations for the American Century.

The perspectives and life experiences of the men who were to fight the war
were, at the outset, narrow. But that would change during the conflict. The
soldiers of the Civil War would witness terrible things on the battlefield that
they would hope never to see again. But they would also travel to faraway
places, developing an awareness of the nation as a whole and a sense of community with people from far-flung locations. Some of these strangers were for
the moment "the enemy," while some earned respect for their bravery and yet
others merited sympathy as victims. As the years passed, old hostilities would
succumb to the overwhelming power of the shared experiences of youth—and
the nation would gradually become united for the first time.

If an American national identity were forged, in large part, through the
changing perceptions of the ordinary men who fought the Civil War, an effort
to understand the experiences, the mind-set, and the day-to-day world of the
soldiers on both sides of the conflict may lead to a fuller comprehension of this
unique nation's character. By reviewing letters and journals that relate the
war's history through a personal perspective—as well as the official documents
that altered the soldiers' lives forever—it may be possible to achieve a better
understanding of how our nation developed into what it is today. And as actual combat was a comparatively unusual event in the life of a Civil War soldier, a key to discerning the true nature of the soldier's experience may be
found beyond the battlefield.

CHAPTER ONE

In the Beginning

Honorable John. B Floyd   Secretary of War
    Sir: I am instructed by the Governor of Virginia to inform you that
there exists in this State an extended and daily increasing apprehension
of insecurity and danger, resulting, among other causes, from manifestations of domestic insubordination; that he feels it necessary for protection and security to arm the volunteer cors [sic] in particular localities
with better arms than we have now at command.[1]

Notes such as the one above, written in December 1860 representing the
concerns of Virginia's governor to President James Buchanan's secretary of war,
reflected the rapid growth of the tension between the North and the South in
the months following the election of Abraham Lincoln. Even before the first
shots were fired at Fort Sumter on April 12, 1861, these communications were
the opening salvos of the war that would change the lives of ordinary Americans forever.

All over the United States, from Maine in the North to Florida in the South
to California in the West, people such as Reverend Essick, J. D. Imboden, and
George Templeton Strong waited—some nervously, others with anticipation.
Over the decades, sporadic violence had erupted over a variety of issues, including states' rights and slavery. But with the election of a Republican president, the standard-bearer of a new political party that the Southerners
believed was dedicated to ruining them, suddenly words were no longer
enough. With a bitter, unself-conscious irony, the Southern states believed
that their God-given civil rights were being abridged by the North. They were
lesser citizens because people in other states were telling them what they could
do and what they could not. The more hotheaded among them may have described themselves as slaves chained to the whim of their Northern masters.

Abraham Lincoln and Jefferson Davis, the leaders of the soldiers

The long-stalled confrontation now seemed inevitable. The Southerners were seriously discussing secession from the Union, and everyone knew that meant war. Both sides of the conflict, however, were confident that justice would serve them well and that they would enjoy a swift victory.

Little more than a month after Lincoln won the presidency, the unraveling of the United States began with the secession of South Carolina from the Union:

> We the people of the State of South Carolina, in convention assembled, to declare and ordain, and it is hereby declared and ordained, that the ordinance adopted by us in convention on the twenty third day of May in the year of our Lord one thousand seven hundred and eighty eight, whereby the Constitution of the United States of America was ratified, and also all acts and parts of acts of the General Assembly of this State, ratifying amendments of the said Constitution, are hereby repealed; and that the union now subsisting between South Carolina and other States, under the name "United States of America" is hereby dissolved. . . . Done at Charleston the twentieth day of December in the year of our Lord one thousand eight hundred and sixty.[2]

With this declaration of secession, the South Carolinians blazed a path that would soon be followed by Mississippi, Florida, Alabama, Georgia, Louisiana, Texas, Virginia, Arkansas, Tennessee, and North Carolina. In the days leading up to the February swearing in of former U.S. Senator Jefferson Davis as president of the newly formed Confederate States of America, the Southerners hastily organized a government, wrote a constitution, prepared for war, and took over several U.S. military bases located on their territory.

In what was left of the original United States there was no less of a furor, but for the moment there was little that could be done. Lincoln's predecessor, James Buchanan, was a lame duck and would remain in office for another four months after the presidential election, until March 1861. Behaving like an uncertain parent, the federal government vacillated while trying to decide upon an appropriate punishment for a misbehaving member of the family. The weakened president did very little during his remaining days in office and left the horror of the upcoming war to his successor.

Not everyone, however, was content to wait for the new administration. Ordinary soldiers and members of local militias were indignant when they realized that the secessionists were beginning the process of breaking up the nation. They would tolerate no delay and were ready to challenge the rebels:

General Stonewall Jackson, the soldier's soldier

January 12, 1861

Hon. James Buchanan:

Dear Sir: Not knowing how soon your honor will need the services of uniformed volunteers to suppress the Southern fire-eating dis-unionists, we hereby tender the services of our company, subject to your order. The following are the names of our members; we number about forty four members.

John A. Wilson
Captain, Washington Artillery[3]

Although the size of the standing federal army was small and many new soldiers would be needed to fight against secession, Buchanan's government did little to remedy the situation. In the South, however, people were preparing for war. Some recognized that a major threat to the Confederate States of America was the imbalance in manufacturing capacity, which heavily favored the North. The mills and factories of Lowell, Massachusetts; Pittsburgh, Pennsylvania; and Buffalo, New York, were the muscles of the federal Goliath glaring at the comparatively diminutive Southern David.

Accordingly, some of the first "battles" of the war were "fought" in Northern territory by men who were not soldiers but traders and policemen. Rebel

Rubble inside Fort Sumter, with a Confederate flag flying over it; an April 1861 photograph

Interior View of FORT SUMTER on the 17th April 1861,
after its evacuation by Maj. Robert Anderson, 1st Art'y U.S.A. Comd'g.
Showing the north end of West Barracks, with the lower tier of Casemates and
Barbette of adjacent north channel face.

agents could move freely throughout U.S. cities and did their best to secure arms and send them south.

For these "troops" life was not very much different from what it had previously been. Rebel buyers sought out armaments, and Yankee law enforcement officials tried to catch them:

> January 23, 1861
> Office of the Superintendent of Police
> Hon. James I. Roosevelt, U.S. District Attorney
> Dear Sir; I beg leave to inform you that I have caused to be seized thirty eight cases, containing about 900 stands of arms, which were about to be shipped on board on the steamer Monticello, for Savanna, GA, thence to be forwarded to Montgomery, ALA., to be treasonably used by parties who are making war upon and armed resistance to the laws and authority of the United States.[4]

Still, it would not be until after the inauguration of Lincoln on March 4 and the subsequent shelling of Fort Sumter in Charleston Harbor on April 12 that the Civil War would begin for the rank-and-file soldier:

> **BY THE PRESIDENT OF THE UNITED STATES: A PROCLAMATION.**
> Wheras the laws of the United States have been for some time past and now are opposed and the execution thereof obstructed in the States of South Carolina, Georgia, Alabama, Florida, Mississippi, Louisiana, and Texas by combinations too powerful to be suppressed by the ordinary course of judicial proceedings or by the powers vested in the marshals by law:
> Now, therefore, I, Abraham Lincoln, President of the United States, in virtue of the power in me vested by the Constitution and the laws, have thought fit to call forth, and hereby do call forth, the militia of the several States of the Union, to the aggregate number of 75,000, in order to suppress said combinations and to cause the laws to be duly executed. . . . I appeal to all loyal citizens to favor, facilitate, and aid this effort to maintain the honor, the integrity, and the existence of our National Union, and the perpetuity of popular government, and to redress wrongs already long enough endured. . . . Done at the city of Washington this fifteenth day of April, in the year of our Lord one thousand eight hundred and sixty one, and of the Independence of the United States the eighty fifth.
> By the President: Abraham Lincoln.[5]

Of the original 75,000, many would die, more would be wounded or fall to disease, some would reenlist, others would desert, and a few would head home as quickly as they legally could. At the end of the Civil War, almost half a million soldiers would never return home. It is estimated that among Union troops 200,000 died from disease while 110,000 died in battle. Among the Confederate armies a conservative estimate suggests that 60,000 died from disease and 75,000 in fighting.[6] All the recruits and volunteers—whether they perished or survived—were on the threshold of an experience that they could not possibly imagine.

A terrible hurricane, growing strong and violent in the humid Gulf Coast and Southern states, had arrived, at long last, in the North. It would level almost everything in its path.

The Men Who Went to War

In the North, the response to Lincoln's call to arms was overwhelming. As in both world wars, and unlike during the wars in Korea and Vietnam, Americans rallied to the declaration of their president. Too many men volunteered, and many had to wait before companies and regiments could be organized for them to join. Who were the men who volunteered? They were farmers, doctors, laborers, aristocrats, immigrants, clerics, clerks, merchants, the impoverished, the unemployed, fathers, grandfathers, sons, and even some women in disguise—in a word, almost everyone—for the initial burst of enthusiasm for the war was powerful. Governor Israel Washburn, Jr., of Maine wrote to the new secretary of war with an immediate response that was echoed by other state leaders:

> Bangor, Me. April 15, 1861
> Hon. Simon Cameron
> Secretary of War
>   Your dispatch is received, and your call will be promptly responded to. The people of Maine of all parties will rally with alacrity to the maintenance of the Government and of the Union.
>   Israel Washburn, Jr., Governor of Maine[7]

How to respond to Lincoln's request for soldiers was not as clear in the states that straddled the new border. For example, while Kentucky stayed in the Union, many of its citizens and soldiers sympathized with the Confederacy. These men confronted a terrible dilemma: while they never questioned the fact that they were Americans, they now had to choose between allegiance to the federal government and allegiance to their neighbors and home territory. Making the determination more difficult was the fact that while they were proud of their history, the concept of the federal government was much more abstract in the nineteenth century than it is today. A substantially weaker institution than in its present form, the federal government offered little in the way of services to or interaction with its people. Just as General Robert E. Lee forsook the offered command of the Union armies to lead the Army of Northern Virginia for the Confederate States of America, so too did common soldiers cross the lines and fight for the new nation that better represented their regional identity:

> Frankfort, Kentucky, April 15, 1861
> Hon. Simon Cameron
> Secretary of War;
>   Your dispatch is received. In answer I say emphatically Kentucky will furnish no troops for the wicked purpose of subduing her sister Southern States.
>   B. Magoffin   Governor of Kentucky[8]

Soldiers relaxing in camp. The seated soldier wears a fez that pegs him as a member of a "Zouave" unit. The French army, its ways and uniforms widely imitated by Union and Confederate troops, fielded elite quick-marching Algerian troops who wore fezes, baggy trousers, and short jackets.

Despite Governor Magoffin's declared intent not to send troops to fight for the Union, Kentucky remained a part of the United States and complied with the president's directive. Many Kentuckians, however, followed Lee's example and fought for the Confederacy.

At this early stage of the war both military forces studiously ignored a substantial source of manpower—the large number of African Americans who were able and willing to fight. In the North some felt that the presence of freedmen would discourage the morale of the troops, while others thought that African Americans were not tough enough to serve. The free African Americans of the North, however, wanted to defend their rights and liberate their enslaved brethren. Prominent leaders such as Frederick Douglass argued for giving them the right to fight, but the feeling was pervasive throughout all strata of the community:

> Washington, April 23, 1861
> Hon. Simon Cameron Secretary of War
>   Sir: I desire to inform you that I know of some 300 reliable colored free citizens of this city who desire to enter the service for the defense of the city. . . . I have been three times across the Rocky Mountains in the service of the country with Fremont and others. . . . I can be found about the Senate Chamber, as I have been employed about the premises for some years.
>   Yours, respectfully, Jacob Dodson (colored).[9]

A great weapon that might have won the war for either side would thus remain constrained within the sheath of prejudice.

In 1862, the First South Carolina Volunteers became the first African-American regiment to fight for the United States after Union troops landed at the fishing community of Hilton Head and occupied the region. Still, the use of African-American soldiers was extremely limited at best. The Confederate troops, who were greatly outnumbered by the Federal troops, nevertheless refused to let African Americans serve until the last month of the war—when it was already too late to save their cause. The fear of an armed revolt of slaves had troubled the Southern states since the institution's inception and proved more persuasive than anxiety about repeated Union successes on the battlefield. In this choice, the Confederacy rejected a source of fighting men that might well have been significant. In Alabama and Georgia, for example, there were almost as many slaves as there were white citizens. Both Mississippi and South Carolina had one hundred thousand more slaves than free Caucasians.

Recruiting: How It Was Done

Who were the men who volunteered one year of service to the Confederacy? According to an Englishman named William Watson who fought for the South, his company was made up of:

> 9 planters, or sons of planters, 11 farmers or sons of farmers, 11 merchants, 13 merchants assistants or clerks, 1 lawyer, 1 engineer, 4 carpenters, 4 painters, 3 compositors, 3 bricklayers, 2 iron moulders, 2 gas fitters, 2 saw millers, 2 gunsmiths, 1 tailor, 1 druggist, 1 teacher, 2 carriage makers, 1 cabinet maker, 2 law students, 1 marble cutter, and 8 miscellaneous.[10]

New Confederate recruits, "Jim and his Pony." This outdoor photo of an Alabama volunteer and his mount is a rare item. Most Southern war photography was done indoors, where photographers could conserve their chemicals.

For those whom the military did want under arms, the bid to get them to enlist was dramatic. While the recruiters had the advantage of a general public who believed in the glory of war and whose dedication to the preservation of the Union or Confederacy was intense, there was still the necessity for a calculated effort to put young men into uniform. For men who had been raised on farms or in simple villages, and even for urbanites, whose normal daily responsibilities ranged from the mundane to the extraordinary, the powerful advertising appeals were influential and enticing:

Shall Licking County Raise A Regiment?

Ho, For the War!

Our County Expects Every Man to DO HIS DUTY!

I have been transferred from the "Regular Army" of the U.S. to the Ohio Volunteers, and am authorized by the Governor to raise and take command of the 76th Regiment, which will go into camp at the Fair Grounds, near Newark.—The men will be sworn in as fast as recruited, and their pay will commence immediately. The following officers have been appointed and the men recruited by them will be mustered into the 76th Regiment to whit:

CHARLES H. KIBLER
L. P. COMAN
H. C. KNOOP
THADDEUS LEMERT
JOSEPH M. SCOTT
R. W. BURT

I call upon the young men of my native county of Licking (and of the adjoining counties) to fill up the ranks of a regiment which will be composed of your neighbors and friends. Your country, in its extremist peril, demands your services: this is the day and hour for the patriotic young men to show their devotion to the cause of their country and its priceless Institutions! Rally, then, under the banner which represents the Constitution and the Union, and symbolizes the honor and glory of our country at home and abroad. Come around the old Flag which has secured to us all the blessings of free government menaced as it is by ingrates and rebels, resolved to maintain it to the end and

"With arm to strike the soul to dare,"
protect it from insult, and carry it forward in triumph until "its sky born glories blaze" on every hill and in every valley of our beloved land!
CHARLES R. WOODS, COL.
Commanding the 76th Reg. O.V. U.S.A.[11]

Volunteer regiments, such as Colonel Woods's, provided the bulk of the fighting men during the Civil War. Generally, a regiment consisted of ten companies, each of which included one hundred soldiers. The most common method of organizing these regiments was for a member of the regular army—which prior to the war had been small and had shared national defense duties with equally impotent local militias—to be given command of a newly formed regiment and the responsibility of recruiting its soldiers. Often these were men of some renown, perhaps celebrated veterans of the Mexican War. If, in a given region, there were no seasoned fighting men who could spearhead an enlistment drive, command would often be given to local community leaders. And as officers were often elected by the troops themselves, the leadership of companies and regiments often reflected the social hierarchy of the communities where

A new Union soldier poses for the camera. He wears a machine-made blue uniform and carries a government-made rifle with a sword bayonet. As time went on, that uniform would wear badly and that bayonet would be thrown away for an iron spike model, one more useful as a tent peg than for threatening an enemy.

they had been recruited. In some cases this would lead to a breakdown of discipline in a company as authority was based on popularity. However, men who had demonstrated a natural ability to lead in civilian life often continued to do so under arms. More commonly, though, the system of electing officers would be replaced by a system of appointments by a higher command.

Advertising was not the only effective tool for inducing men to fight for their country. The popular sentiment of both nations was fervent in its support of a decisive war. The thrill of martial valor permeated all levels of society. Authors, poets, and songwriters reflected this attitude in their work, and any young man who might be a reluctant soldier could not escape the constant cultural din encouraging him to fight:

> In Freedoms name our blades we draw,
> She arms us for the fight!
> For country, government and law,
> For Liberty and Right.
> The Union must—shall be preserved,
> Or flag still o'er us fly!
> That cause our hearts and hands has nerved,
> And we will do or die.
>
> Then come, ye hardy volunteers,
> Around our standard throng,
> And pledge man's hope of coming Year,—
> The Union,—right or wrong!
> The Union,—right or wrong—inspires
> The burden of our song;
> It was the glory of our sires—
> The Union—right or wrong! [12]

The recruiting songs of the Confederacy were equally provocative:

> Rally round our country's flag!
> Rally boys, no do not lag;
> Come from every vale and crag,
> Sons of Liberty!
>
> Northern Vandals tread our soil,
> Forth they come for blood and spoil,
> To the homes we've gained with toil,
> Shouting, "Slavery!"

Traitorous Lincoln's bloody band,
Now invades the freeman's land,
Arm'd with sword and firebran,
'Gainst the brave and free.

Arm ye, then, for fray and fight,
March ye forth both day and night,
Stop not till the foe's in sight,
Sons of Chivalry.

In your veins the blood still flows,
Of brave men who once arose—
Burst the shackles of their foes;
Honest men and free.

Rise, then, in your power and might,
Seek the spoiler, brave and fight;
Strike for God, for Truth, for Right;
Strike for God, for Liberty! [13]

If some recruiting songs appealed to a young man's patriotic sense of duty, one anonymous song written to encourage enlistment was more quietly manipulative and worked on a more personal level:

Don't stop a moment to think, John,
Your country calls—then go;
Don't think of me or the children, John,
I'll care for them you know.
Leave the corn upon the stalks, John,
Potatoes on the hill,
And the pumpkins on the vines, John—

But take your gun and go, John,
Take your gun and go,
For Ruth can drive the oxen, John,
And I can use the hoe.
And if it be God's will, John,
You ne'er come back again,
I'll do my best for the children, John,
In sorrow, want and pain.

In winter nights I'll teach them all,
That I have learned at school,
To love the country, keep the laws
Obey the savior's rule.

    Then take your gun and go, John, etc.

And in the village church, John,
And at our humble board,
We'll pray that God will keep you, John,
And heavenly aid afford;
And all who love their country's cause
Will love and bless you too,
And nights and mornings they will pray,
For freedom and for you.

    Then take your gun and go, John,
    Take your gun and go,
    For Ruth can drive the oxen, John,
    And I can use the hoe.[14]

For those who could resist such appeals and still balked at the idea of fighting for their country, the eminent poet Oliver Wendell Holmes wrote a poem called "The Sweet Little Man" that was aimed at humiliating men into joining the armed forces:

Now while our soldiers are fighting our battles
Each at his post to do all he can
Down among Rebels & Contraband chattels
What are you doing, my sweet little man?

All the brave boys under the canvas are sleeping
All of them pressing to march with the van
Far from home while their sweethearts are weeping
What are you waiting for, sweet little man?

Bring him the buttonless garment of a woman!
Cover his face lest it freckle and tan;
Muster the Apron-string Guards on the Common,
That is the corps for the sweet little man.

Give him for escort a file of young misses
Each of them armed with deadly rattan
They shall defend him from laughter and hisses!
Aimed by low boys at the sweet little man.

Now then nine cheers for the stay at home ranger!
Blow the great fish horn and beat the big pan!
First in the field, that is farthest from danger,
Take your white feather plume, sweet little man! [15]

The effect of all these pressures was an explosion of enlistments. Anticipating a short war, many young men were afraid they would not be able to get into uniform in time to grab their share of the glory. Tens of thousands simply could not wait to sign up:

Chapel Hill, North Carolina April 28 1861
    Dear Sister: It was with great delight and pleasure I perused your very kind and interesting letter, which I now hasten to answer. There is great excitement here. Everybody talks, thinks, and dreams of war. The students are leaving daily. The village military departed yesterday, accompanied by twelve or fifteen students who joined them as privates. There is another company being formed here composed mostly of students. They wish to go to Washington City. I desire very much to join them and will do so, if Pa and Ma are willing. I shall await their answer with impatience, hoping it will be in the affirmative. . . . Lavender Ray [16]

The enthusiasm of the young recruits was not theirs alone. In both nations the citizenry turned out to celebrate the soldiers as they went off to fight what everybody expected to be a short, triumphant war. Each side believed that its cause was justified and that its moral authority would ensure it victory. Similarly, each felt it had certain advantages that its enemy could not overcome. In the North people referred to the edge that the defense of their ancestors' legacy provided. They also recognized the benefit of their superior industrial capability and vastly more extensive transportation network. Southerners thought that Yankee soldiers were coarse and inferior in every way to the more refined Confederate. They also appreciated the value of fighting, to a large extent, on their home territory.

Believing that they were well dressed in the armor of their convictions, both

Union and Confederate supporters were, in fact, appallingly overconfident—naive, would-be "emperors" without a stitch of clothing to share among them.

After years of steadily increasing tension, the departing soldiers were celebrated with an enthusiasm that revealed a societal sense of relief that the untenable situation would finally be dealt with. As the farmers, clerks, students, lawyers, tradesmen, and others donned their first uniforms and made their first attempts to march in formation, the atmosphere was more festive than military. As Union troops headed south and Confederate regiments marched north, their dreams of glory seemed to be coming true:

Richmond, Virginia   May 31, 1861
My Dear Mother:

The people of Virginia excel everything that I have ever heard in their favor. . . . Our advance from Savannah to this place was one continued ovation. In Charleston we were received by the citizens and military. After a fine supper at the Charleston Hotel we were addressed by Governor Pickens. . . . At Petersburg, Virginia, there are more pretty women that I ever saw in one place. They gave us an enthusiastic reception. The windows and balconies were crowded, and, as we marched by to the tune of "The Bold Soldier Boy," "The Girl I Left Behind Me" &c., "God-bless-the-boys" was heard on all sides. Banners were thrown out by fair hands. Handkerchiefs waved, bouquets showered upon us, rosy lips quivered and bright eyes were filled with tears, as the boys filed past. And, indeed, we

A Mississippi volunteer holding cavalry weapons. When Yankees and rebels first signed on for the war, many borrowed weapons from a photographer's studio props to pose for a picture. But this soldier's pistol and saber look to be his own.

looked like boys, with our handsome blue uniforms smooth faces. Every-
where we stopped, the ladies cheered and joined "the company of bachelors" as they call us. The ages of the men average from 16 to 25, not a
married man among us. We tell them that if we go back bachelors it
won't be our fault.[17]

War fever swept the nation, and sometimes men got carried away by the
hoopla and excitement. Perhaps it was the novelty of leaving an isolated life
on a rural farm. Maybe some signed up to avoid the difficulties of an impoverished urban life. Cases of drunken men enlisting and then regretting their enlistment after sobering up were not unheard of. Mostly, however, people were
carried away by a sense of intense patriotism and the belief that their nation
was in imminent danger. Children under eighteen lied about their age to enlist. Stories abound of young men who wrote the number "18" on a scrap of
paper, stuck it into their shoes, and then felt comfortable in telling recruiting
officers that they were, indeed, "over eighteen." Equally, hardy men over the
cutoff age of forty-five lied in order to be allowed to serve. Some, such as rejected Union volunteer James Leonard, would not bend the truth and complained bitterly that they were not allowed to fight:

> After accepting several men over 45 years of age, and several infants,
> such as a man like me could whip a dozen of, I was rejected because I had
> the honesty to acknowledge that I was more than 45 years of age. The
> mustering officer was a very good looking man, about 35 years old; but I
> guess I can run faster and jump higher than he; also take him down, whip
> him, endure more hardships, and kill at least three rebels to his one.[18]

Some men, however, caught up in the electricity of the early days of the war,
evaded the enlistment restrictions, regretted their impetuous decisions, and
later petitioned for release from their obligation:

> To CP Buckingham Adjutant General:
> Dear sir, the undersigned represent that on the 10th day of December
> 1861 being considerably excited in behalf of his adopted country he un-
> thoughtfully volunteered and was sworn in to serve in Captain Samuel
> W Spencer's Company 78th Regiment. . . . Your petition represents that
> although he is 54 years old he would willingly continue in said Company
> and fight for the flag of the Union was it not for the following considera-

tions which have forced themselves upon his mind since he volunteered, to wit: he is a German naturalized citizen, a blacksmith by trade and has a family of 6 minor children at home whose mother is dead, all depending on him for their daily support . . . under such circumstances the undersigned is anxious to be released from service.[19]

"I Have My Doubts as to Getting a Company Made Up"

As ardent as most men were to volunteer, however, there were some who wanted no part of the fighting. Some objected to war on religious grounds. In the South, some were loyal to the Union and considered the Confederates to be traitors. In the North, some felt the rebels had the constitutional right to secede and others were not willing to lay down their lives to free African Americans. Similarly, many living in the Confederate States of America believed the war was being fought to protect the interests of the wealthy and had no interest in dying to defend the institution of slavery. To those who were anxious to fight, the position of those who did not agree was completely objectionable:

> May 17, 1861
> My Dear Father,
>   I am ashamed for the people of Jackson County. . . . They are dead in ignorance and sloth. They have neither energy or patriotism . . . the only way to get men in this part of Jackson is to draft them. It is discouraging to ride day after day and have men to render such frivolous excuses, as having had broken arms, legs, and ribs and fingers and toes cut off, &c. &c. A goodly number of men whoere going to join this company have joined elsewhere, but a certain set of liars who informed them that my company had fallen through. I have no one to assist me in this enterprise. . . . I now have on my list seventeen names and, if was nearer filled out several others would join. I have my doubts as to getting a company made up.[20]

The Union forces were so confident of defeating the secessionists swiftly that the initial enlistment period for soldiers was only three months. Confederate soldiers signed up for a one-year tour of duty, which, if slightly more realistic, soon proved to be impractical. President Lincoln would soon call for more troops and the reenlistment of the original volunteers. If in the early stages of the war there was a surplus of men willing to volunteer, the recruiters had to work harder to get enough bodies in uniform when it became clear that the war would in fact last for a long time.

In some cases it was not a lack of willingness to serve but a less carefree approach to joining up that evolved. If in the spring of 1861, prior to the Union disaster at Bull Run (Manassas, according to the Confederacy), some men enlisted without considering the ramifications for their families, by the following winter some were a good deal more circumspect:

> Summerfield. 12.2.61
> M. D. Legget Esq.
> Dear Sir,
> Your note was duly received. Is there any possibility that I could obtain a commission as a Lieut. in your regt? I wish to go to war if I can do so consistently; I have a family to maintain which I could not keep on the pay of a *private* or I would go as such. I was urged to go as captain of the first company that went from our county. But I could not possibly go at that time. . . . I could raise 30 to 40 men who would go with me if they were certain that I was to be one of their officers. . . . [I]f recruits could receive a months pay in advance it would be quite an inducement. Has any arrangement of that kind been made? If you think there is any chance for me to get a commission in your Regt. I will get a recommendation from the "County Committee" and come [indecipherable]. I would rather join your regt than in any other I know.
> Yours very respectfully [indecipherable] Wheeler[21]

Others discovered after a few months away from their loved ones that they had joined the army for the wrong reasons. If some men had enlisted out of patriotism or sheer excitement, others were serving because of peer pressure or the mistaken belief that a loved one had wanted them to do so:

> Winchester July 15, 1861
> My Dear Annie: Yesterday I received your letter by Dr. Dodd . . . but was very much disappointed that I did not hear from you sooner. . . . In your letter by Dr. Dodd you say you are proud that I am in the service of my country and in the last you seemed distressed and probably surprised that I am in the Confederate Army for twelve months if my services are needed. I thought you expected me to stay when I left. I done everything I could to honorably get out of the volunteer service . . . you did not seem

satisfied and wounded my feelings several times in regards to the substitution. I thought you preferred me to go in my own place.[22]

As the war defied everyone's expectations and continued into 1862, the military authorities discovered that they had to work even harder to get men into uniform. If enthusiasm had filled the ranks in the previous year, now there would have to be a little more in the way of showmanship and spectacle. In Boston young men might read a flier for an upcoming recruitment rally that was designed to motivate them into enlisting complete with celebrity speakers and entertainment:

TO ARMS! TO ARMS!!
GREAT WAR MEETING
IN ROXBURY

Another meeting of the citizens of Roxbury,
to re-inforce their brothers in the field,
will be held in
ELLIOT SQUARE, ROXBURY,
THIS EVENING AT EIGHT O'CLOCK

Speeches from
PAUL WILLIARD, REV. J. O. MEANS, JUDGE RUSSELL,
And other eloquent advocates

The Brigade Band will be on hand early.
Come one, Come all!

GOD & YOUR COUNTRY CALL!![23]

At a rally a potential recruit could expect to be subjected to musical entertainments, waving banners and flags, and general pageantry. According to Union soldier John Billings, an ancient veteran of the War of 1812 might make an appearance, followed by one from the Mexican conflict. Inevitably an "old-timer" would "shout his willingness to go again" and a "patriotic maiden lady would go in a minute if a man." When the young men were sufficiently roused, "at proper intervals enlistment rolls is presented for signature."[24] And when patriotism could not be stirred with speeches, music, and production values, as was the case when the war dragged on, the regiments offered generous financial rewards and a questionably mercenary credo for anyone who joined them:

These new Union volunteers are being housed in barracks in the Washington, D.C., area. Most combat troops wouldn't see this kind of housing again for the rest of the war.

GENERAL POPE'S ARMY

"Lynch Law for Guerrillas and No Rebel
Property Guarded!"
Is The Motto Of The
SECOND MASSACHUSETTS REGIMENT

$578.50 for 21 months' service
$252.00 State aid for families of four.
$830.50 for short service
$125.00 cash in hand.

This regiment, although second in number, is second to none in regard to discipline and efficiency, and is in the healthiest and most delightful country. Office at Coolidge House, Bowdoin Square.
Capt. C. R. Mudge
Lieut. A. D. Sawyer[25]

In most cases, once a recruit signed up he would have some time, perhaps days or more commonly weeks, to settle his business before becoming a full-time soldier. Sometimes in the interim, the recruit would muster up with his future company for training during part of the day and return home to do his chores. When the time came for the men to join their companies full-time, there would often be a parade and they would be cheered by their neighbors. Uniforms and weapons would be dispersed, when they were available, and the recruit would then take an oath of loyalty:

> I John Doe do solemnly swear that I will bear true allegiance to the United States of America and that I will serve them honestly and faithfully against all the enemies and opposers whatsoever and observe and obey the order of the President of the United States and the orders of the officers appointed over me according to the rules and articles for the government of the armies of the United States.[26]

"A Soldier Was Simply a Machine"

As the war progressed, more and more soldiers were needed to take the place of those who had fallen on the battlefield or succumbed to disease. While a steady stream of men continued to volunteer and reenlist, neither military could keep its ranks filled. Accordingly, in the summer of 1862 President Jefferson Davis of the Confederacy created a law that modified the duration of his soldiers' enlistment, making their obligation open-ended until the end of the war. He also initiated conscription—the drafting of all able-bodied men between eighteen and thirty-five years old for a period of three years. Sam Watkins of Company H of the First Tennessee Regiment recalled bitterly:

> A law had been passed by the Confederate States Congress called the Conscript Act. . . . From this time on till the end of the war, a soldier was simply a machine, a conscript. It was mighty rough on rebels. We cursed the war, we cursed [Confederate General Braxton] Bragg, we cursed the Southern Confederacy. All our pride and valor had gone, and we were sick of war and the Southern Confederacy.[27]

The following year, President Lincoln, needing an additional 300,000 men, also initiated conscription for the Union armies.

In both cases exemptions were offered to those men who could afford a deferral. Three hundred dollars bought a "commutation fee" for men trying to stay out of the U.S. military. The wealthy of the Confederacy had to pay up to five hundred dollars to escape service but also had the advantage of an even more provocative escape clause: any man who owned twenty slaves was automatically exempt from service. To those Confederate soldiers who resented fighting for the privileges of the wealthy, this was just another demoralizing perk of the well-to-do:

> A law was made by the Confederate States Congress about this time allowing every person who owned twenty negroes to go home. It gave us the blues; we wanted twenty negroes. Negroe property suddenly became very valuable, and there was raised the howl of "rich man's war, poor man's fight." The glory of the war, the glory of the South, the glory and pride of our Volunteers had no charms for the conscript.[28]

"The Drain upon the Army Is More Than I Can Bear"

The most popular way to avoid service, however, was to provide a substitute. For a fee, often of a thousand dollars or more, men who had not been drafted would serve in the place of the wealthy. Apparently the guilty feelings of those who could afford more than the lesser commutation fee was eased by the fact that they had not deprived their nation of a body in uniform.

Among those who could not afford to avoid the draft, there was an increasingly large group who wanted to stay home. Stories from the front lines regarding the conditions of war revealed that it was not such a glorious enterprise after all. The variety of reasons for men to avoid the army of both nations was wide, and their rationalizations stymied any number of recruiting quotas:

> Penfield, Georgia; February 26, 1862
> My dear friend:
> . . . You have seen, doubtless, the Governor's proclamation calling for twelve additional regiments, declaring that he would resort to a draft were the said 12,000 men not forthcoming on the 4th of March, prox. Well, we were all determined never to stand a draft and we thought to volunteer on the 4th. . . . All of our class . . . concluded to go to the same company and were quite ready to start, when, all at once, came a notice from the Governor exempting the students of Mercer University from the draft and from militia duty . . . and the mighty ebullition of our patriotism suddenly cooled down to the freezing point. . . . And now here we are and here we will remain for some time to come, plodding the daily

round of college life, boring and being bored to the best of our ability. As our only design was to evade the draft, should one be found necessary, of course we very readily embraced the opportunity afforded by the exemption of putting a terminus to our connection with these halls of science in the usual manner. We suddenly found it impossible to tear ourselves away and . . . to tell the truth and shame the devil, I was very glad to get off from going. . . .

Louis Crawford[29]

The rules regarding exemption were different in different places. Men who belonged to a state militia, the equivalent of today's National Guard, did not have to serve. Men who performed necessary jobs on the home front, such as blacksmiths and civil servants, also did not have to serve. As the war carried on endlessly and tens of thousands of soldiers died, would-be recruits tried harder to avoid service by acquiring a "special application for exemption." The bureaucracy charged with supervising and providing dispensations was, however, vulnerable to corruption and gullibility—so much so that both governments were obliged to establish new standards to prevent the hemorrhaging of their manpower:

Circular #3.   Confederate States of America
Bureau of Conscription
Richmond, Virginia. January 19, 1864

In view of the great increase of special applications for exemption and the facilities with which signatures are obtained, it has become necessary to prescribe regulations for proceeding in such cases to prevent the allowance of exemption in cases specially presented and supported by many signers with some show of testimony, but without real merit. The officers of conscription will therefore be governed by the following instructions:

I. Every application should be sworn to by the applicant and verified by the affidavits of at least two respectable citizens who are personally acquainted with the facts testified to by them.

II. Applications so verified should be carefully, particularly, and vigilantly investigated by the local enrolling officers and a report of the facts, with their opinion in approval or disapproval forwarded through the proper official channel. . . .

C. B. Duffield
Assistant Adjutant General[30]

Despite the best efforts of both militaries to limit the number of men avoiding service, the problem was intractable. Even men who were due to return to their regiments after a furlough were reluctant to go. Their loyalty to their friends under arms was tempered by their knowledge of how dangerous a proposition war really was, as recorded by Bostonian doctor John Perry:

> Falmouth, April 15, 1863
>
> I have felt dazed and benumbed since my arrival here, probably from the effort I made before leaving home to suppress all gathering emotions. On the Sound boat I gave way, and I confess to behaving as I did when a child for the first time away from home. I cried as I did then,—all night long. I thought Harry Abbot in the berth above me was fast asleep, when suddenly he rolled over and looked down upon me. I felt for the moment thoroughly ashamed of myself, but he said nothing and settled back into his place, and then I heard him crying also. We had talked things over a bit, and I knew the poor fellow passed safely through so many battles he could hardly escape unscathed again.[31]

Toward the end of the war many simply deserted their companies or ignored their draft notices. There was not much that could be done to punish those who refused to fight. Deserters could be executed, and many were, but those who made it home were relatively safe. The U.S. government was exhausted and focused its attention on ending the war as quickly as possible—not tracking down men hiding from duty. The Confederacy was in even worse condition, and its infrastructure was crumbling. Men who wanted to stay home could do so because there was no one left to pursue them. Even at the highest levels of government, leaders could only register their frustration with a system that was so easily corrupted and taken advantage of:

> Headquarters Army of Northern Virginia. September 10, 1864
>
> Honorable Secretary of War Sir: . . . the drain upon the strength of the army by exemption of civil officers, postmasters's clerks, and mail carriers . . . is more than I can bear. . . . A large number of able bodied men are taken from the Army or kept out of it as mail contractors. In many instances these contracts are made for the sole purpose of evading service in the Army.
>
> The case of one Leftwich, of Richmond, has been reported to me as a flagrant instance of this kind. He has a contract to convey the mails of an unimportant route in Alabama. He resides in Richmond, where he is car-

rying on his business, and has never seen his route, as I am informed. Yet the court discharged him. . . . Another instance has been reported to me of a young man in Louis County, whose name I cannot now recall, but who obtained a contract to carry the mail from the obscure post-office of Mechanicsville . . . and was discharged from the service. He is the son of wealthy parents, and I am told remains at home, and employs someone else to carry the mail. . . . I am constrained to say that while it is important that all the interests of the people should be regarded by the Government their preservation from subjugations is the greatest of all, and in my opinion the emergency requires the sacrifice of every other consideration to the vital question of the public safety.

Very Respectfully, your obedient servant, RE LEE [32]

As the war neared its end, and the Confederacy's defeat became inevitable, desperate men proposed radical solutions to the problem of fielding an army:

Raleigh, North Carolina January 29, 1865

His Excellency Jefferson Davis: . . . How this war can be successfully managed brought to a speedy and honorable end, bringing us independence are questions that are on every tongue. . . . I propose to give you my plan briefly: Declare by law that every soldier who has or will enlist in our army, and who at the time of such enlistment was not a slave owner or landowner shall receive a bounty, or pension at the end of the war, upon being honorably discharged, of one negro slave and fifty acres of land . . . and further shall have all the negroes which they can capture from the enemy. . . . Lincoln has tempted thousands of men into his Army by offering reward. I now propose to out bid him. . . . If we make it to the interest of the world to fight on our side, men from all quarters of the globe will take up arms in our defense. . . . We can command thousands of men from Ireland, Germany, Poland, Austria, England, and France by offering them a home in the sunny South, and servants. . . .

J. W. Ellis [33]

Such ideas, of course, were never pursued, and within four months of J. W. Ellis's letter the war was over. Tens of thousands of men began the process of leaving military life and started out on long journeys back to the farms, towns, and cities they had left years earlier.

But back in the early days of the conflict, when the nature of battle was unknown and the promise of fighting was an opportunity, not a terrible hardship, the men happily left behind the lives they knew, convinced they would soon return home covered with glory and filled with memories of wonderful adventures. More often than not, they willingly passed their medical examinations, swore their oaths of allegiance, and traded their farm clothes and bookkeeper's suits for woolen military uniforms of many designs. They kissed their families good-bye and marched off, assured in their convictions and enthusiastic about the experiences that lay ahead of them.

In the years that followed, those who survived would be deprived of their innocence—for the world of the soldier would challenge them in a way that was more profound than anything they could possibly have imagined.

CHAPTER TWO

The New World: Military Life and Camp Conditions

*T*he journey to the battlefield often was the first interaction a soldier had with the world beyond his home, and some faced the expedition with trepidation. More men were excited by the prospect of an adventure, though, and embraced the idea of exploring parts of their own country that were, to them, strange and new places. A trip from Connecticut to Baltimore is today accomplished in less than a day on Interstate 95. In the 1860s, however, it was a lengthy affair, required a variety of transportation, and ended up in a place inhabited by vastly different people from those whom the soldiers knew at home. For the men who were interested, their travels were an eye-opening experience that had the potential to show them exactly what and who they were fighting for. Private James Sawyer of South Woodstock, Connecticut, described what it was like to leave for the south in a letter to his family:

Fort McHenry. Baltimore Maryland
Dear Father, Mother & Sisters,
I take this opportunity to drop you a few lines to let you know we have arrived at our destination.... [O]n Thursday the 21st, our cook had orders to cook up 3 days rations and at 3 on Friday, the regiment was in line with everything ready to start.... [W]e embarked on the steamer "City of Boston" bound to New York. We had a pleasant ride across the sound. We arrived in New York at 5 and after a cup of coffee went on the steamer "Kill von Kill" . . . [A]t 9½ we started for Elizabethport, NJ. We got there at half past ten and took the cars for Baltimore. We rode from 10½ Satur-

Officers of the Eighth New York State Militia, some of the first Union troops called up by Lincoln. Their tent and camp equipment is far better than what most soldiers on the other side had available.

day to 11½ Sunday. . . . They stopped frequently on the way. . . . [S]ometimes we stopped near an orchard so we could help ourselves to apples. We entered the state of Maryland at about 9 o'clock Sunday morning. You could see the difference between the free and slave states very soon. We could not see near as much cleared lands as we did in other states.

The niggers were plenty enough and at the door of every log cabin near the railroad, they stood as thick as bees, shouting and waving their hats as we passed along . . . we came across a number of secesh houses as we went along. At all the loyal houses the inhabitants were out cheering and waving their hats and handkerchiefs at us as we passed their houses while the rebels stood around their houses without giving a cheer or wave.

[Fort McHenry] is a very pleasant and healthy place and I am glad that we are stationed here. We have a good sea view and convenient places for bathing.[1]

Among the first aspects of their new lives the Civil War soldiers had to adjust to was living in a clamorous environment. Especially for men raised in small towns or on remote farms, the change was both surprising and stimulating:

My dear Mother:

Two weeks ago today, at this hour, I was with you in old Georgia. Today I am in Virginia, the land of battles, surrounded by armed men and myself metamorphosed from a quiet citizen to a soldier, the difference between which two positions cannot comprehend unless you should experience the change. For instance, two weeks ago scarcely a sound fell upon my ear from the time I left my bed until this hour, except the voice in common conversation. Today from almost every QUARTER comes the sound of the drum from Pig's Point, from Newport News, Craney Island, or batteries on this point and also from the direction of Norfolk. With this music as a bass accompaniment can be heard every now and then the deep tones of a Columbiad gun from one of the many batteries close to this place. I find this place at once dull and exciting, dull because we lie inactive, exciting because we lie at the same time like a lion at bay, watching a game in which we may soon play an important part.[2]

Tent Life and Other Substitutes for Home

Another major change for new soldiers to adjust to was moving from a family home to living communally in crowded tents with strangers. At the beginning of the war, both armies housed their men in tents designed by an officer previously assigned to fight the Plains Indians named Henry Sibley. Sibley, who took his inspiration from the Native Americans' tepees, created a twelve-foot-high, conically shaped, canvas-covered structure that could house a dozen men. Some Sibleys were supported by an external structure of poles, while others utilized an internal tripod that was adjustable according to the terrain. The soldiers slept on the bare ground with their feet at the center of the tent, where in winter months a small stove was placed. Piping led up to a hole at the top of the tent to allow fresh air in and smoke from the stove out.

It was not long before the Sibleys were determined to be too expensive and unwieldy for the frequent moves required by the military. In their place the army supplied the men with "A," or wedge, tents. Simpler than the Sibleys, wedge tents housed four to six men in a cramped space. One Union soldier wrote in complaint:

"[F]ive in one tent six feet square! We lie down on the same side, either right or left, parallel; as one turns all must."[3]

These men of the Third New Hampshire Regiment were sent to the beach near Beaufort, South Carolina, to save it for the Union. This was not tough duty for men used to rough New England winters.

Other soldiers slept on the ground, protected from the cold and damp by only an oilskin sheet. The thin canvas tenting that protected them from the elements hung from two six-foot vertical poles and a horizontal crossbar.

As the war continued, wedge tents were commonly replaced by "dog" or "pup" tents that housed only two men and barely managed to do even that. Massachusetts trooper John Billings measured the length of such a tent to be five feet, two inches. While the men of this period tended to be shorter than those alive today, the pup tent was still insufficient for its task.

Designed for maximum portability and to be carried on a man's back, the pup tent was actually supplied by its manufacturers in halves. Each soldier would carry his share of a tent while on the march. In the evening, when camp was being set up for the night, he would button his section to that of his tentmate. Wisconsin trooper Philip Cheek recalled his first encounter with the most commonly used shelter of the Civil War:

> While on this march there was issued to us what the Government called shelter tents but what the boys called "Pup Tents." Each man was given one half, which was 5½ feet sq. of heavy sheeting; on one edge were buttons, the other button holes. We used them in pairs, buttoning the two pieces together, then get in, if you could . . . peg the sides down and there you were . . . the only way you could crawl in was to get on

This abandoned camp shows how troops would arrange things to make themselves comfortable. The empty oven was used by army bakers, and the appropriated Southern home in the background kept officers warm and dry. The tent to the left of the oven was the most typical shelter.

your knees, then if you were 6 ft. or over you stretched out, either one end or the other of you would be out of doors, and if you turned over, you each had to agree and turn over together or you would both be out of doors, they were open at the end.[4]

Officers generally had better accommodations than enlisted men did, and they also had the use of "wall tents." Also known as "hospital tents" because they were often employed to house the sick and wounded, these dwellings actually boasted four canvas walls upon which the peak of the tent sat. The advantage of this layout was that officers could actually stand upright inside, conduct business, and enjoy a more civilized environment. On occasion an officer's wall tent might be well finished, complete with a wooden floor and real or improvised furniture:

> The accommodations here are about as liberal as there [a previous camp], two wall tents being placed end to end, for office and bedroom, and separated at will by a "fly" of canvas. There is a good board floor and mop board, effectively excluding dampness and draughts, and everything but sand, which on windy days penetrates everywhere. The office furni-

ture consists of a good desk or secretary, a very clumsy and disastrous settee, and a remarkable chair. . . . [T]he chair is a composite structure: I
found a cane seat on a dust heap, which a black sergeant combined with
two legs from a broken bedstead and two more from an oak bough. I sit
on it with a pride of conscious invention, mitigated by profound insecurity. Bedroom furniture, a couch made of gun boxes covered with condemned blankets, another settee, two pails, a tin cup, tin basin. . . .
[T]oday it rains hard, and the wind quivers through the closed canvas,
and makes one feel at sea. All the talk of the camp outside is fused into a
cheerful and indistinguishable murmur, pierced through at every moment
by the wail of the hovering plover.[5]

Common soldiers were not always condemned to spend their nights in
flimsy, cold, damp tents, though; there were times when they enjoyed more
substantial accommodations. Usually this was during the winter, when both
sides effectively observed an informal truce. Regiments would stay in one winter camp for months at a time, and the men had both the need and the opportunity to construct homes that could better hold the elements at bay. When
possible, soldiers constructed homes made of logs, scavenged wood, fence

Union troops in
"winter quarters."
Confederate and
Yankee soldiers were
often permitted to
build huts or cabins
from logs to keep
them warm until the
spring military
campaign season
opened. The log
homes were turned
into firewood when
warm weather came.

posts, bricks, mud, and sod. Illinois soldier C. W. Wills wrote home to describe his first winter quarters in a wood cabin during December 1861. While his new home was an improvement upon living outside in a tent, Wills made no pretense that the conditions were anything but primitive:

> We are at last established in our quarters and thoroughly "fixed up" with all the modern improvements in the housekeeping line, coupled with the luxuries of the ancients and the gorgeous splendor and voluptuousness of the middle ages. We have a chimney whose base is rock, the age of which man cannot tell, whose towering top is constructed of costly pecan wood boughs embalmed in soft Missouri mud cement. We have a roof and floor, beds, and door, of material carved or sawed from the lofty pines of Superior's rock bound shores. . . . We have tables and chairs and shelves without number and a mantle piece, and crowning glories, we have good big straw sacks, a bootjack and a dutch oven.[6]

Still, log huts were a luxury. In regions where wood was available but not abundant, the soldiers would "stockade" their Sibley or wedge tents, creating a significant improvement in their living conditions. To do so, they would usually dig a hole so that their quarters were actually a foot or two below ground level, which helped keep them warmer by providing the natural insulation of the earth. The stockade itself was a wooden foundation from two to five feet high, made of logs, the space between them being sealed with mud. The canvas tent would sit on top of this foundation and sometimes even boasted a real door built onto a frame with hinges. If bricks were available, a fireplace and chimney might be built into a space where the canvas was trimmed away for this purpose, as Dr. John Perry wrote home:

> Mountain Run. November 11, 1863
> . . . I have been working hard today, pitching my tent upon a log foundation. It will be warmer, and will allow me to sit up. Tomorrow I shall build an underground fireplace, for the wind blows so hard here in the winter that it is impossible to keep warm by an outside fire, for while your front is warming your back is freezing, and if the fire is very near the tent, the smoke blows in and smothers you. My eyes are now almost put out by the smoke; my hands are covered with pitch from handling pine logs; my feet are soaking wet; and I am cross.[7]

The soldiers were ingenious when it came to improving their creature comforts with what few supplies were available to them. Chimneys were constructed with mud-lined barrels and primitive floor heating systems were created, as described by Vermont soldier E. F. Palmer while serving in the Green Mountain State's Second Volunteer Brigade:

> The morning is cold and windy. By 8 o'clock it begins to snow. . . . [T]he soldiers are disappointed not expecting it so early in the year, and then their tents are not fitted for it. . . . [S]now and sleet fall all day and by night it is five inches deep. . . . [T]hey dig a channel under the tent some three feet long, brick up the sides, cover these with flat stones or pieces of iron; and at the end of chimney. Some of these worked finely; others intolerably. Now you see the boys, tears streaming from their eyes, coming out of their tents the smoke rolling after them.[8]

Problems such as fireplaces and chimneys that did not draw well were, however, a luxury that soldiers often wished they had. Even with its great advantages as a manufacturing powerhouse, the North could not always supply its soldiers with the most basic of commodities—usually because of transportation failures, as C. W. Wills discovered:

> We have had it sweet the last day and two nights. Rained like sixty and we have no tents. There is no shelter but a few trees and you know they amount to nothing in heavy rains. It is amusing to see the boys figure at

A Federal officer enjoys luxury camp equipment that most Union and rebel troops could only dream of. As well as the spacious tent, there are folding camp chairs and a table.

night for dry bed. Everything, gates, cordwood, rails, cornstalks, weeds, and panels of fence and boards are confiscated, and genius is taxed its utmost to make the sleeping as comfortable as possible. . . . Milo Farewell, Hy. Johnson and myself sleep on an armful of cornstalks thrown on a floor of rails with nothing between us and the clouds.[9]

Even more poorly supplied, Confederate soldiers constantly suffered from exposure to the elements and coped as best they could in adverse weather conditions. Virginian Carlton McCarthy later remembered:

Tents were rarely seen. All the poetry about the "tented field" died. Two men slept together, each having a blanket and an oil cloth; one oil cloth went next to the ground. The two laid on this, covered themselves with two blankets, protected from the rain with the second oil cloth on top, and slept very comfortably through rain, snow, or hail as it might be.[10]

Occasionally, the rebels would be able to make use of tents captured in battle, as recorded by surgeon Spencer Welch:

Camp on Rappahannock River, Va., January 11, 1863
    Yesterday was a very wet day, but we can keep fairly comfortable with the little Yankee tents we have captured during the summer campaign. . . . Wood is very plentiful where we are now encamped and we have rousing fires.[11]

Neither the Union or the Confederate army was especially egalitarian, and Jedediah Hotchkiss, assigned to make battlefield maps for Southern general Thomas "Stonewall" Jackson, used his financial resources to make sure that he did not suffer in the same way as the rank and file. When his unit was encamped near a boardinghouse, Hotchkiss rented a room and stayed out of the bad weather:

April 24, 1861
    The rain is now beating against our windows and it is dark without. I pity our poor shelterless men. I am enjoying excellent health; am not exposed any at night and do not intend to go into a tent until the weather is better, although it costs something more to live as we do, paying for your board, but one's constitution is saved and that is of more value than a few dollars.[12]

The Quality of Camp Life—or Lack Thereof

Although he may have been resented for his privilege, Hotchkiss was right about protecting his health. Even when soldiers had good tents or log cabins to live in, the fundamentally poor conditions of many army camps were difficult to overcome. During the course of the war, armies traveled back and forth repeatedly across the same territory, denuding it of trees and leaving muddy, polluted quagmires. The strategic demands of war did not always match the requirements of selecting healthy campgrounds, and the soldiers suffered accordingly:

> We are encamped on soil so saturated with water that I sent a protest to General Warren today asking him if we could move to a drier spot, but he answered we should have to go several miles to find such, and that, of course, was impossible. We are evidently to remain here for the winter. I have the whole regiment out today, cutting down trees to let the sun in,

These soldiers even enjoy being waited on by camp servants. But the camera also reveals they knew how to set up a camp. Trimmed pine branches are used as a wind and weather shelter behind the tents. Soldiers also used soft pine to produce makeshift mattresses.

and digging trenches to drain the water off, but as it is only necessary to dig a few inches to come upon more water, the task is rather a hopeless one.[13]

Compounding the damp soldier's misery were the subfreezing temperatures that came when night fell. In the morning the men would wake and find that

> My sweet potatoes froze; meat shared the same fate, as likewise the water in our canteens.[14]

Seeking shelter inside a tent was often a futile gesture when winter winds began to blow. Confederate Lieutenant Richard Lewis wrote home to describe a frigid November night when his regiment's quarters were not nearly strong enough to stand up to the fierce gales:

> The last two days have been very cold; the wind blowing with such terror that nearly all the tents were blown down, and a great deal torn. The wind blew so very hard that Harry had to keep rocks on the ovens to keep them from blowing off while he was cooking.[15]

The combination of incessant cold and wet conditions led to inevitable results: illnesses that swept through the camp:

> The nights are cold. This morning, when I went to wash [basin] . . . I found it frozen an inch deep. If you wake any hour of the night, you hear the strokes of a dozen axes; and what is really painful, many coughing—coughing deep and hoarse. The cold has crept through the tent and blanket and, thief like, robbed the soldier of his sleep.[16]

The sicknesses caused by the damp conditions varied in degree (see Chapter 9). Coughing was commonplace. Ground itch tormented many soldiers as white pimples filled with pus broke out on the body. Compelled to scratch, soldiers soon found their wounds bleeding, leading to scabs, which, in some instances, covered the entire body. Wounds would not heal, and minor respiratory diseases would settle in the soldiers' lungs, becoming serious. Anxious to remedy the situation, Confederate General James Longstreet gave creative orders to help his men stay warm in November 1862, when they were unable to construct adequate shelters:

General Orders, No. 47:

The inclement season having set in, commanders will take every method of protecting and guarding their men from the weather in their present exposed situation. . . . To this end company and regimental commanders will take care that the fires are kept burning during the entire day, and will at night see that they are moved to a short distance so that the men can make their bivouacs on the earth thus warmed during the day. . . . The bivouacs made in this manner are warmer and dryer than any can at present be devised.[17]

In addition to the problems created by disease, the debilitating effect of long exposure to cold on the men's morale was serious. In December 1862, Union soldier Henry T. Johns witnessed a riot triggered when his regiment was not given fuel to keep warm. The Massachusetts Forty-ninth Volunteers destroyed a gunpowder storage facility and a food warehouse:

A building containing a large quantity of powder was partially destroyed, and boards carried off for fuel. I don't blame them for that. Put soldiers, half starved, among loyal citizens in canvas tents with the mercury near zero and you have all the ingredients for a riot. Such was our condition. . . . I contend we had a right to run the government in debt for all the loose boards we could find . . . we were . . . in a deserted horse shed and because there were 8 tons of powder in the adjoining shed we were not allowed to have a fire. Making up our minds that it were pleasanter to be blown up than to freeze—fire we had in defiance of orders to the contrary.[18]

Lice, Heat, and Other Constant Companions

Cold was not the only natural enemy challenging the comfort and welfare of the soldiers. A significant annoyance for soldiers of both armies was the constant onslaught by a variety of insects. Mosquitoes, fleas, lice, ants, spiders, and other biting creatures made tens of thousands of soldiers miserable. Although the soldiers did not know it, bug bites could also transmit disease, making what was considered a terrible annoyance into an unseen but deadly threat. Mosquito netting and smoking offered some respite but not nearly enough. A Union soldier noted his suffering in a letter:

There is one consolation to be drawn from the cold, it stops the "chigres" from biting us. I would rather have a bushel of fleas and a million of mosquitos on me than a pint of "chigres." . . . [T]hey are a little bit of a red thing, just an atom bigger than nothing, they burrow into the skin and cause itching that beats the regular "camp" all hollow. . . . [T]he ants here also have an affinity for human flesh and are continually reconnoitering us. . . . I do manage to keep clear of greybacks [lice] though.[19]

As miserable as the soldiers were made to feel by the constant assault of hungry insects, there was another natural phenomenon that made them even more unhappy. The summer heat, especially in the Southern camps, was a greater trial than carnivorous bugs and was often considered to be worse than the cold of the winter months. This was especially true when the armies were in transit—which was often. Parched and covered in dust, the men rarely had reliable access to pure water supplies, shade, or rest. Heatstroke, sunburn, dehydration, intestinal diseases, madness, collapse, and death could follow.

In the heat of summer or in winter's cold, troops were always consumed by camp chores. These men use a summer afternoon to catch up on mending their uniforms, cleaning brass buttons, and getting off some letters home.

"The Amateur Barber"; view of a soldier getting a haircut

While in camp, Northern soldiers, unfamiliar with Southern temperatures and humidity, suffered during drill sessions and broiled in tents that were oven-hot. Only when the heat was intolerable were guards allowed to sit under protective awnings instead of marching their beat. Yankees did not have exclusive rights to suffering from the heat, however. Confederate doctor Spencer Welch wrote home to his family:

> The bitter cold of winter does not compare in severity with the hard marching of a summer campaign, and I should prefer six winters in camp to one summer on the march.[20]

At the peak of a Southern summer the opposing armies refrained from battle or strenuous activity, as correspondent to *The Jewish Messenger*, J. Cohen reported:

Camp Near Clear Creek, New Corinth, Miss.
August 1, 1862
Dear Messenger:

Here in the temporary cessation of hostilities, which the heat of the weather renders imperative on both sides . . . we have commenced a thorough course of drill and instruction, doubtless—if no unforeseen circumstances transpire—to continue through the remainder of the summer, . . . we rest at present in undisturbed quietude. No marches, scouts, reconnaissance, etc., diversify the monotony of camp life. . . . Could you have been in camp last night you would have seen several squads of soldiers grouped together on the grass beneath the bright starlight of these Southern skies, busily engaged in relating their experiences of the past. At times they were merry and seemed to enjoy various recollections of the past year, again a shade of sorrow would flit across their countenances as they spoke of the absent dead . . . and then, when their thoughts would revert to "home,"—"Home, home, sweet home," then would seriousness pervade the circle, their conversation would become more hushed, a sense of loneliness, of being far from mother, wife, sister, or daughter, or that dearly loved one, would cause a deep drawn sigh to escape their manly bosoms, and the sounding of "Tatoo" would be a relief that is better imagined than described. "Roll Call" would follow, one by one these sterling patriots would retire to their canvas habitations . . . and no sound was to be heard in the camp, but the occasional "who goes there?" of some vigilant sentinel patrolling his beat . . . such is our military life; day after day passes by, the events of one being but a repetition of the other.[21]

A great danger posed by the terrible summer heat was its effect upon sewage. In the military camps, which suffered from poor sanitary conditions, the accumulating waste festered and created a pestilent miasma.

Still, camp hygiene was important year round and in all weather conditions. Few other facets of life in a military camp had as much influence upon the well-being and happiness of the soldiers as its systems for maintaining a clean environment. Assigned the responsibility of inspecting the cleanliness and maintenance of Union camps, Doctor J. S. Newberry of the U.S. Sanitary Commission reported from the Valley of the Mississippi:

I found camp streets, tents, spaces between tents, drains, and edges of the tents filthy. Refuse slops were buried in trenches; but the trenches were nearly filled before the dirt was filled in. . . . The men were undisciplined. The horses tied very near the tents, and their dung not removed. The cooking bad. The men dirty. In short, by want of cleanliness and attention to the requirements of civilized life, the men were in danger of losing all self respect.[22]

Conversely, Newberry described the nearly ideal circumstances of the camp belonging to the Sixth Indiana Regiment:

> This was in excellent condition. The colonel is a gentleman and a soldier, alive and active in his duties. The surgeon, Dr. Charles S. Schussler, is eminently well qualified, and devotes himself untiringly to his duties. Guided by science he is saving many lives by taking those precautions necessary to prevent sickness . . . the streets of the camp are beautifully turnpiked and well drained. The tents are struck or raised from the bottom often. The slops are carefully disposed of, so as not to be in the least offensive; the men clean, their clothing well washed. The sink was on the leeward side of the camp, in the woods, at a proper distance, neither too far nor too near . . . most of the companies have built log houses, with fireplaces and chimneys.[23]

Daily Schedules and Camp Routine

Policing the camp was only one part of the schedule that defined a soldier's day. Although a camp's routine might be altered because of severe weather, holidays, marches, or battle, under normal conditions the timetable was rigidly followed, and each event was announced by the bugler's differing calls.

A military camp day began before sunrise. During the winter months, the soldiers would be awakened at six, but for the balance of the year reveille was an hour earlier:

> At five, the drummers and fifers, whilst the stars still shine, march around camp beating drums. Sleep is frightened from every eye; a stir, a bustle in every tent. The boys creep out with their woolen night caps on, and attend roll call. Then some go back, wrap themselves in the blankets and await the coming day.[24]

At roll call each company would line up and the sergeants would make sure that the men they were responsible for were present. After that was accomplished, the day would unfold according to the needs of the particular regiment. In John Billings's Massachusetts artillery regiment, roll call was followed

*Soldiers at rest
after drill*

by stable call, when the horses were fed; breakfast call; sick call at eight in the morning, when those who required medical attention visited the doctors' tent; water call, when horses were led to rivers or other water sources; fatigue call, when a camp was cleaned of waste, wood and water were gathered, and equipment was cleaned; drill call, the rehearsal of military procedure and movement; boots and saddle call, the practicing of artillery movement; dinner call at noon; afternoon drill, water call at 4 P.M.; stable call; retreat call, indicating the end of the working day; dress parade, similar to the morning roll call except that soldiers were dressed in formal uniform and officers provided information about and gave lectures on various subjects; supper; tatoo call, the last roll call of the day, held at 8:30 P.M.; and taps, when lights were extinguished and soldiers were forbidden to talk in their tents after 9:00.[25]

Defying minor regulations and irritating commanders was a common occurrence, and pranksters were known to imitate rooster calls, cat cries, and dogs barking late into the night.

Connecticut infantryman James Sawyer's regiment lived by a slightly different schedule:

I have plenty to do here. We stand guard every other day. When not on guard we drill. We have to get up at 5, breakfast at 6. Then comes cleaning the tents and washing dishes. At 7 if on guard we go on duty if not, drill from 7 to 9 am. Then it takes us from 9 to 11 to scour our guns and equipment. At 11, drill until 1 pm, when dinner is ready. Drill again from 2 to 3. At 4¹/₂ comes dress parade. Then supper. And by that time it is dark. Lights are put out at 9¹/₂. So our time is pretty well occupied.[26]

The quality of a common soldier's camp life depended on luck, circumstances, and the assignments he received. The same was true for officers. Some were sent to establish posts in diseased swamps or lead suicidal charges, while others enjoyed an existence that they would later write about wistfully. No doubt each man's character also contributed to his perceptions of his experience. Thomas Wentworth Higginson, who bravely chose a task rife with potential trouble—leading an African-American regiment in a prejudiced army—remembered certain days of his wartime duty with unmistakable fondness:

> We used to have reveille at six, and breakfast about seven; then the mounted couriers began to arrive from half a dozen different directions with written reports of what had happened during the night, a boat seen, a picket fired upon, a battery erected. These must be consolidated and forwarded to headquarters with the daily report of the command, so many sick, so many on detached service and all the rest. . . . [T]hen we scattered to our various rides, all disguised as duty; one to inspect pickets, one to visit a sick soldier, one to build a bridge or clear a road, and still another to headquarters for ammunition or commissary stores. Galloping through green lanes, miles of triumphal arches of wild roses, roses pale and large and fragrant, mingled with great boughs of the white cornel, fantastic masses, snowy surprises—such were our rides, ranging from eight to fifteen and even twenty miles. Back to a late dinner with our various experiences. . . . After dinner to the tangled garden for rosebuds or early magnolias, whose cloying fragrance will always bring me back to the full zest of those summer days; then dress parade and a little drill as the day grew cool. In the evening, tea; and then the piazza or the fireside, as the case might be,—chess, cards,—perhaps a little music by aid of the assistant surgeon's melodeon, a few pages of Jean Paul's "Titan," almost my only book, and carefully husbanded,—perhaps a mail with its infinite felicities. Such was our night.[27]

But the majority of soldiers would remember their war days with less nostalgia. For many, the most pronounced memory of camp life would be the terrible

A laundress in camp. When camped near a community, troops were allowed to use their own funds to hire locals to help them with the endless rounds of chores. Though low paying, being a camp laundress was honorable work.

boredom that grew out of the monotonous routine. Life in camp was an endless series of repetitive chores, few of which provided excitement or enlightenment. Men who had left their families and homes to engage the enemy in heroic battle spent most of their days cleaning camp, digging latrines, tending horses, doing laundry, gathering wood or water, constructing roads, slaughtering cattle, and preparing for rigorous Sunday inspections. Soldiers complained that they found

> Today's duties so similar to those of yesterday that it is difficult to recall the day of the week, to realize that you are mentally stagnating.[28]

Although the soldiers and officers organized diverting amusements to keep the men's spirits up (see Chapter 3), the tedium of daily life often led to declining morale and resentment in the ranks. Officers would be blamed for the dull and difficult conditions the men had to endure. James Sawyer wrote home to his parents:

> We have no officers that care at all for the interest of the men. Major Peal is hated by the regiment.[29]

Officers were scorned for insisting on drills and chores that the common soldier regarded as useless, poorly thought out, and unpleasant:

> Last night I had a little more experience in soldier life. . . . I had slept but a little when an officer came around [and] ordered us to put on knapsacks and load our muskets. After all this had been done we stood in line about five minutes, when we were ordered back to bed again and to keep our guns with us. So I went to bed again having my loaded musket as a bedfellow.[30]

Inexperienced officers who did not know their business were looked upon with contempt, and the mood of a regiment could border upon the mutinous. Equally, camps serving under officers who were considered to be overly ambitious seethed with discontent, as Union soldier Onley Andrus described in a letter home to his family:

> Now I don't believe there are any cowards in the 95th Regt, except it be your Humble Servt, but I believe there are very few men who would rush into a fight alone on account of their patriotism, I hardly think Col Humphrey would, but he is looking for Stars and is willing to sacrifice every man in his Regt to accomplish his aims. You may not know what is meant by "looking for stars." I will tell you. A Lt. Col wears on his shoulders two simple leaves, a Col wears a Spread Eagle, Big Genl wears on Star, and Major Genl wears two Stars. Well our Col being very anxious for promotion we call it "looking for Stars." And in his anxiety to find them he would, I think, forget all about comfort of his men.[31]

For the most part, soldiers lived an outdoor life while performing their chores, and the tenor of their days was heavily influenced by the weather. While their routines were altered during the worst of summer and winter, Civil War soldiers often had to do their jobs under adverse conditions:

> We have been seeing and feeling the roughest side of camp life, ever since my last [letter]. Rain in double headed torrents; lightning that will kill easily at five miles; thundering thunder; and wind from away back. But the mud dries like water on a hot brick, and six hours sun makes our parade ground fit for drill. Afternoon when the sun is out it's hot enough to scorch a phoenix; yesterday we drilled from 1 to 3. I was almost crisped, and some of the boys poured a pint of grease out of each boot

after we finished. Up to 10 last night when I went to sleep it was still boiling, but at five this morning, when we got up, we shivered in coat, vest, and blankets. Bully climate! And then the way that the rain patters down through the roof, now on your neck; move a little and spat it goes, right into your ear, and the more you try to get away from it the more you get, until disgusted you sit up and see a hundred chaps in the same position.[32]

Among the most important subjects announced at dress parade was the assignment of camp guard duty for the following day. Those men performing picket duty (see Chapter 5) would patrol the camp's perimeter, often in close proximity to the enemy, and sound the alert if an attack was made. It was not always an enviable task:

The names of those that are to be guards are read off the night before. Last night my name was in the list. Morning came and with it the various rounds of duties, reveille, roll call, hanging up the things in the tents, policing the ground, washing, breakfast, squad drill, then guard mounting. A 110 privates, six corporals, 3 sergeants, one lieutenant, have been detailed to guard the camp. This is their duty 24 hours. They are divided into 3 reliefs, each on 2 hours, off 4. None but privates walk the beats, which are from four to 10 rods. [A rod is equal to 5.5 yards.] The corporals run at their calls. Strange did it seem at first to be awake at midnight, hearing half a dozen screaming "corporal of the guard, no. 1" or 5 as it may be. Two large tents is the guard house. As night grows darker and colder, the dew heavier, a whole relief, 33, crowd into them, some standing, some lying parallel, others horizontal on the legs of the first tier. Towards midnight faces grow sober, "This is pretty raw" says one; "little tough" another, "one must be drunk or mad" continues a third, "to enlist."[33]

Conversely, Henry Johns of the Massachusetts Forty-ninth Volunteers found picket duty a welcome relief from the everyday pressures and cacophony of camp life. While walking the picket, soldiers escaped from the numbing chores that normally occupied them:

> For two Sabbaths I have been on guard and I enjoyed it especially at night. A man has so few chances to be alone while in camp, that I could but hail with pleasure my nightwatches. After the bustle of the day there was something very soothing in the quietness. To be in the midst of a thousand sleeping men, hearing no thing save the measured tread of your fellow sentries, is like the solemnity of a large city in the small wee hours of the night.[34]

Even for the men who remained behind in the heart of a crowded military camp, the nighttime hours before taps offered a pleasantly different atmosphere from the frenetic daytime. In a world of drilling and chores, the night allowed the men to enjoy reflective moments, as John Perry noted in October 1863:

> Last night the moon was brilliant, campfires blazed in every direction, and with our blankets spread around a huge mass of burning embers and our pipes lighted, we lay listening to music from the bands; I, for one, dreaming of matters and things far enough away from where I was . . . music is a tremendous help. Our own band is not here, but the two other brigades have theirs, and as the camps adjoin we enjoy the benefit of both. One band generally plays two hours after breakfast, and the other from sunset until half past nine.[35]

As serene as a particular night might be, however, the men lived with the dread knowledge that the situation could rapidly change at any time. War obeyed no schedule, and, as James Sawyer wrote home to his parents, his superiors made sure that his company did not become complacent:

Back River   Baltimore   Md.   April 3, 1863
My dear Father, Mother, and sisters:
    We had quite a surprise party the other night. It happened this wise. We turned in as usual at 9 O'clock. I went to sleep, and awoke about midnight. I had been awake but a few minutes when I heard the sentinel out by the guardhouse challenge and immediately after several guns were fired. The next minute the corporal of the guard was into the barracks shouting, "Turn out the guard! Turn out the guard! The camp is attacked." The guard immediately sprang from their bunks and ran out. I jumped up and commenced dressing as quick as I could and most of the boys were doing the same. Before I was dressed the captain came in and turned out the drummer who sounded the long roll. By that time I had hurried on my clothes and equipment, and awoke Clarendon who had not awoke up yet. I took down my gun and ran out to fall into line.
    When I went out the guns were flashing and crashing up on the hill by Col. Standbury's. Thinks I we are in for a fight now I guess. The order came to load and fix bayonets. We obeyed and the next minute were marching off at Double quick toward where the fighting was. We arrived at the top of the hill by Colonel Standbury's, made a half wheel and

Men of Company E of the Fourth United States Colored Troops in Fort Lincoln in the defenses of Washington

halted then came the order, "Rear Flank, ready—aim—fire." I was in the front rank, and while the rear rank were aiming I turned my head to see if any were so excited as to shoot those before them, but everything was right.

After we fired we smelt a rat. We had been fooled. It was a ruse of the captain to see how quick we could turn out and how we would act when we thought were in danger. He said we did well and that he could rely on us in case of a real attack. . . . [I]t did look a little war like to be suddenly risen from sleeping, go out in a dark night and see the flash of guns as they were snapping like a bunch of fire crackers, to hear the old drum rattling, the captain giving orders in a hurried and excited manner, and the boys seizing their guns and equipment and hurrying out to fall into line. I did not feel frightened but was some excited. My hand trembled in spite of me while I was loading my musket and the thought passed through my head, "I wonder if any of us will get shot." I made up my mind to do my best.[36]

Fear of Fighting

Concern about combat was never far from the mind of the Civil War soldier. Although the atmosphere in a military camp could be one simultaneously of joviality, determination, boredom, and resentment, fear was omnipresent—perhaps suppressed, but never vanquished.

While drilling was a preparation for battle and the various entertainments, sports, and other recreations were intended to distract the soldiers, certain truths were discovered in combat that lingered upon their return to camp. Memories of terrible sights and the behavior of others affected the mood of many men and the camp itself:

> A fierce fight is a wonderful builder up and tearer down of reputations. Heroes vanish and the underrated step up in the confidence of their comrades . . . blustery commanders reveal "hereditary heart disease" which "alone" prevents him carrying out his repeated threats against the enemy. The boys know why the Captain is sick and he can never control them again. . . . [I]t is curious to note the diseases affecting certain soldiers on receiving news of an impending battle. Sick ones leave the hospitals and well ones seek to occupy their beds just vacated. The bully of the squad is sick. He has a terrible pain in his right arm and his legs feel queer, his head reels.[37]

Try as the men might to avoid thinking about the dangers of war, it was impossible to do so in the hours prior to battle. In the moments leading up to fighting, the spirit of the camps varied. Some officers worked their men up into a fever. Others encouraged reflection and prayer. Before one particularly dangerous mission, Henry Johns watched a group of men prepare themselves:

> You could find many penning messages to the loved ones at home. On boards, on knapsacks, in secluded places they were writing and if some cheeks were white and tears rolled down manly faces, I think you will credit them to some other cause than fear.[38]

For Union soldier Elisha Rhodes the anticipation of combat was the most difficult challenge, as he noted in his diary:

> We have spent nearly a month in ordering our camp and now have orders to leave. In fact we are all packed up and some of the troops are moving towards the river. This looks like another attack upon Fredericksburg. . . . Tomorrow I suppose we shall try to shoot a few rebels. I wish it was over for it is worse for a soldier to wait for a battle to begin than it is to do the fighting.[39]

The rebels Rhodes would soon face in combat were confronted by the same fears. Writing home to his family in Georgia, Confederate trooper Shepard Pryor described his apprehension and sadness on the eve of an encounter with the Yankees:

> My dear Penelope,
> I sit down to write this morning under circumstances that are peculiar to me to write under. We have orders to march this evening with five days' rations on a toilsome and dangerous march over mountains in the woods for the distance of perhaps 30 miles to get there for the purpose of attacking the enemy in the night on Cheat Mountain. This letter may be the last that you'll ever get from me. . . . It is awful hard for me, my dear, to think of not seeing you and those dear little children. Oh, how it pains my heart to write this! . . . You must try to raise our children to the best of your ability, and I am satisfied if you do that they will be raised right. Learn them to love and fear God. Oh, don't let them forget that they had a father and my dear boy speak of me frequently and learn him to love

me, though I may be dead to this world. I cannot help but crying, to write you thus, thinking perhaps it may be the last time, and to think of what you'll have to undergo with a house full of fatherless children. . . .

I have one remark to make as regards Lou. I know your sentiments as regards her, as I've heard you express yourself. I want you to take care of her and raise her as your own. Raise her for my sake. She is mine and my first child. . . . Give all our children such an education as your pecuniary affairs will admit of. . . . I'll close, though knowing I'll perhaps have to meet the enemy before I see you. I am ready to, thank God, obey my country's call.[40]

Confederate soldier Ira Woodruff wrote to his cousin Mattie, acknowledging his fear of death but tempering his concern with the promise of eternal life in a better place:

Cousin Mattie,

The time draws near when perhaps we will bid each other a long farewell, for the decrees of fortune are uncertain and no one with our limited capacity can penetrate the murky curtain that veils our fortune. . . . [I]f it should ever fall to my lot to face the instruments of my death, where perhaps cannon balls may rain around me, I shall think of my own sweet friends that I have left behind me. . . . [I]f I never meet you again in this world, I hope we will meet each other in that land of love where our names will glitter like sparkling diamonds upon the tables of eternity!

Your Affectionate Cousin,

Ira Woodruff[41]

On the eve of battle, many would seek consolation in the soothing words of favorite biblical verses, as S. H. Dent noted in May 1864:

We have just received orders to be ready to march at any moment . . . nearly everyone thinks the collision so much talked of here cannot be postponed a great deal longer. I can not think that the enemy will attack us up front . . . be cheerful darling about the result. I think General J[ohnston] will be victorious when he fights and I trust the same kind Providence who had hitherto protected me will continue to do so. . . . I am reading 2nd Kings also—I will read to morrow morning beginning at the 21st chapter.[42]

Aware of their vulnerability, soldiers feared many things, but it was not always the most apparent threats of injury, pain, and death that troubled them. Writing to his family in Massachusetts, John F. L. Hartwell worried most about dying away from his native soil and loved ones:

> If I was to die at home it would not have the dread to me as the death that stares for me in the face but to see thousands of men rotting unburied on the field of battle unburied & unknown & if buried, thrown in a heap & covered with a little earth to moulder them back to dust. If I could banish all such thoughts & be sure if dying to be in the presence of my beloved family & receive their last kiss, to once again feel the gentle pressure of the hand of those at home I do dearly love I could go to battle with a brave heart & steady hand but No alas my lot is now vested in a hand of strangers to us & our noble intentions.[43]

Almost all the soldiers experienced moments of fear, but for many the great challenge, in the moments leading up to actual combat, was not to panic. Gaining confidence from the righteousness of their cause, the soldiers of both sides also found strength in the prayers of their loved ones. To these men the performance of duty was a goal worth working toward. Joshua Callaway, serving in the Army of Tennessee, wrote home to his wife, Dulcinea:

> Now, my Dear, it will perhaps surprise you when I tell you that in the very midst of all this terrible thunder, blood, carnage, slaughter, with my heart lifted to God in prayer and my trust in him and knowing that my wife and a host of others were praying for me, I felt perfectly calm and secure, knew all that was passing around me. Never lost my wits a single moment. And I am proud to say that I don't think I did anything of which you or I or any of my friends need be ashamed.[44]

In time some men became jaded to the terrible sights witnessed on the battlefield. Marion Hill Fitzpatrick, serving in the Army of Northern Virginia, described his own lack of affect in a letter to his wife, Amanda:

> I have changed much in my feelings. The bombs and balls excite me but little and a battlefield strewed with dead and wounded is any every day consequence.[45]

Most, however, felt a fresh sense of horror every time they were confronted by the appalling results of the fighting. Confederate artilleryman Robert Stiles recorded his horror at seeing the "mementoes" left behind the retreating Federal forces, "the ghastly leavings of numerous field hospitals; pale, naked corpses and grotesque piles of arms and legs."[46]

Soldiers also knew that war offered many terrible ways to die other than simply falling in combat. The battlefield was a hazardous place even after the fighting was done. As recorded by Warren Lee Goss, a Union prisoner held by rebels, Confederate and Union troops were known to help each other out when confronted by a common enemy:

> Using my musket for a crutch, I began to turn away the burning brushwood, and got some of them out. I tell you, it was hot! Them pines was full of pitch and rosin, and made the fire as hot as a furnace. I was working away, pulling out Johnnies and Yanks, when one of the wounded Johnnies . . . toddled up and began to help. . . . The underbrush crackled and roared, and the poor devils howled and shrieked when the fire got at them. We were trying to rescue a young fellow in gray. The fire was all around him. The last of that fellow I saw was his face. . . . I heard him scream, "o, mother! o, God!" It left me trembling all over like a leaf. After it was over my hands were blistered and burned so I could not open or shut them; but me and them rebs tried to shake hands.[47]

The soldiers of both sides were all too aware that death would come in many forms: bullet, artillery, fire, or bayonet. For men who went off to war seeking glory, accomplishment, and adventure, the new knowledge of the true nature of fighting brought them to their senses. It did not take many experiences of combat for them to realize that despite the righteousness of their cause, war was no respecter of personal dignity. Union private Frank Wilkerson noted in 1864:

> One veteran told the story of the burning of some Union soldiers who were wounded during Hooker's fight the battle of Chancellorsville . . . as they lay helpless in the woods. It was a ghastly and awe inspiring tale. As we sat silently smoking and listening . . . an infantry soldier who had, unobserved by us, been prying into the shallow grave he sat on with his bayonet, suddenly rolled a skull on the ground before us and said in a deep low voice, "That is what you are all coming to, and some of you will start toward it tomorrow!"[48]

Certainly, many men took their concern for the well-being of their respective nations into battle with them. After the initial glamour of military service dissipated, however, this began to change. The real fear in the hours before an assault by the enemy was not for countries, governments, or political institutions. It was inspired by the terrifying glimpses of their own terrible fragility that taunted them from the corpses of those who had gone before them:

> [T]he dead bodies of men and horses had lain there putrefying under the summer sun for three days. . . . I recall . . . the shocking distension and protusion of the eyeballs of the dead men and dead horses. Several human and inhuman corpses sat upright against a fence, with arms extended in the air, and faces hideous with something very like a fixed leer, as if taking a fiendish pleasure in showing us what we essentially were and might at any moment become.[49]

Life on the March

Marches such as the one undertaken by Shepard Pryor's Georgian regiment were not uncommon in the months when travel was possible. Indeed, the movement of troops, whether in pursuit of the enemy or toward targeted locations, was the essence of the war. During these marches the camp life the Civil War soldier had grown familiar with changed almost completely. Frequently traveling twenty miles a day and sometimes going as much as thirty or forty, these regimental maneuvers tested the soldiers' endurance, sanity, and even survival skills. While the basic command structures of camp life were maintained while on the move, many of the support systems the men depended upon were suddenly absent.

Soldiers generally traveled carrying light packs in order to make the march less grueling and quicker. Often they took little more than half a pup tent, a blanket, a pair of socks, a gun, two hundred rounds of ammunition, and rations that had already been cooked. Personal belongings were left behind. When possible, supply wagons followed the troops, hauling only limited quantities of food, ammunition, and grains for the regiments' horses and mules. But as Union General William Tecumseh Sherman noted, "No army could carry food and forage for a march of three hundred miles."

In theory, soldiers would prepare enough food for several days of marching, at which point they would be resupplied. Seemingly practical as this concept was, it relied upon the ability of each military to fulfill this basic obligation. If the shipping of rations to permanent and semipermanent camps was a process that often failed, it was nearly impossible to ensure a steady supply of food to regiments that were moving swiftly through war-ravaged or remote territories.

Army cooks tackle the thankless task of cooking for the troops.

Compounding the problem, armies did not always follow their prescribed routes, and transportation in the 1860s was haphazard under the best of conditions. In wartime the result was chaos. Thin as the survival margin was for soldiers in camp, the odds against them while in transit were even greater. Hunger was as fierce an enemy as anything an opposing army could offer, as Spencer Welch wrote home to his wife:

> Ox Hill Ca. [presumably Carolina], September 3, 1862
> . . . I stood the late terrible march surprisingly well, but I have learned what hunger and hardships are . . . we have had some dreadful sufferings especially on these forced marches. The fatigue and pangs of hunger were fearful . . . we marched fast all day Monday and all day Tuesday and until late Tuesday night, when we bivouacked in a field of tall grass near Bristow Station . . . and went to sleep without supper. The country was a waste, and I heard no sound of chicken, cow, or dog during the night.[50]

The men of the rebel armies endured unimaginable privations while moving through the land they were trying to defend. Patriotic as they may have been, their constant hunger wore down their morale. They deserted when they could, and those who stayed resented the leadership that was letting them down so appallingly. Sam Watkins of the First Tennessee Volunteers recalled the reaction of his fellow soldiers when confronted by the president of the Confederacy during the November 1863 siege of Chattanooga:

> In all the history of the war, I cannot remember of more privations and hardships than we went through at Missionary Ridge. And when in the very acme of our privations and hunger, when the army was most dissatisfied and unhappy, we were ordered into line of battle to be reviewed by Honorable Jefferson Davis. When he passed by us, with his great retinue of staff officers and play outs at full gallop, cheers greeted them, with the words, "Send us something to eat, Massa Jeff. Give us something to eat, Mass Jeff. I'm hungry! I'm hungry![51]

Although generally better supplied, the Union soldiers faced similar deprivation once they left the relative abundance of their established camps. Making matters more difficult, they were commonly moving through hostile territory. While Confederate troops could expect to enjoy goodwill and a seat at the dinner table of a local family if there were food to be shared, the Yankees were usually less welcome. In their hubris, Union officials boasted that theirs was the best-prepared and best-provisioned army in the history of the world, but the rank-and-file soldiers found reality to be different indeed:

> Camp near Warrenton. October 25, 1863
> We do not stay long in one place but go marching on. We have stopped here only temporarily; yesterday it rained so hard, and our supplies are so far gone, that we cannot move again for at least 24 hours, for the men have literally almost nothing to eat. The supper last night for our own mess consisted of maggoty hard bread and brown sugar (alias sand).[52]

If hunger was one of the great demoralizing forces of the common soldier during a march, it was closely matched by other miseries of the road. The inability of either military to supply its men with the necessary items to shelter themselves left soldiers hopelessly exposed to the elements. Heat, cold, rain, ice, snow, mud, and dust conspired to weaken those already exhausted by their exertions and chronic hunger. War was an urgent business, and armies ignored bad weather unless it was absolutely impossible to continue:

Falls Church September 19, 1861

There was every appearance of rain when we started—but we have no regard for the weather when we are ordered to move—and, sure enough, we had not marched more than a quarter mile before it commenced raining, and it was one of the heaviest falls of rain I have ever experienced. The roads being flooded with water and all of us drenched to the skin, making no halt to seek shelter from it, and further we had no dry clothes in our possession to put on when we camped for the night.[53]

Unpassable roads were no excuse for stopping, and although Spencer Welch was stretched to his limit of endurance, a glimpse of his determined regiment offered temporary inspiration. He kept marching:

Orange County, Virginia. August 18, 1862

We started last Saturday about dark and continued to travel over the bad, muddy roads all night. We had a very tedious march and did not stop except to get the artillery out of the mire, and at one time to eat and rest a little. Whenever the men would come to mud holes and fords of rivers they would plunge right in without hesitating a moment. This is necessary because an army must never be allowed to hesitate at anything . . . our division is about 15,000 strong . . . it extended several miles, and whenever we would get into a long straight piece of road where I could look back, the sight was most amazing. The compact mass moved four deep, and, with their glittering guns, looked like a river of human beings.[54]

But a momentary boost of the spirit was not enough to get soldiers through the life-threatening conditions they faced on the road. Absent tents, Confederate soldiers such as Theodore T. Fogle slept unsheltered from cold weather:

Dear Father and Mother,

Well, here we are, after a march of two days and a half. We left Aquia Creek last Saturday morning about 6 o'clock, marched 14 miles the first day. The road for part of the way was awful. The wagons would mire up to the hubs of the wheels, and we would have to pry them out . . . so we did not get to our first camping place until about an hour before sunset. We did not camp. We just built fires, made coffee, ate a dry biscuit or two and slept under the trees with only enough shelter to keep off the dew. . . . I did not sleep well, was too cold, woke up about 12 o'clock and went to a fire and sat there and talked until 3 o'clock and then laid down with my feet to it and slept for but little over an hour. Then the drum beat for us to prepare for the march. We started by sunrise.[55]

Marching through winter storms presented a terrible test for men who had already withstood the challenges of battle. For soldiers from the Deep South, the snow and ice of Virginia, Pennsylvania, and Maryland could be as deadly as the bullets fired from Union guns:

> Snow and rain and sleet and tempest seemed to ride and laugh and shriek and howl and moan and groan in all their fury and wrath. The soldiers on this march got very much discouraged and disheartened. As they marched along icicles hung from their clothing, guns, and knapsacks; many were badly frost bitten, and I heard of many freezing to death along the road side.[56]

Despite their superior transportation infrastructure, Union soldiers also suffered from shortages of camp essentials while marching toward the Confederacy. The deprived regiments' commanders and the congressmen representing them did what they could to entreat assistance from the government:

> His Excellency A. Lincoln:
> My Dear Sir: If the union is to be maintained the loyal people of the border slave states must be sustained. . . . Our men who have enlisted have been lying out without even a blanket, destitute of tents and camp equipage, destitute of arms and ammunition, for weeks and weeks.[57]

The U.S. government did what it could to race the necessary equipment to the men who desperately needed it. Like their rebel counterparts, however, many Yankee soldiers were forced to sleep outside in snow and slush with little more than an oilskin for protection:

> March 24, 1864
> . . . We have marched . . . some 35 days during this time. . . . I think I never suffered on a march as I did on the Sand Mountain in Dekalb County. I wore a thin blouse, and had no overcoat. I'd lie so close to the fire nights that the clothes on my back would scorch and my breath would freeze on my whiskers.[58]

As harmful as freezing temperatures were for soldiers on the march, heat was even more debilitating, for there was no escaping the sun and little relief for a man's thirst:

> In summer time the dust combined with the heat caused great suffering. The nostrils of the men filled with dust, became dry, and feverish, and even the throat did not escape. The "grit" was felt between the teeth, mouth, ears, and hair. The shoes were full of sand and the dust, penetrating the clothes and getting in at the neck, wrists, and ankles and mixed with perspiration, produced an irritant almost as active as cantharides . . . their heavy woolen clothes were a great annoyance . . . the sun produced great changes in the appearance of the men; their skins tanned to a dark brown or red, their hands black almost, and long uncut beard and hair burned to a strange color made them barely recognizable.[59]

Pushed beyond endurance, hungry, parched, and susceptible to disease because of their weakened condition, many soldiers on both sides were unable to go on. Some fell back and became stragglers, but many were too ill even to do that. A large number of soldiers were incapacitated by sunstroke, and many died, even if they were transported to field hospitals or makeshift infirmaries. In May 1864, it is believed that "hundreds of men dropped dead from lack of proper precaution in the intense heat"[60] while Union troops made a grueling march to the Pamunkey River in Virginia.

Under these conditions the men did whatever they could to relieve themselves of extraneous baggage. They left whatever was not absolutely necessary by the side of the road to lighten their burden. Later on, many would regret having abandoned a blanket, a coat, food, or most disastrously—their shoes and boots.

Limping Soldiers and Crippled Armies

Marching almost twenty miles a day required the men to have shoes that could stand up to the poor roads, high rivers, and abuse that came with such a pace. Few were fortunate enough to have decent-quality footwear, however. After a short time on the march, a great many soldiers lacked even the most fundamental protection for their feet and suffered greatly:

Charleston, Jefferson County, W. Va., September 24, 1862
    . . . If I should tell you what our army has endured recently you could hardly believe it. Thousands of the men now have almost no clothes and no sign of a blanket nor any prospect of getting one, either. Thousands have no shoes at all, and their feet are now entirely bare. Most of our marches were on graveled turnpike roads, which were very severe on the barefooted men and cut up their feet horribly. When the poor fellows could get rags they would tie them around their feet for protection. I have seen the men rob the dead of their shoes and clothing, but I cannot blame a man for doing a thing which is almost necessary in order to preserve his own life.[61]

Aware of the Confederacy's inability to provide its armies with shoes, General James Longstreet ordered his men to improvise:

It having been found impracticable, at the present juncture, to fully supply the army corps with shoes, the attention of commanders is directed to the advantageous employment of the raw hides of slaughtered cattle in the manufacture of a strong and warm covering for the feet . . . experience has shown that an excellent substitute for the shoe can be made out of this material. Hides are hereby authorized to be used for this object and the energy, and practical judgment, and the experience of the commander will always be shown in making the most of small resources for the comfort and protection of his men.
    By command of Lieut. Gen. Longstreet.   G. M. Sorrel, A.A. Genl.[62]

While shoes could not win battles, as perhaps a technologically advanced artillery piece might, armies were greatly debilitated by their shortage. Armies had to move and soldiers had to be fit to fight. Barefoot soldiers were walking wounded even before the first shots of a battle were fired. Emphasizing the importance of shoes, Geoffrey Ward has written, "The greatest battle ever fought on the North American continent began as a clash over shoes."[63] It happened when the armies of both the North and South converged on the town of Gettysburg, Pennsylvania, when word spread that a warehouse of new shoes was there for the taking.
    As the war drew to a close, the brutal years of hardship took their toll. The great mobile army camps, columns of soldiers that once stretched for miles, were reduced to straggling lines of emaciated men whose survival had more to do with their own willpower than anything the army could offer them:

The winter of 1864–65 was the coldest that had been known for many years. The ground was frozen and rough, and our soldiers were poorly clad, while many, yes, very many were entirely barefooted. . . . [T]he once proud army of the Tennessee had degenerated to a mob. We were pinched with hunger and cold. The rains, and sleet, and snow never ceased falling from the winter sky while the winds pierced the old, ragged, grayback Rebel soldier to his very marrow. The clothing of many were hanging around them in shreds of rags and tatters.[64]

For the hopeful young men who marched off to war in 1861 with shining equipment and elaborate uniforms, seeking glory, the degeneration into poverty and debility was a shocking humiliation. The process of deterioration, however, was not a quick one, and during the course of the war the soldiers exercised the whole of their limited ability to stave it off. Despite the adversity of fixed and mobile camp life, the men found relief and rediscovered the pleasures of being alive in games and entertainment (see Chapter 3). Further, by working endlessly to improve their living conditions, the Civil War soldiers affirmed their personal sense of dignity and worth as human beings.

Certainly, these men demonstrated their strength and grit on the battlefield, but it may be that an equal triumph—an unlauded one at that—was resisting the constant pressure of entropy. If by the end of the war their physical condition was much reduced, the Civil War soldiers deserve recognition for withstanding the assault upon their souls.

CHAPTER THREE

Fun, Games, and Other Matters of Life and Death

Confronted by physical and emotional challenges that would have once been unimaginable to them, it is not surprising that the Civil War soldiers had a desperate need for diversion. Viewed from the perspective of a reader at the beginning of the twenty-first century, however, what is unexpected is the insidious, constant root cause of their craving: boredom. One could hardly be blamed for assuming that the soldiers had enough on their minds. That was often not the case, however.

History books generally focus on battles, acts of heroism, cowardice, magnanimity, and treachery, creating the impression that soldiers spent the majority of their time fighting. As Confederate soldier Carlton McCarthy recalled, reality was a different matter:

> Another fancy notion was that the principal occupation of a soldier should be actual conflict with the enemy. He didn't dream of such a thing as camping for six months at a time without firing a gun.[1]

In our era of diversionary overload provided by the Internet, cell phones, cable television, satellite television, MTV, movies, videocassettes, radio, books on tape, compact discs, DVD, and computerized play stations, it is difficult to comprehend how much of a challenge empty hours posed to the off-duty Civil War soldier.

For most men, once the day's drilling was done, the camp policed, the meals cooked, and their weapons maintained, there was literally nothing to do. This was especially true in winter camp, where weather conditions restricted the amount of time a man could dedicate to his normal responsibilities and the day stretched out even longer. To some extent this was not novel for men of the mid–nineteenth century, as their entertainment options had been limited under the best of circumstances compared to what we enjoy today. At home, however, unlike in military encampments, they had a recreational infrastructure in place in which they could participate: theatrical groups, bands, orchestras, baseball teams, football clubs, athletic competitions, religious organizations, and various social societies.

The endless boredom of camp life presented the authorities with a profound morale problem and threatened the smooth operation of the armies. As C. W. Wills noted in a letter home early in the war, idle soldiers were liable to get into trouble:

> We have had some fighting in camp lately. An artillery man stabbed one of the 9th and got knocked, kicked, and bayoneted for it. The artillery have sworn to have revenge and every hickory man (the 9th have a fatigue suit of hickory) they see they pounce onto. They have a skirmish every day.[2]

With some cooperation from the military command, the rank-and-file soldier took it upon himself to provide his own recreational opportunities whenever possible. Doing so was no easy task, as soldiers lacked supplies and were on the move often enough that any equipment ordered might not ever catch up with them. Regardless of the impediments, the soldiers persevered, and the level of sophistication of many of the entertainments organized by the troops showed a level of ingenuity that was equal, or in some cases superior, to that of the military strategists.

Conversation and Political Discussion

To begin with, not all of the soldiers' amusements were complex. For many who faced boredom on a daily basis, small distractions were the first line of defense. The soldiers' most fundamental diversion for was simple conversation. Topics of conversation ranged widely, especially during a casual smoke, cup of coffee, or tobacco chew. Common subjects included the ineptitude of their superiors, the draft, the poor quality and quantity of their rations, and men who were considered "jonahs" (those who had bad luck and were accident-prone) or "beats" (those who were skilled at avoiding their duties); there were also political conversations in which the men discussed what they were fighting for and the qualities of their national leaders.

The debates were lively and might carry on for days and nights at a time.

Foreigners supporting the Union cause. Pictured from left, they are the Duc de Chartres, the Prince de Joinville, and the Comte de Paris, all titled members of the same French family who served on Major General George McClellan's staff in 1862. Aristocrats to the bone, they didn't think much of President Lincoln and were great supporters of McClellan, a presidential candidate in 1864. Foreign observers also traveled with the Confederate armies.

ed according to Act of Congress, in the year 1862, by BARNARD & GIBSON, in the Cl
the District Court of the District of Columbia.

Men who were fighting and dying for political beliefs held them strongly and did not shy away from vituperative discourse. The scornful opinion of Union supporter Adam Gurowski regarding Abraham Lincoln might be surprising to us today, but during the war his ideas would have been met with as many nods of assent as voices raised in dispute:

> Lincoln is a simple man of the prairie, and his eyes penetrate not the fog, the tempest. They do not perceive the signs of the times—can not embrace the horizon of the nation. And thus his small intellectual insight is dimmed by those around him. Lincoln begins now already to believe that he is infallible; that he is ahead of the people, and frets that the people remain behind. Oh simplicity or conceit![3]

The dictatorial tendencies of C.S.A. President Jefferson Davis were also the subject of vigorous discussions around rebel campfires, especially after he introduced the Conscription Act of 1862. Later, as the war approached its conclusion in the spring of 1865, other topics became the focus of conversation. The Confederate soldiers' conversation at this time would have reflected their fatigue and hopelessness of troops, as described by a soldier named Jim in a letter back to his family:

> Deer sister Lizzy; i hev conkludid that the dam fulishness uv tryin to lick shurmin Had better be stoped. We have bin gettin nuthing but hell & lots uv it ever sinse we saw the dam yankys & i am tirde uv it. shurmin has lots of pimps that dont care a damn what they doo. and its no use tryin to whip em. if we dont git hell when shirmin starts again i miss my gess, if i cood git home ide tri dam ard to git thare. my old horse is plaid out or ide trie to go now. maibee ile start to nite fur ime dam tired uv this war fur nuthin, if the dam yankes Havent got thair yit its a dam wunder. Thair thicker an lise on a hen and a dam site ornraier.
>
> you brother jim.[4]

Salvation, Dirty Pictures, and Other Solitary Pursuits

Information and editorials that molded the troops' political opinions may have been found in the variety of reading material they enjoyed. While rarely supplied on a steady basis unless in winter camp, soldiers could subscribe to papers from home, buy local journals, and sometimes even trade over the picket lines with the enemy to get the perspective from the other side:

> We are pretty well supplied with news here; all the dailies are offered for sale in camp, but we are so far out of the way that the news they bring is two days old before we get them. TRANSCRIPTS and UNIONS are sent to us by the office free. I wish you would send me the REGISTER once and a while, and put in a literary paper or two, for we have considerable time to read.[5]

Other popular reading material included the Bible, fine literature, dime novels, serialized books, religious tracts offered by Christian organizations, and pornography. Obscene books, drawings, and photographs were procurable by mail, and their relatively easy availability concerned a number of officers, preachers, and pious enlisted men. Richards & Roche, a company based in New York City, offered "New Pictures for Bachelors," including, "Mermaids wearing only mist and foam."[6]

A wagon used by newspaper reporters in camp. Newspapers and magazines from home were one of the great wholesome camp amusements. Confederate troops often passed around the Southern Illustrated News, *a Richmond, Virginia, weekly that carried engraved illustrations.*

But reading was not the only solitary pursuit for less sociable, more introspective soldiers. Bostonian doctor John Perry of the Twentieth Massachusetts Volunteers whiled away the hours of a December afternoon in his tent daydreaming:

> It is raining and blowing fearfully, but I am snug and dry under my canvas shelter, where, in a little space ten feet square, is combined bedroom, sitting room, and office; for I am still living in a tent as I cannot find sufficient wood to build a hut. It is dull enough with nothing to do and nothing new to hear. I spend hours alone in my tent, thinking of the future; questioning and answering myself. This seems to be a desert that I am now passing through, which must be crossed.[7]

In better weather Perry would escape from his endlessly melancholy chores in the regimental hospital to enjoy the fresh river breezes and the simple glories of a summer evening's setting sun:

> Last night the heat was intense, and it seemed to me that a puff of pure air, free from the atmosphere of the hospital wards, would be worth a kingdom; so, finding a few spare moments, I drew a mattress out on the

Army bandsmen, a handy source of entertainment. These men carried saxhorns, musical instruments that are no longer used.

cottage piazza, upon which I threw myself. The situation of our hospital is quite at the edge of the bluff over the water, so that we have the beautiful bay almost beneath us. The sun was just setting; sky and water were aglow with color, and while smoking my pipe I saw passing below a large force of transports loaded with soldiers whom I knew were commanded by General Burnside. I knew also that the President and General Scott were aboard. Bands were playing, flags flying, and all seemed gay and brilliant. On they sailed with the sunlight upon them, on into the purple and gray. "Ah!" I thought, solaced by my pipe, "Behind me in the stifling wards is the night of that which has passed."[8]

Another solitary pursuit was carving or whittling. Soldiers on both sides passed many hours sculpting ornaments and jewelry out of any material they could get their hands on, including wood, bone, corncobs, leather, shells, stones, roots, coins, and even horses' hooves. The production of intricately hewn chess pieces, bracelets, rings, crucifixes, charms, letter openers, and pipes, among other things, consumed numerous empty hours.

Music and Singing

Although some men preferred the opportunity for reflection provided by private pastimes, a great many soldiers seized the chance to socialize and participate in communal activities. In a highly regimented world that offered hardship, danger, homesickness, and boredom, distraction and fun were of premium value.

Perhaps the most common and least formally organized of the soldiers' amusements involved music and singing. A great many of the companies had men with some musical proficiency who might be able to play a violin, banjo, guitar, spoons, or Jew's harp. Musicians would sometimes play instrumental pieces and on other occasions would accompany the men's singing. Popular songs of the era were often sentimental or patriotic. Soldiers would often sing their favorites, and not always with positive results—for emotional ballads would often remind them that they were far from home and the women they loved. Renowned songs among the Civil War soldiers included "All Quiet

Musicians pose with a horn hanging from a tent pole and a pair of cymbals out front.

Along the Potomac," "Home, Sweet Home," "The Girl I Left Behind," "The Bonnie Blue Flag," "The Battle Hymn of the Republic," "My Old Kentucky Home," "The Old Canteen," and "The Union Right or Wrong."

Soldiers were also partial to songs with a political edge that reinforced their sense of righteousness by lambasting their opponents. The pseudonymous rebel lyricist "Ole Secesh" wrote one of the more venomous attacks on President Lincoln, entitled "The Despot's Song":

> With a beard that was filthy and red,
> His mouth with tobacco bespread,
> Abe Lincoln sat in the gay white house,
> A-wishing that he was dead,—
> Swear! Swear! Swear!
> Till his tongue was blistered o'er;
> Then in a voice not very strong,
> He slowly whined the Despot's song,—
> Lie! Lie! Lie!
> I've lied like the very deuce,
> Lie! Lie! Lie!
> As long as lies were of any use;
> But now that lies no longer pay,
> I know not where to turn;
> For when I the truth would say,
> My tongue with lies will burn!
> Drink! Drink! Drink!
> Till my head feels very queer!
> Drink! Drink! Drink!
> Till I get rid of all fear!
> Brandy, and whiskey, and gin,
> Sherry, and champagne, and pop,
> I tipple, I guzzle, I suck em all in,
> Till down dead-drunk I drop.
> Think! Think! Think!
> Till my head is very sore!
> Think! Think! Think!
> Till I couldn't think any more!
> And it's oh! to be splitting of rails,
> Back in my Illinois hut;
> For now that everything fails,
> I would of my office be "shut"!

Jeff! Jeff! Jeff!
To you as a suppliant I kneel!
Jeff! Jeff! Jeff!
If you col my horros feel [*sic*]
You'd submit at discretion,
And kindly give in,
To all my oppression,
My weakness and sin! [9]

But Confederate songwriters could be equally harsh in criticizing their own leadership. Coming under withering satire was the plan of Captain Jonathan Harrolson, "Who sent tank cars around the southern cities collecting urine from which ammonium nitrate could be extracted for use in gunpowder": [10]

John Harrolson! John Harrolson!
You are a wretched creature,
You've added to this bloody war
A new and awful feature.
You'd have us think while every man
Is bound to be a fighter,
That ladies, bless the dears,
Should save their pee for nitre.

John Harrolson! John Harrolson!
Where did you get the notion,
To send your barrel round the town
To gather up the lotion?
We thought the girls had work enough
Making shirts and kissing,
But you have put the pretty dears
To patriotic pissing.

John Harrolson! John Harrolson!
Do pray invent a neat;
And somewhat more modest mode
Of making your saltpetre;
But tis an awful idea, John,
Gunpowdery and cranky,
That when a lady lifts her skirts,
She's killing off a Yankee! [11]

Union soldiers also employed music and lyrics to make their feelings known when they felt they were being treated shabbily by the military command. The declaiming of editorial poetry around a fire, or before a more formal audience, was also a technique for protest or simply getting frustrations off a soldier's chest:

Increase our Pay & Rations

Respectfully dedicated to Hon. Gideon Welles.
(Secretary of the U.S. Navy.)

Oh! Uncle Gideon, hear my prayer
Give ear unto my supplication,
Let master's mates have a better share,
Of the "Greenbacks" of the nation.
For pity's sake, oh! "Uncle Gid"—
Increase our pay and ration,
And we'll freely swear none ever did
With half the wisdom fill your station.
The times are hard and goods are high,
And as for food; upon my word.
On less than a double XX it's no use to try,
To get our grub lockers stores.
Oh! "Uncle Gid" indeed its hard,
That we poor fellows should suffer so,
While you've got the greenbacks by the cord,
And we're just the boys to make em go,
Then ponder well ere you refuse,
The boon we all so humble crave,
An increase of 35 per month would infuse,
Fresh courage even into the brave,
And you, oh! Most august body,
The Congress of our Nation,
Give less cash for contracts shoddy
And more for our pay and ration,
We would not ask our pay increase,
Could we but supplant our station
But as things stand we think the least,
You can do is to increase our pay and ration.[12]

Thomas Wentworth Higginson, commander of one of the first African-American regiments, enjoyed the spontaneous singing and dancing of his men. He was particularly fascinated by the uninhibited and foreign nature of their performances, which were indeed different from the formal and restrained dancing he had experienced while growing up near Boston:

> December 3, 1862, 7pm: . . . From a neighboring cook fire comes the monotonous sound of that strange festival, half pow-wow, half prayer meeting, which they know only as a "shout." These fires are usually enclosed in a little booth, made neatly of palm leaves and covered in at the top, a regular native African hut. . . . [T]his hut is now crammed with men, singing at the top of their voices, in one of their quaint, monotonous, endless, negro Methodist chants, with obscure syllables recurring constantly, and slight variations interwoven, all accompanied with a regular drumming of the feet and clapping of the hands, like castanets. Then the excitement spreads: inside and outside the enclosure men begin to quiver and dance, others join, a circle forms winding monotonously round some one in the centre: some "heel and toe" tumultuously, others merely tremble and stagger on, others stoop and rise, others whirl, others caper sideways, all keep steadily circling like dervishes, spectators applaud special strokes of skill; my approach only enlivens the scene; the circle enlarges, louder grows the singing, rousing shouts of encouragement come in, half bacchanalian, half devout, "Wake 'em brudder!" "Stan' up to 'em brudder!"—and still the ceaseless drumming and clapping, in perfect cadence, goes steadily on.[13]

Theatrical Productions

Although unplanned entertainments were a fixture in camps during the war, many regiments also devoted a great deal of energy to more organized events. In the winter of 1862, the Confederacy's Washington Artillery Regiment debuted a new society dedicated to entertainment, performance, and education:

> Our newly organized "Literary and Dramatic Association" gave their first entertainment in this camp. An immense fire was built, around which logs were placed, in horseshoe form, for the audience. Upon a platform, seated in an arm-chair improvised from a flour barrel, sat the President Corp. R. Mck. Spearing.

The President opened the meeting by stating the objects of the society, which were, by the contribution of whatever varied talent the boys possessed, to assist, upon station occasions (when we were at leisure), in the amusement and instruction of the command. A certain number were booked for the opening night, and in all sincerity it can be recorded, the entertainment was highly creditable. George Meek was especially praised for his recital of Poe's "Raven." . . . [A]s cold weather comes on apace we will have different amusements to help pass the idle hours of winter camp.[14]

As the war progressed, some of the soldiers' entertainment became more sophisticated. J. Cohen, correspondent to *The Jewish Messenger* newspaper, reported that he had attended a vaudeville variety show while in Corinth, Mississippi, during April 1863:

In this line . . . may be included the stage, which, strange as it may appear, has been eminently successful at Corinth. There is now a regular troupe engaged nightly at "Corinth Music Hall,"—an old frame building, formerly used for storing forage—in showing to the admiring military population of this garrison wonders of sleight of hand, negro minstreling, jig dancing, comic and sentimental songs, etc. The admittance fee of fifty cents will admit you to the luxury of a front seat, which is rough pine board, supported about a foot from the floor, all innocent of any back or railway whatever. . . . A night or two since, another "theater" opened to a crowded house in front of the "Tishomingo Hotel." It is somewhat to the credit of the discipline of the troops here, that no bad effects are traceable to these nightly amusements.[15]

Attending a performance was not the only way a soldier could participate in a regiment's theatrical presentations. Especially during the quieter months of winter camp, soldiers became involved in the writing, editing, and staging of plays. It was not long before the reputation of the soldiers' cooperative theatrical evenings spread and the audience included the most influential members of society:

You have heard, I presume, of the second performance of the "Washington Artillery Varieties Company." It was a complete success; even better than the one we had just prior to the battle of Fredericksburg. In fact, the army has declared the "Varieties" an institution. It was attended by a score of ladies from the surrounding country, a special railroad train having been run for their accommodation. Gen. Longstreet and staff were present. Gen. Lee was prevented by business from being present, but sent his regrets in an autograph note, thanking the managers for their kind invitation, and wishing them success in their efforts to introduce these entertainments into the army.

Representatives from all the divisions of the army were present, some of Jackson's men walking twenty miles, so great was their desire to see the show.[16]

Great attention was paid to detail. The "Washington Artillery Follies" was not a rough presentation but the culmination of a great expenditure of energy on costume design, stage sets, rehearsals, musical accompaniment, and even the preparation of programs:

> The stage was tastefully decorated with the Battalion colors and the guidons of the four batteries. . . . [T]he whole scene was illuminated, not by the "soft light of alabaster lamps," but by tallow dips hung in Chinese lanterns, that some thoughtful fellow managed to bring from Maryland last summer.
>
> The united bands of the Twelfth and Sixteenth Mississippi regiments under the leadership of Professor Hartwell, furnished delightful music. . . . The programmes were handsomely printed in Richmond, and distributed throughout the army.[17]

Casting these spectaculars presented challenges beyond the obvious problem of placing battle-scarred men in the roles of romantic female leads:

> The programme opened with "Pocahontas, or Ye Gentle Savage,"—a demi savage, semi-civilized extravaganza, with music dislocated and reset through the instrumentality of Seignor [sic] Knight. . . . Private W.P. N———, of Third Company sustained the part of "Powhattan, first king of the Tuscaroras." . . . Private Bob Many, of Third Company, was capital as "Pocahontas" and Corp. W———, of First Company, as Capt. John Smith, was excellent. . . . "Toodles" was the after piece,—Corp, H.——— of Second Company as Toodles, and Sergt. B———, of Second Company, as Mrs. Toodles. . . . Of course through out the play the house came down any number of times, and the audience appeared delighted. . . . The band played the "Bonnie Blue Flag" and the audience scattered to their camps.

The bills announce that the "Lady of Lyons" is to be performed again, but, as "Pauline" was wounded at the battle of Fredericksburg, and is now confined to the hospital, it is puzzling the managers who is to cast for the part. The choice will fall upon Bob Many, we suppose.[18]

Distraction from the sorrows and fears of war was not the only motive for staging such productions. Especially as few soldiers were ever paid their combat salaries on time or supplied with sufficient rations, it is an all the more impressive display of charity that the box-office receipts were often contributed to a worthy cause:

They are getting up in the brigade a regular theater, for the amusement and pleasure of the mind, having already one in the division . . . and the most striking feature about it is that money which they accumulate is contributed for the benefit of the sick and wounded soldiers in the army, and is attended by some of our most prominent generals.[19]

Dramatic presentations were not the only performance-based entertainments enjoyed by Civil War soldiers. Both Union and Confederate troops were also entertained by compatriots who participated in glee clubs, debate societies, magic shows, lectures, and improvised circus performances. A frequent and popular diversion was instrumental shows put on by regimental bands. Occasionally bands would move through a camp to play for particular officers or into towns, where local citizens could view their performances.

Philip Cheek of Company A in the Sixth Wisconsin Regiment recalled a unique gathering of bands that occurred while the Sauk County Riflemen were camped on the banks of the Rappahannock River near Fredericksburg, Virginia:

One of the nicest things that occurred while in the service took place here. It was a beautiful moonlit night, the evening was warm and balmy and as the evening shadows fell after dress parade, our bands played our national airs and then war songs, including Yankee Doodle, Star Spangled Banner, etc. Alternating would come from the rebel side of the river their songs, including Dixie and The Bonnie Blue Flag. Winding up this duel of bands by both sides playing "Home Sweet Home." Both armies joined and sang that grand old piece together and when the great hush fell over, methinks if you could have seen them all at that time, you would have noticed that there was a tear for the old homes on their sturdy cheeks.[20]

The Party Circuit

Precisely to prevent soldiers' dwelling upon melancholy thoughts of home, other kinds of diversionary entertainments were organized by the military command to be enjoyed in the camps. The purpose of these activities was to raise the spirits of the men by offering them food, drink, and, most especially, a situation that imitated a normal social setting as much as possible. St. Clair Mulholland, a member of the 116th Pennsylvania Volunteers, attended a picnic held for officers on Saint Patrick's Day, 1863:

> It was one o'clock when General Meagher announced that all further operations would be postponed for half an hour, and invited the ladies, the generals present, and staffs, to a collation, prepared and awaiting destruction at his quarters, and thither the goodly company proceeded. In front of the quarters two Sibley tents had been pitched, separated by a space of ten yards, which space was enclosed by an awning. In and under these the guests thronged. Mountains of sandwiches disappeared, no doubt filling up those voids which nature is said to abhor. With the precision and promptitude of file-firing, pop, pop, went explosions that preceded copious draughts of rich wines. In and out, in fact everywhere, went the attentive officers of the brigade, attending to their visitors. What attracted most attention however and gratified every appreciative palate were potations of spiced whiskey punch, ladled by Captain Hogan, the Ganymede of the occasion, from an enormous bowl, holding not much less than thirty gallons.[21]

When their regiments were camped near population centers, soldiers took advantage of the various entertainment opportunities the cities and towns offered. Attending balls and visiting with local women was a favorite pastime—and often led to a soldier being punished for missing the evening curfew. Still, most men thought the penalty worth it if their homesickness and boredom were relieved momentarily:

> Though it may cause a laceration of the feeling of the tax-payers, and old Abe may shake his head disapprovingly, yet it be known that in Corinth balls are gotten up, balls are attended, and dancing progresses night after night in the "wee sma' hours of the morning." Much to the chagrin of those lovers of the Terpsichore, who, on returning to camp, find themselves detailed for picket duty for the ensuing 24 hours. The lat-

est and best ball of the season here occurred last Tuesday evening, being given under the direction of the military authorities, in commemoration of the anniversary of the battle of Shiloh; it was well gotten up, and, together with the supper, passed off very pleasantly. Another military ball, under the auspices of the officers of the Ohio Brigade, is on the tapis, and promises to be a fine affair.

It is only by thus methodically annihilating time, that we can dispel the home thoughts which are ever crowding our minds, giving us the blues to such an extent as to make us feel decidedly uncomfortable.[22]

Enlisted men did not always enjoy the same entitlements as officers and at times had to resort to improvisation if they wanted to partake in a celebration—or the company of women:

Now we were all talking about how we should celebrate "Mardi Gras" for we did not mean to let the carnival go by without paying it due respect; it would remind us of home, if such reminder were necessary.

It was determined that we should give a grand fancy and masked ball, a grand supper, and such other "Divertisments" as the occasion demanded. . . . [T]he day at last came, and, in spite of short rations and of cold, the ball was given, and never did more gayety prevail in any assembly, whether under the "gilded panels of a "palace" or the "Green foliage of a kingly park." Ladies impersonated by our youngest fellows, and showing right pretty arms and necks, were there with their girlish chat and their coquettish flirtations: and under improvised masks and dominos one might believe they were the genuine article. . . . Corporal Bob Many was so pretty and girlish with his plump neck and rounded arms that he was voted the "belle of the ball" and had a train of admirers following him the whole evening. The boys actually wanted to hug him, but the floor committee wouldn't permit such infractions.[23]

Similarly, when soldiers went home on furloughs, they pursued pleasure and fun with great energy. The women who waited for them at home understood their needs. They made sure that the soldiers' time away from the battle front or military camp was busy and filled with a holiday spirit, as recounted by Ellen S. Elmore of Columbia, South Carolina:

Sad as these days were, taken as a whole there were plenty of happy hours. Concerts, fairs, and bazaars gave relief from the strain upon our hearts and brains, and when our soldier boys came on furlough and wanted to dance and sing, who of us would refuse to do their bidding, even though there were some croakers who talked about the sin and shame of such proceedings when calamity was so near. My good wise mother was of a different mind, and opened her hospitable doors to all the social calls of the situation.[24]

Sports

As popular as music, theatrical presentations, and social gatherings were, there were still other activities that were of equal importance to the morale of the Civil War soldier. Most prominent among these were sports and athletic competitions. Sports, it was believed, contributed greatly to the physical and mental health of the troops, keeping the men in shape, happy, competitive, and fostering a sense of team spirit among the many companies and regiments. In order to encourage officers to organize athletic competitions, the U.S. Sanitary Commission performed a study on the benefits of such vigorous communal activities and noted the declining character of the regiments lacking such options:

> In 42 regiments systematic athletic recreations: football, baseball, &c were general. In 156 there were none. . . . [W]hen there are none, card playing and the other indoor games generally take their place. There is some evidence of serious mischief from gambling. Sharpers are believed to have enlisted for the purpose of making money as professional gamblers.[25]

The passion for athletic activity was held equally by the rebel armies. Although the Confederate men did not have an organization such as the sanitary commission to formally recommend that they participate in sports, the soldiers did so instinctively. During some quiet periods of the war, games became the focus of their lives and created an atmosphere very different from what they might have expected. Lieutenant Richard Lewis wrote home to his mother about the environment of a camp established near Fredericksburg in January 1863:

> All the boys appear to be perfectly delighted that they have remained so long undisturbed and are to pass off the monotony of camp life in all kinds of sports and pleasures. It reminds me very much of my school boy days.[26]

Among the best-liked sports was baseball. Although still in its formative stages as a game, baseball was well enough known that it could cross the regional boundaries that might have separated regiments and bring them together. Those who were unfamiliar with the game quickly caught on, and it was played frequently and with passion. Wherever and whenever possible, soldiers picked up a bat—or a near facsimile, such as a fence post—and attempted to leave the horrors of the battlefield and the stupefying boredom of camp life behind:

> Since the ground has become dry, many are the amusements. After the drilling is over, towards evening, the wide level space in front of the camp is crowded with soldiers. Many are playing ball. The most expert choose up, and one is to keep tally; now they strip off coats and sweating and eager as to the result, push on the lively game.[27]

The game played by Civil War soldiers was substantially different from baseball as we know it today. For the most part, they soldiers chose between two versions of the game: the New York and Massachusetts. Although the New York game would go on to be more popular among civilians and eventually evolve into modern baseball, the rank-and-file troops of both sides preferred the Massachusetts rules.

Also known as "townball," the Massachusetts approach to baseball employed teams of up to fifteen men defending a square infield. Bases were located at each of the four corners. In lieu of flat bases, wooden sticks would be driven into the ground to take their place. Instead of standing at a home plate, the batter would stand between fourth and first base and run around the infield, as we do today, in a counterclockwise direction. Pitchers threw overhand, there was no such thing as a foul ball, and an inning had only one out per side. If three missed pitches were caught, the batter would be out. A fly ball, if caught, was an out. Fielders attempted to throw out a runner by hitting him with their throw. Finally, there was no nine-inning limit to the game. Instead, the team that reached a previously agreed-upon number of runs would be the winner. During the Civil War, baseball was an offensively minded game, and the scores were more suggestive of those of modern football than what one would expect to witness on the diamond today:

> On the 12th of March we had a game of baseball with some of the 104th N.Y. Regiment. As opportunities for indulging our love of this pastime were not very frequent, we got a great deal of pleasure out of it. Score: 10th N.Y.—20, 13th Massachusetts—62.[28]

The skills that are treasured in modern baseball were sometimes a liability for the Civil War athlete. Strong pitchers, the foundation of today's championship teams, were in some cases unwelcome and were invited to leave the game, as one Confederate hurler discovered:

> As card playing was prohibited in camp, and the boys had to do something to amuse themselves, a mass meeting was called to provide means, ways and [indecipherable], and [indecipherable]. After much discussion and flaming oratory, they decided on Base Ball. A ball was soon improvised, some of the boys giving their yarn sox for the purpose, and the game commenced, the entire mob joining in, except the Captain, who owing to the great dignity of his office, refrained from participating in the sport, well we have had some boss players. The game got to be all the rage, for there was nothing else to rage, the game did not run very long, until Frank Ezell was ruled out, he could throw harder and straighter than any man in the company, he came very near knocking the stuffing out of three or four of the boys, and the boys swore they would not play with him so he was laid off.[29]

Although gambling was officially frowned upon in the context of card playing and other "vices," money was often wagered on ball games. Officers who feared the moral corruption of their men were assuaged by the improvement of morale fostered by friendly competition and the communal spirit that followed:

> While in at Falmouth [Virginia] the baseball fever broke out. It was the old fashioned game, where a man running the bases must be hit by the ball to be declared out. It started with the men, then the officers began to play, and finally the 19th [Mass.] challenged the 7th Mich. to play for sixty dollars a side. Capt. Hume and myself were the committee of our regiment in the brigade. The game was played and witnessed by nearly all of our division, and the 19th won. The $120 was spent for supper, both clubs being present with our committee as guests. It was a grand time and all agreed that it was more fun to play base than minnie ball.[30]

Less prevalent but the forerunner of contemporary baseball, the New York version introduced the diamond-shaped infield with three bases leading to home plate. Although pitchers threw underhand, the New York game instituted the concept of foul balls and eliminated the goal of hitting the runner to make an out. For the first time, an inning was defined by three outs, and the length of a game was determined by a number of outs instead of runs.[31]

In its early days as "America's game," baseball demonstrated an unusually strong hold on the attention of both Confederate and Union men. Officers who might have been expected to be insistent on the need for their men to display their drilling skills surprised their underlings by giving different orders. In late January 1864, one member of Rhode Island's Light Artillery battery recalled:

> We had a fine game of ball in honor of General Hays, who had sent to Washington for balls and bats to enable us to play to good advantage. When the general and his wife came galloping into camp, with a number of officers and ladies, our Captain went out to greet them and said, "Oh, General, I suppose you would like to see the battery on drill." The general quickly replied, "No, I want to see them play ball, which they can do better than any men I ever saw."[32]

Legendary stories of baseball teams crossing picket lines and playing their enemies are widespread but not necessarily verifiable. As enemy soldiers did fraternize on numerous occasions for trade, gambling, and general socializing, it is not unreasonable to assume that such games were in fact played.

A game with a very different, less harmonious attitude was recorded by George Putnam (author of Civil War memoirs) to have taken place in Texas. During the course of the game, the Union ballplayers came under attack by Confederate troops:

> Suddenly there came a scattering of fire of which the three fielders caught the brunt . . . the center fielder was hit and was captured. The left and right field managed to get into our own lines.[33]

A prototypical version of modern football was another favored game and highly valued by the military command because it offered physical conditioning, distraction, and relaxation to soldiers suffering from the stresses of military service:

> We had a diversity of sports and recreations; in fact, our ingenuity was taxed to devise means for relaxation and enjoyment. We had a large ball, composed of rubber, from which we extracted much sport and merriment; with it we played the game of football. It caused a vast amount of fun

when some luckless fellow, full of earnestness, would launch forth his foot to kick the ball, but before his foot, though it went straight for the mark, could reach the desired object, the ball would be kicked away by feet more active than his own, and he would measure his length on the ground, to the infinite amusement of spectators. He found that kicking into vacancy, with all of his might, was attended with disaster, like the recoil of a gun when it is overcharged. It is apt to kick back and do injury. The merry laughs which often resulted from our rubber ball exercises, were loud enough to startle the natives.[34]

The commanders of both sides also believed that football had other beneficial effects on their men. In its violence, a vigorously played match was as close to actual combat as possible short of the real thing:

At two o'clock, the regiment turned out on the parade ground. The colonel procured a foot ball. Sides were arranged by the lieutenant colonel, and two or three royal games of foot ball—most manly of sports, and closest in its mimicry of actual warfare—were played. The lieutenant colonel, chaplain, and other officers mingled in the crowd; captains took rough-and-tumble overthrows from privates; shins were barked and ankles sprained; but all was given and taken in good part.[35]

Civil War football was quite different from the modern game and more closely resembled contemporary soccer. A ball would be thrown into a large crowd of players, and they would try to kick the ball down the field, eluding the opposing team, and, using their feet, get it across a goal line. Requiring little more than a flat, cleared plot of land upon which the soldiers could play, football was often a casually organized game that soldiers could play at whim:

"Come boys, let's have a little game of football," said a big fellow, and he walked out, a large football in his hand, to an extensive field adjacent. About 200 followed the proposer, which comprised the "little" game proposed. I was of the number. We were soon divided off, and stretched out in two opposing lines across the field; also the goals, which were the extreme ends of the field. Soon the ball was going—kick, bat, spang, and away it would go—now back, now forth—now to, now fro—hither and thither. At last it received an impetus that brought it near my end. Another like that and it would be out of the field—the game would be lost. I ran toward it and kick it back. At the same moment a powerful fellow of the opposite side ran for it. We are equal distances from it; I saw that he was running desperately, and I ran desperately. Our course lay at right angles. As we arrived within ten feet of the ball, we knew that all now depended on a single desperate effort. Simultaneously, we made that desperate effort. We both reached it at once, coming together with a force that sent me sprawling at quite remote distance from the ball. At the same time, the collision so staggered my opponent, that after all, one of my comrades succeeded in reaching and kicking it first; which he did, sending it a hundred paces from immediate danger. The game was not yet lost. It grew more desperate. The ball seemed to be struck alternately by someone of each side every second, so it was kept spinning backward and forward within a small sphere, in a manner truly delightful. The opposite side gained a momentary advantage; the ball was once more sent spinning almost to the goal, but it stopped right at my feet. It was decidedly useless for anyone to attempt to reach it now before I could kick it; all stood still. Now was an opportunity for me to both exhibit my prowess to the admiring crowd, and, at the same time, do much for our side of the game. Now, I would last show them how to kick a ball—how to send it the whole length of the field. I poised myself on my left, swung my right foot backward, drew a long breath, and executed a kick that a mule might have delighted in. But, oh, horror! I aimed too low, and my unfortunate toes came in sheer contact with a rough root which protruded from the ground.[36]

Another immensely popular activity for the soldiers of both sides was boxing. Boxing had the advantage of requiring not many participants and little in the way of equipment, as the contests were most commonly fought with bare fists. On the occasions when gloves were used, the contestants often had more trouble dealing with the unfamiliar gear than with their opponents:

A crowd was collected around two pugilists who, with boxing gloves to protect their knuckles and prevent them from being barked against each other's faces, were batting away at each other's heads most delightfully. It was amusing to hear the cheer and plaudits of the Crowd. When the pair of novices got tired—and it wasn't long until they did—another couple tried it, making, as usual, many ludicrous motions, and calling forth peal on peal of laughter . . . after quite a number of them had tried it to their satisfaction, the gloves were thrown down and none seemed to try it any more.[37]

Unplanned boxing matches occurred frequently as a way of settling arguments among the soldiers and might be held in a field near a company's tents or even on the streets between their tents. Soldiers of both nations may have fought side by side against their regimental compatriots when in battle, but they also fought regularly among themselves:

> Occasionally there was a downright fist fight, the result of some quarrel. It was not considered the thing at any time in the 27th to part two men at all equally matched, until one or the other said "enough." In fact it was not safe to quarrel unless one wanted to fight. A ring was often formed, with the two quarrelling fellows inside, and they were almost compelled to knock it out or quit quarrelling.[38]

Organized boxing events had enormous audiences and were always heavily promoted. Large amounts of money were often wagered on the fights, and even the officers approached these extravaganzas with a sense of ceremony, creating a festive atmosphere:

> Pat informed me that a prize fight was on between Charley Austin, of the Vermont Brigade, and a man named Purcell, from one of the Pennsylvania Regiments in Wheaton's Brigade, catch-weight, for a purse of $500, made up by subscription. Austin belonged, I think to the First Vermont Heavy, though he had sailed two or three whaling voyages out of New Bedford. Purcell was a Pittsburgh iron molder, and my recollection is that he was from Col. Jim Patchell's 102nd Pennsylvania.
>
> The Rhode Islanders pitched the ring on a small level plot of ground near Rock Creek, a short distance from Blagden's old mill, and Austin and Purcell 'shied their castors a little before noon the last Sunday in July 1864.
>
> The referee was Serg't Wilcox, of one of the batteries. Nearly 1,000 spectators were at the ring side, among whom were several officers, who, in parade uniform, would have worn eagles on their shoulder straps and one who was entitled to wear a star.
>
> At this time they had been fighting 38 minutes by my watch. When they came up for the 12 round Austin led for Purcell's heart, but was cleverly countered on the chin and barely escaped a knockdown. But Wilcox said: The men will observe time. The fight is under London rules, and I am here to see that carried out. I decide that Mr. Austin has lost the fight

by a foul. I am capable of enforcing that decision. The fight is ended. If the principals agree to it, side bets may be declared off, but the fight must stop here.[39]

Athletic Events

More involved sporting events were often held during holidays, when a break from the normal routine offered the opportunity to enlist judges, give awards, and even create ceremony. Horse racing and jumping were favored activities and also served the purpose of keeping riders and animals in top condition. On Saint Patrick's Day, 1863, the 116th Pennsylvania Volunteers advertised the running of a "Grand Irish Steeple Chase":

> To come off the 17th of March, rain or shine, by horses the property of, and to be ridden by, commissioned officers of that brigade. The prizes are a purse of $500; second horse to save his stakes; 2½ mile heat, best two in three, over four hurdles four and a half feet high, and five ditch fences including two artificial rivers fifteen feet wide and six deep; hurdles to be made of forest pine and braced with hoop.[40]

Irish-born soldiers and descendants of earlier Irish immigrants were reputed to be the best horse jumpers of all.

Despite the terrible risk of injury and even the loss of horses, these soldiers entertained their compatriots and enjoyed the glory that grew in response to their fearlessness:

> General Meagher, wishing to keep up the spirits of his men, organized a steeplechase and a mule race and numerous prizes were offered. . . . The preparations are made by building a hedge or brush fences, digging ditches six to eight feet wide, etc. . . . The gentlemen (in this case officers exclusively), mounted in jockey dress, ride over the round, and jump the fences and ditches they come to. Six, perhaps as many as eight, enter the contest and go abreast. As the jumping is very hazardous, it becomes exceedingly exciting. . . . It was certainly a great novelty to many of us, who born in the states had never before seen such recreation, which must unquestionably have been the invention of wild Irishmen, who did not know what fear is. It was an or-

dinary occurrence to see men with dislocated arms, broken shoulder blades and black eyes; and, in some cases the horses were killed outright or disabled so that they were shot to put them out of pain.[41]

When time and living conditions permitted, sporting events sometimes evolved into something more elaborate that involved pageantry. Tournaments that evoked the chivalry and competition of the romantic past were performed by Confederate troops. Involving citizens from the community, they were more than simple competitions; in their own way, they were a kind of theatrical performance:

> I will describe as well as I can the grand Tournament and Coronation Ball given by the officers of the third Corps . . . the tournament was to have taken place on the 5th of this month and then the Ball was to have been given on the evening of the 6th at 7 o'clock in honor of the Queen of Love & Beauty and her Maids of Honor (of whom there were 4).
>
> Owing to the rain and bad weather it had to be postponed until last Monday and the Ball until last Tuesday evening. . . . Each Knight had to put in $30 a piece (and there were 30 Knights) and 50 Gentlemen subscribed $30 a piece for the privilege of attending the ball. The whole sum subscribed was $3,000, we sent the money to Richmond and foraged around in the surrounding country and got up a splendid Supper.
>
> All of the Knights having assembled, we proceeded to Register our names alphabetically and out of the 50 there were only 5 privates (myself among the number), we were to ride 5 times a piece (and all had sabres we had to first cut off a head on a post), next take a ring then cut a head on the ground and last off a bag of straw (about the size of a man's head) from a pole, on the point of your Sabre. The Knights having registered they were formed in a line and addressed by Gen. Davis. That being done we commenced writing Gen. Wright calling out their names alphabetically and we starting at the Sounding of the bugle. Each Knight had told who [what young lady] he was riding for and she would send him a Rosette to designate her Knight. I was riding for Miss Kate Willis, an elegant and accomplished young lady of Orange. . . .
>
> I mounted my Charger, the bugle sounded and I was off like the wind (for recollect we all had to ride at full speed). I took the first one, took the ring, cut off the lower head and took the last one making a clean through (and by far the best ride that had been made) amid the cheers of the whole crowd and waving of the Lady's handkerchiefs.[42]

A wide variety of races and contests would be offered at holiday times, mixing bona fide athletic challenges with more lighthearted activities. A New York volunteer infantryman recalled a spontaneous footrace in Falmouth, Virginia, at Christmastime 1862:

> Among other things, an impromptu foot-race was gotten up between the Fourth New York and our regiment. The former regiment, with which we are now brigaded, was from New York City, and its general make up was decidedly "Sporty." They had in their ranks specimens of all most kinds of sports such as professional boxers, wrestlers, fencers, and runners. One of the latter had been practising in the morning, and some of our boys remarked "that he wasn't much of a runner" whereupon they were promptly challenged to produce a man who could beat him, for a cash prize of $20 in gold. Win or lose, our fellows were not to be bluffed, and so promptly accepted the challenge. Back they came to camp with their "bluff," to look up a man to meet this professional. So far as our men were concerned, it was another case of the Philistine defying the armies of Israel. Where was our David? All hands entered into the fun, from the colonel down. The race was to be a 100 yard dash from a standing mark. We found our man in Corporal Riley Tanner, of Company I. He was a lithe, wiry fellow, a great favorite in his company, and in some trial sprints easily showed himself superior to all others. He, however, had never run a race except in boys' play, and was not up on the professional tactics of such a contest. It was decided that the affair should take place at 5:00 p.m. on our regimental front, and should decide the championship of the two regiments in this particular. The course was duly measured and staked off, and was lined on both sides by a solid wall of men, nearly one whole division being present, including most of the officers. If the championship of the world had been at stake, there could hardly have been more excitement, so much zest did everyone put into it. On the minute the Goliath of the bloody Fourth appeared, clad in the most approved racing garb. He was a stockily built young Irishman, and looked decidedly formidable, especially when our poor, little David appeared a moment later, with no other preparation than his coat and cap off and pants rolled up. Nevertheless, our boys thoroughly believed in him, and we all gave him a rousing cheer. The signal was given and away leaped our little champion like a frightened deer, literally running away from the professional from the start and beating him leisurely in the end by more than a dozen feet. Great was the furore which followed. The victor was

carried on the shoulders of his comrades of Company I triumphantly back to his quarters and afterwards through all the company streets, the victim of immense popularity.[43]

Not all victorious athletes were so much admired or financially rewarded. More often, the winner of a footrace might enjoy a measure of dignity and pride, but his prizes measured up unfavorably with that of the winner of a chase of a soaped pig: the man who caught and held the animal got to keep it:

> Another object of amusement was a slushed pig, with his tail shaved and greased, and which was turned loose to be caught by the slippery appendage. The men formed a circle with the pig placed inside, together with those who desired to have a hand or foot in the chase. The animal was very fat and could not run fast, but seemed to have little difficulty in eluding a capturing grasp. After being chased thus for some time the pig became weary and Sergeant Moore of Company E stepped up and caught him by the tail. Thus ended the pig chase, and Company E that night made a sumptuous dinner on the pig.[44]

Other more traditional contests included the throwing of ten- to fourteen-pound weights, jumping hurdles, and the tossing of quoits, a game similar to modern-day horseshoe pitching. Competitions designed to entertain the soldiers included blindfolded wheelbarrow races, three-legged races—"[T]he men were in pairs, with one leg of each man tied together, and the efforts made by each pair of men to get a progressive gait on by using the three legs was ridiculous"[45]—and sack races.

Among the less traditional contests were a challenge to determine who was a regiment's best dancer of Irish reels, jigs, and hornpipes and a sport called "ganderpulling." Ganderpulling involved suspending a goose from the limb of a tree and men galloping by on horseback, attempting to pluck the head off the unlucky bird.

Improvisation was an important skill for soldiers seeking diversion through sports as conditions were often not conducive to familiar organized games. Rhode Island's First Light Artillery created a competition called "Scratch a little":

> A stake was driven into the ground, then two men were tied, each by the left wrist, with a cord ten feet long. One had a stick cut with notches and a plain one, and he rubbed the two together making a noise. The other had an old stocking stuffed to pound with. Both were blindfolded

and placed at rope's length. When the game began one tried to find the other so as to pound him, while the other was trying to keep clear. Sometimes they were together listening to each other's movements. The German kept saying, "scratch a little; I see where you are." Sometimes they would be nearly touching. I thought there was more fun in it to look at than any game I ever saw. General Hays was in camp and saw us play ball; also saw the scratch game and was evidently pleased with both.[46]

For soldiers camping at a distance from other regiments and away from potential opponents, the simplest of games could provide fresh air, exercise, and, if nothing else, diversion from less wholesome activities:

It was a sign of a healthier state of morals as well as physics, when the men began to seek recreation in the open air in trials of physical strength . . . and when, in the exuberance of their spirits, a delinquent mess mate was placed on a blanket made taut by the grip of a score of hands, and bounded ten feet into the air, to come down again in the midst of the merry group, only to make a second and third involuntary flight—it was always more pleasant to hear the hearty laugh, over these rough out door camp sports, than to reflect that, for want of the spirit to engage in more manly recreation many were dissipating body and soul around the card table or the dice table.[47]

Wrestling and boxing were other popular sports and were enjoyed in both a casual, "pick-up" manner among friends and more formally. Wisconsin rifleman Philip Cheek recalled a novel match that he witnessed:

Boxing was in great vogue, and it was comical to see George Washington of another company, 6 ft. 6 in. tall, put on the gloves with Larry O'Neil, the little drummer, about 4 ft. in height.[48]

Epic Snowball Fights

While men's inclination to participate in various sporting activities seemed to be influenced by their social position—officers liked fencing and challenges to their horseback-riding skills, while enlisted men enjoyed rowdier contests—there were times when men from all ranks joined together in play. During the winter months, enlisted men engaged in snowball fights that were frequently fierce and involved entire regiments. The men took the mock warfare seriously, even to the point of taking prisoners and paroling them. In the early spring of 1864, it was reported by one Southern soldier that two men had actually been killed in playful combat.

The officers' corps saw the usefulness of snowball fighting on a large scale and sometimes provided strategy and leadership on the field. Not only did the colonels and generals enjoy themselves, but they used the massive snowball fights to experiment with strategy and to keep the men's battlefield skills sharp:

> Considerable snow fell that winter, and every time it snowed the soldiers would turn out and have snowball battles. One day our division challenged Rodes' Division to battle in a large field. They came out, and the battle raged with various success until towards evening, when a great many of our division got tired of it and went to camp. When Rodes' men saw our line weakened they brought up fresh troops and made a charge and ran us into our quarters. It looked rather bad for us to be defeated in that way, so some of the boys went to General Walker and got him to come out and take command.
>
> It was fun for Walker, so he mounted his horse, collected his staff, and sent conscript officers all over camp and forced the men out. We had signal corps at work, took our colors out in line, had the drummers and fifers beat the long roll, and had couriers carrying dispatches and everything done like in a regular engagement with the enemy. . . . .[W]hen General Walker got everything in readiness, and the line formed, he ordered us to charge up close to Rodes' men and then wheel and fall back, so as to draw them after us and away from the piles of snowballs they had made. When the drums beat we were to wheel again and charge them and run them over the hill and capture their snowballs. . . . At the same time the Louisiana brigade slipped around through the woods and struck them on the left flank, by surprise, and the rout was complete. . . . We captured several stands of colors. . . . [O]fficers would be captured and pulled off their horses and washed in the snow . . . but all took it in good part. After the fight was over we went out with a flag of truce and exchanged prisoners.[49]

Swimming Holes, Leapfrog, and Explosive Bowling Balls

Less competitive athletic events were also important opportunities for the men to keep fit, work off their frustrations and fears, and have some fun. When near a suitable river or lake, soldiers would dive in for a swim as soon as they were allowed to. For Northern troops marching through Southern territory, however, the water sometimes offered surprises that they would not have found back at home:

> No sooner was the coffee cooked than almost every man in the command was swimming about in the stream. The pleasure of the bath was much lessened by the enormous quantities of water snakes that infested the vicinity. After dark a group of officers were enjoying the welcome swim, their clothes piled on the shore, when someone cried out that he felt something moving around his feet. A match was lit and a sight met the bathers' eyes that horrified and amazed them. The whole strand was a mass of writhing, squirming serpents! Snakes of all sizes, short and long, thick and lean, in groups and tied in knots . . . snakes by the hundred, countless and innumerable. What a scramble for clothes before the match went out! What an embarrassing predicament when it did! . . . How everyone got back to camp with enough clothes to cover their nakedness is a mystery.[50]

Other less competitive pastimes included variations on games that in normal circumstances would have been the exclusive province of children. Either men were seeking comfort in the recreations of their youth, or the extreme monotony inspired them to play hopscotch and leapfrog.

Try as the men might to fill their off-duty hours with games they knew from home, they could not always do so. The challenges were various, including bad weather, lack of men to field a team, or topography that did not cooperate with their need for a level playing field. Still, facing long, empty hours, the men became more clever in adapting games to fit their circumstances or invented entirely new entertainments. "Hot jackets" was such a creation that involved soldiers attacking the opposition with hickory whips.[51]

More innovative and truly surreal were improvised bowling matches in which the men rolled explosive shells meant for the artillery, as Union soldier William H. Sallada remembered:

> Those of us who were posted in the game of ten pin . . . were anxious to invent some substitute for it. At length we discovered a plan that would work. A destructive implement of war, called a spherical case shell, weighing about twelve pounds, would answer for the required ball. Dangerous as they were a number of these were employed for the purpose. Alleys of the rudest formation were made and in a short time we were up to

our eyes in this new play . . . we knew that a very slight cause might explode one of these engines of death with which we were playing carelessly, but lives were cheap in the army. . . . [O]n a certain occasion one of these ten pin shells filled with elements of destruction resented the violence with which it was handled, by bursting, suddenly & awfully. . . . [A] quick sulphurous flame shot from it, mingled with that appalling sound which is the signal of its disruption and then flying bullets and fragments of the parting shell, hurtled through the air.[52]

Hobbies, Seeing the Sights, and Entrepreneurs

Despite all the energy devoted to sports, theatricals, and music, the Civil War soldiers still faced the tedium of several long years away from home. Needing relief, they continued to seek out other forms of diversion. Many regiments organized their own newspapers or took over established journals in the towns they were occupying. Publications such as *The Zouave Gazette, Missouri Army Argus, The Rebel Banner, The Camp Hudson Times,* and *The Waltonville War Cry* reported on stories of interest to the soldiers and editorialized in favor of their respective political positions.[53] Many men whiled away the long hours by writing letters home to friends and family (see Chapter 8). Others would leave camp to hunt or fish.

Excursions into cities and towns near military camps offered the soldiers a chance to enjoy a taste of civilian life and, if appropriate, even do a little sightseeing. Nineteen-year-old E. F. Palmer enjoyed his first look at the nation's capital:

> The streets are patrolled by soldiers but no one asked for our pass. Two hours at the patent office, two hours at the Smithsonian Institute, a glance at the President's House, a stroll through the spacious capital.[54]

Few soldiers were as earnest a tourist as the young Vermonter. A trip to town provided a variety of diversions, including theaters, bordellos, museums, stores, and restaurants. Although the therapeutic value of a visit to a brothel should not be underestimated, to the way of thinking of a Civil War soldier a simple change from normal rations was quite welcome and certainly a safer way to spend time.

The Oriental Restaurant in Richmond, the Confederate capital, offered meals at prices listed in rebel dollars, although customers paid with English sovereigns. Soup was $1.50 a plate. Turkey or chicken cost $3.50. Rockfish cost $5.00. Roast beef or pork was served for $3.00. Ham and eggs could be purchased for $3.50. A dozen fried oysters cost $5.00. A glass of fresh milk was $2.00. A bottle of champagne cost $50.00. A pitcher of ale cost $12.00. The only item that was offered at a price that might be familiar to restaurantgoers today was a cup of coffee for $3.00. Considering that most volunteers made less than $40.00 a month, a meal on the town was quite an extravagance.

New technological innovations such as photography appealed to the soldiers, and while visiting local cities they spent many hours prepping their uniforms and posing. Traveling photographers also migrated between camps looking for customers, and the men would wait in line for hours for their turn:

> Artists—picture takers—positively coin money, if that expression is permissible in this age of "Greenbacks." It is true that they suffered a fearful probation, while the Paymasters were yet a great way off. But no sooner had the first Regiment been supplied with their "spondoolux"

Wagons of Samuel Cooley, an entrepreneur photographer who maintained a studio in Beaufort, South Carolina. He made a very good living taking pictures of the Union troops that occupied that part of the South for most of the war.

than their studios were thronged with officers and soldiers in full uniform and armed to have the magic sunshine fix their lineaments for the benefit of "Friends at Home." Day after day, the busy artists are engaged to the full extent of their abilities, and then are obliged to turn many away. Cartes de visite are furnished at the moderate cost of six dollars per dozen, or four dollars per half dozen—such as Brady or Anthony would ask two dollars per dozen for. Common ambrotypes that in New York cost 25 cents, are put up in Corinth for one dollar and fifty cents. Cases sell proportionately high.[55]

Pursuing pleasurable activities was only one way men spent their free time. Some took advantage of the empty hours to improve their lot or make money. Georgian soldier William White wrote to a friend of his, proposing to set up a sutler's business in which he would be a partner:

> Friend Thomas . . . First, I want to know if you are engaged in any permanent business. If not, if you desire to make money, I shall put you on the road to a small fortune to be gained in a short time. I propose for you to come here, buy a one horse vehicle and peddle in the army on just such produce as may be secured in the country. In that way you may realize from $100 to $200 a day. . . . [I]f you can raise $100 that will be sufficient, as I can furnish $300 and I consider $400 an ample sum to commence with. I am anxious for you to come as I wish to be your partner and divide the profits with you. . . . Everything that is brought into camp finds very ready sale. I have several times made $10 a day by buying and selling apples and that, too, when I had to pay around $70 a barrel for apples. If you can accede to my proposition and wish to enter into a co-partnership of that kind, let me know immediately.[56]

At holiday times, when the normal daily camp routine was suspended, some men left camp to wander through the countryside, appreciating its beauty, relaxing, and attempting to understand the local customs and people. James Sawyer wrote home to his parents in Connecticut about how he had spent Christmas 1862:

> I will tell you how we spent Christmas in Maryland. . . . Christmas in this part of the country is as great a day as Thanksgiving with us. . . . [W]e were excused from drill and had liberty to go where we pleased so

Gero. Bartlett of Woodstock and myself thought we would take a walk around the country. There is but few houses round here; and most of them are negro cabins. As we were travelling along through the woods we came to a nigger cabin and as we were passing an old woman came out and said "Christmas gift to you, gentlemen." Now around here when a person says that to you—you are expected to come and take something, a piece of cake, or glass of beer or anything they happen to have . . . if you refuse it is a sign of enmity. We went in and took some egg nog and sat and talked with the family. They consisted of two old women, a young man, a son of one of them, and a little girl. Everything in the room looked neat and tidy. We staid [sic] and talked with them about an hour. They thought a great deal of "Mass Lincoln" as they called him, and rejoiced the first of Jan was so near at hand [when the Emancipation Proclamation would take effect]. . . . [D]uring our rambles we were treated to quite a number of Christmas gifts; even the lowest and poorest people had a little something to give.[57]

Getting into Trouble

Nevertheless, it was impossible to fill all the hours of all the days, months, and years of a soldier's service. Men were inevitably confronted with idle time, and some handled it better than others. Unfortunately, there were those who did precisely what the command structure tried to steer them away from doing: getting into trouble (see Chapter 7) or simply wasting time with mischief.

Civil War soldiers engaged in a wide variety of tomfoolery, some activities completely harmless, others less so. A new arrival in a company was often the victim of tricks that tested his mettle or simply offered a good laugh. Sam Watkins recalled the joke of taking a new man "larking":

At this place we took Walter Hood out "A larking." The way to go "A larking" is this: Get an empty meal bag and about a dozen men and go to some dark forest or open field on some cold, dark, frosty or rainy night, about five miles from camp. Get someone who does not understand the game to hold the bag in as stooping and cramping a position as is possible, to keep perfectly still and quiet, and when he has got in the right fix, the others to go off to drive in the larks. As soon as they get out of sight, they break in a run and go back to camp, and go to sleep, leaving the poor fellow all the time holding the bag.[58]

Other practical jokes were tests of the officers' patience, played on them by usually good-natured enlisted men. At times, however, the gags strayed out of control:

> We extracted a good deal of fun at times; for instance, one night Captain Malloy was entertaining some officer friends in his tent about the time "taps out." They were feeling good, all standing, glasses lifted singing, or trying to sing, Benny Haven's Ho. About that time the tent ropes were all cut; the tent catches them in a mass and tent takes fire. Official dignity was gone, and the most unceremonious scramble took place.[59]

Alcohol often contributed to the more outrageous pranks. Confederate soldier Earle Lewis and his friends ran a risk of prison time and the anger of their associates for a binge during which they pretended to be members of the provost marshall's organization in January 1863:

> We had a terrible spree in camp one night during Christmas week. The boys nearly all getting drunk and kicking up a terrible hurrah! Earle Lewis, of my company, organized a so called Provost Guard, and, after I lay down that night, slipped my sword and uniform out of my tent and doffed himself with it, and went around to different stations that night, where he knew some of the men in the Virginia Brigades had whiskey to sell, and captured it and brought it into camp that night, under pretense that he was a Provost Guard from Longstreet's headquarters, arresting the men, but turning them loose, all being glad to get at liberty rather than go, as they thought, to headquarters.[60]

As the military commanders feared, some bored soldiers engaged in practical jokes that were cruel, racist, and dangerous:

> Today some of the 6th Iowa filled an oyster can half full of powder, set a slow train to it and planted it in the ground. They then set a cracker box over it and got a negro to dancing on the box. A coal was then touched to the train and the nigger was blown full 20 feet. He landed, fortunately, without injury, but so badly scared he was crazy for an hour.[61]

More alarming to the military authorities than the occasional knavery that veered out of control was the pervasive addiction of soldiers to gambling. Although technically prohibited, gambling may have been second only to food gathering in the hearts and minds of the Civil War troops. Gambling was good entertainment, took up a lot of time, and offered the hope that a poor soldier could make an instant "fortune."

Most common were card games, and in the military camps soldiers could be found playing endless matches of blackjack, poker, keno, and euchre. When the men did not have enough money to bet with, they used substitutes: rations, liquor, magazines, or whatever else was of value to them. Other traditional wagering contests included chuck-a-luck, faro, and raffling games in which soldiers bought tickets on the chance of winning a variety of items.

Confronted by an endlessly repetitive routine, the soldiers eventually found that even their diversions became boring. Seeking new and more interesting pursuits with which to entertain themselves, they began to engage in less conventional pastimes. They bet on children's games, such as marble shooting. Some built toy boats, launched them into bodies of water, and gambled on which would cross a finish line first. Others staked their money on cockfighting, and some soldiers, absent the luxury of using birds for sport, turned to other less valuable creatures for diversion:

> The boys would frequently have a louse race. There was one fellow who was winning all the money; his lice would run quicker and crawl faster than anybody's lice. We could not understand it. If some fellow happened to catch a fierce looking louse, he would call on Dornin for a race. Dornin would come and always win the stake. The lice were placed in plates—this was the race course—and the first that crawled off the plate was the winner. At last we found out Dornin's trick; he always heated his plate.[62]

Spiritual Solace

Trapped as the Civil War soldiers were in an environment of surreal contrasts—a mixture of daily horrors and tedium—it was natural for them to distract themselves to escape reality. There were times, however, when no amount of game playing or entertainment could provide deliverance. At moments such as these, many men turned away from the real world and sought solace in the spiritual realm.

The troops' attitude toward religion during the war was generally inconsistent. In a reflection of societies both past and present, some soldiers and regiments pursued a religious life, while others ignored it completely. Far from the social influences of home, threatened with death by bullet or disease every day, and exposed to the corruptions of more worldly compatriots, many Civil War soldiers' behavior was altered, as soldier H. H. Penniman noted:

> War is a dreadful evil and the army is a school of bad morals, about nine tenths of the troops entering the army irreligious become worse and worse. A great crowd of men without the restraints of society and no influence from women become very vulgar in language, coarse in their jokes, impious and almost blasphemous in their profanity. . . . [I]t is dreadful to see how much worse a mess or squad will become after one of their number is killed . . . to pass away time, to play cards, to drink, to eat, to run around, to do anything that will hinder the serious thoughts of eternity. . . . Sabbaths come and go unheeded.[63]

Religious activities were not always encouraged by the military command. Regiments' attitudes toward religion often mirrored the sentiments of their leaders; some preferred not to have preachers among their men and made it difficult for soldiers to attend services:

> Sergeant John Whipple wants to go to church but needs 3 signatures. If not back by 4 pm he may be arrested by the Provost Guard and jailed over night. Without a good excuse, I might hear at the next dress parade something like the following: Sergeant Whipple of Co. I for unsoldier like conduct on the 26th of April 1863 is hereby reduced to the ranks . . ." He went to a black church and found "150 members . . . all dressed decently and fashionably."[64]

While some military leaders were religious men and required their regiments to be equally so, a number of military leaders embraced religion as a means of protecting their soldiers from moral decline. Both the Union and Confederate armies had a Christian Commission, or charitable organization, that contributed money for Bibles, revival meetings, and religious reading material. The purpose of organizing such events and distributing Christian articles was to discourage soldiers from participating in any number of sins, most notably drinking, gambling, stealing, and swearing. A great many men ignored the religious lectures, but others found comfort in the words and rituals that were familiar from home. In the 1860s, the church played a prominent role in the lives of ordinary Americans, and after having been catapulted into a chaotic

Religious services dispelled for a while the dread and hardships of earthly activities; they were a kind of safe harbor that weary soldiers could look forward to.

world of violence, scores of soldiers—Edward Boots, among them—sought re-assurance in Christianity:

Plymouth, North Carolina. September 8th

Dear Mother. . . . We have been having preaching every night for some days by McGraves, an agent of the Christian Commission. He is a pretty good old fashioned preacher. It is a great pleasure to listen to an old fashioned sermon once more. We have a Bible class that meets every Sabbath. I have attended several times & have found it very pleasant. The teacher is a Sergeant of the Artillery. Last Sabbath a boy came into class that I had never seen before. Last night he was at church, after ser-vice he came up to me & introduced himself saying that he wished to be-come acquainted with me. He said that he belonged to the cavalry & that they were such a wicked set that he had no pleasure with them. . . . [H]is is a hard lot for the cavalry are a terribly rough set.[65]

Religion was also an important part of preparing for battle, and ministers urged their flock to do their duty. Facing death, soldiers found comfort in the promise of Heaven and courage in the reminder of their righteousness:

Sunday August 3, 1861

Wrote my wife early in the morning then went to church with the General to hear Reverend Dr. Stiles preach, in the camp of Lawton's Brigade of Georgians, in the woods a mile from our camp. The text was "Show thyself a man." . . . He prayed that there might be no straggling when we again went forth to battle, and said, "O Lord, when we go out again to fight give us the biggest kind of victory." The old man was eloquent and his voice thrilled like a trumpet and perspiration rolled down his face.[66]

Aware that religion could be used to bolster the spirits of his patients and staff, Dr. John Perry of Massachusetts encouraged those under his care to participate in the singing of religious hymns:

June 15th, 1862

This afternoon I collected all my convalescents in the kitchen of the cottage, placed them about a blazing fire,—for it was chilly and raining hard outside,—and started the singing of Methodist hymns. The music caught like an epidemic, and soon from every side came doctors, nurses, patients, negroes, until we had a rousing chorus. All of them sang with their whole souls, each one asking for his favorite humn, and the concert ended with "Old Hundred." How I did enjoy that![67]

As the war progressed and the soldiers were exposed to continuing hardships, tragedy, and loneliness, their religious sensibility grew even stronger. As Rhode Islander Elisha Rhodes noted, the soldiers around him began to pursue religious activities even when the formal guidance of ministers was not available:

Camp Near Warrenton, VA. September 6, 1863

We are having considerable religious interest in our regiment, and I pray God that it may continue. Soldiers are not the worst men in the world but they are very careless in regard to matters of religion. We have had no Chaplain for many months and consequently no regular services. Our last chaplain never did any good in the regiment. . . . About three weeks ago three of our men who are Christians attended a religious meeting at one of the camps. . . . On the way home they kneeled down in the woods and prayed that God bless our Regiment. The next week six of them met for prayer, and last week about 30 were present. Tonight I was invited to join them. I accepted and made an address. About 50 men were present at first but they soon began to come into the grove and soon nearly every officer and man of our Regiment was listening to the service. I never saw such a prayer meeting and I know the Spirit of the Lord was with us.[68]

The religious urge was especially intense among the soldiers of the Confederacy. During the last years of the war religious tent revivals were held that offered prayers, songs, sermons, professions of religious awakening, and baptisms. They were attended by tens of thousands of soldiers at a time.

Southern officer Jedediah Hotchkiss recalled the seriousness with which his regiment observed a day of fasting and spiritual reflection in his diary:

Friday March 27th 1863
    There was a heavy white frost and the sun came up clear and bright and we had a glorious day; warm and pleasant. This was the day appointed for fasting and prayer and it has been well obeyed in the army;— a Sabbath, a peace Sabbath, quietness has prevailed and worship has in almost every camp, over 50 sermons were preached in our Corps. Dr. Lacy preached at Hd. Qrs. to a good audience,—from Matthew 21st, 44th. An excellent sermon on national responsibility to God;—he read, in connection to the 20th and 23rd Psalms. We had prayer by General J. in the morning at 8, and in the p.m. at 5 we had prayer meeting. May much good come to us, O Lord, from our united prayers this day. I wrote to my wife and daughter in the evening.[69]

Union soldier David Close enjoyed a similarly pious atmosphere among his company of Ohio volunteers:

Camp McCook Cumberland Maryland November the 4th Ad 1862
    Dear Aunt and Uncle. . . . We have a remarkable civil and religious company. There is scarcely any wicked or profane persons among us. We can go to church every Sunday for our chaplain always preaches two sermons on that day. We have also prayer meeting every night in our tents. I attend them regular and I think that they tend to keep a young man from falling into bad company. And I think it is a providential circumstance that I enlisted in this company for I hear that there is a desperate sight of wickedness in the very regiments that I came so near enlisting in.[70]

On occasion the diligent pursuit of religious services by military men led to unexpected results and behavior that was distinctly not spiritual:

> On Sunday while at Fredericksburg the company got permission to go to church. Having come off Sunday morning inspection we presented a very neat appearance. The church was filled with soldiers and citizens. They hesitated to pass the contribution box but were quietly informed we wanted to participate in that part of the service and we did. When it came to the place in the prayer where you all pray for the President of the United States and all having authority over us, the Parson announced, "We will now join in silent prayer." After the service was over we appointed a committee to wait on the parson and told him we would be there next Sunday and that if he failed to pray for the President and others according to ritual audibly we would burn the church.[71]

Then, as now, Christmas was one of the highlights of the religious calendar and was celebrated with good cheer by the soldiers of both armies. Amid the death and destruction, even men who were not religious could find peace and hope on this holiest of Christian days. On Christmas Day, fighting stopped, the normal routine of drilling was suspended, and men contemplated issues greater than themselves. Even those who were not interested in spiritual refreshment enjoyed the pleasures of a day of rest and the spirit of giving, as Union trooper St. Clair Mulholland recalled:

> Christmas Day 1862 was celebrated in the camp, many boxes of good things from home were received, and shared by the recipients with comrades less fortunate. Some of the boys were a little homesick, to be sure, but enough were sufficiently light of heart to drive dull care away. A large Christmas tree was erected in the centre of the camp, and peals of laughter and much merriment greeted the unique decorations, tin cups, hardtack, pieces of pork and other odd articles being hung on the branches. At night the camp fire roared and blazed, the stars shone above the tall pines, the canteen passed around and care banished for the hour.[72]

Secret Societies

Organized religion was one way in which soldiers pursued spiritual or communal reassurance. In addition, secret societies such as the Masons thrived during the course of the war as men who found their experiences to be dehumanizing tried to bring dignity and order into their lives. In a war that pitted neighbors, brothers, and relatives against one another, some organized secret societies dedicated to a peace that transcended nationality. A wary report from an intelligence operative to Confederate General Braxton Bragg in 1864 described a secret society that he believed was undermining the resolve of the army:

> General: I returned yesterday from my tour of investigation as to the secret treasonable society alleged to exist in this state [Alabama]. . . . I am satisfied that the society embraces more than half the adult males of Randolph, Coosa, and Tallapoosa Counties . . . it extends into portions of Georgia . . . the society is nameless . . . its designation is the Peace Society. No records are kept. Each initiate is an independent, dissevered link in a perfect chain. He is told by his eminents who are his associates or brethren, but meets them at no "convocation" of the order. You prove one man to be a member, but outside of his statements you have no other proof of other memberships. It is a society without officers, a community without members.
>
> But it is no less singular in its objects than its organization. Its obligation and its professed object, peace, are not objectionable but its real teachings are as varied as the communities or even the men to which they are imparted. If the initiate is an ignorant but pure man he is told that the object of the society is to procure an honorable peace; if disaffected as to the policy of the Government he is told that the aim is to procure a change of rulers; if a traitor, to produce mutiny among our soldiers, to destroy our loyal citizens, and to take the State back into the Union on any terms.[73]

Aside from whatever intentions may have been assigned to the Peace Society members, they concentrated a great deal of their energy on a complex system of greetings and signals with which they could maintain secret communication. For soldiers enduring the endless tedium of camp life, practicing and understanding ritual gestures and clandestine passwords must have absorbed many empty hours:

> The grip of the order is given by taking hold of the hand as usual in shaking hands, only the thumb is turned with the side instead of the ball to the back of the hand, when the following dialogue ensues, "What is that?" "A grip." "A grip of what?" "A constitutional peace grip" "Has it a

name?" "It has." "Will you give it to me?" "I did not receive it, neither can I so impart it." . . . [After agreeing to talk, they continue their coded conversation.] Then they spell the word peace by calling a letter alternately, beginning with any letter except the first. This is the password. The ordinary signs of recognition are given as follows: The party giving the sign takes up a stick or something of the kind in his hands, holding it in both in front of the body and carelessly throwing it to the right, using both hands. This is to be recognized by putting the right hand to the lock of the hair on the right side of the head as if pulling off something and throwing it to the right. . . . [T]he sign to be given by the soldier on the battlefield is by the soldier carrying his gun with the muzzle inclined to the right, or an officer carries his sword with the point inclined to the right, and if on horseback, with the hilt resting on the thigh. The sign of distress is given by extending the right hand horizontally and then bringing it down by three distinct motions, or, if the sign cannot be given, the words, "Oh Washington!" are substituted for it. An expression used as a means of recognition is, "I heard that the boys are all coming home."[74]

For all of the Civil War soldiers' efforts to distract themselves and escape the horrors of the battlefield through games, entertainments, religion, and other activities, ultimately, they were only stopgap measures. Despite the men's many temporary reprieves from the reality of the world provided by their diversions, when the fun was over they were still at war. They may have wanted desperately to believe otherwise, but there was no escaping the truth. Soldiers are transformed by their experiences, and not always for the better. No better example of such a decline in the human nature of a soldier can be found than an incident that occurred in a town called Petersburg and was recorded by Doctor John Perry. If most games and entertainments the Civil War soldiers participated in demonstrated a determination to survive, others illustrated how deeply cynical and hopeless many men were:

June 20th 1864
    Yesterday another brave officer, Lieutenant G——— of the Twentieth Regiment, was killed, and uselessly so. . . . [W]e had been fighting for several days in the most advanced trenches amidst persistent firing from both sides, which, however did little damage, except to prevent all rest and sleep. Finally both armies saw the folly of such warfare and desisted. Towards noon yesterday, weary, I suppose of the inaction, a Confederate

sharpshooter mounted his earthwork and challenged any one of our sharpshooters to single combat. Lieutenant G———, a fine fellow, standing at least six feet two in his stockings, accepted the challenge and they commenced what to them was sport. Life is cheap in this campaign! Both fired, and the Confederate dropped. G———'s great size was so unusual that this opponent had the advantage, and our men tried to make him give way to a smaller man. But no! He would not listen, became very excited as his successes multiplied and when darkness stopped the dueling he remained unscathed, while every opponent had fallen victim to his unerring aim.

The lieutenant was so exhilarated that he claimed with much bluster a charmed life; said nothing could kill him; that he could stand any amount of dueling, and this he could prove in the morning. . . . [W]e officers used every argument and entreaty to convince him of the foolhardiness . . . of such a course. He would not yield his determination, and when we left him was simply waiting, as best he could, for daylight to begin the dueling again. As we all foretold, he was finally killed.[75]

Chapter Four

Rations, Recipes, and the Ravenous

*F*or young men raised on the valorous wartime exploits of George Washington, Andrew Jackson, William Henry "Tippecanoe" Harrison, and Zachary Taylor, a soldier's life quickly proved itself to be something less exalted than what the men were hungering for. Romantic visions of battle and glory were quickly replaced by the reality of a numbingly repetitive schedule in camp, mixed unpredictably with spasms of violence and incoherent moments of terror, pain, and sadness.

Games and entertainments that were designed to ease their psychological burdens were effective but not completely so. With little variation in their suddenly regimented lives, the few pleasures of life the soldiers were allowed grew in importance to them. The acquisition of fundamentals, such as food—and its preparation, which may have been taken for granted amid the plenty and comfort of home—now became the focus of a tremendous expenditure of effort.

When the men were successful in finding something decent to eat and had the luxuries of time and supplemental provisions to help them prepare their meal with care, it was no small triumph. It was, in fact, a highlight in a trying existence that challenged them far beyond anything they had been led to expect. More commonly, however, the men made do with inadequate rations, for the availability and quality of food changed constantly and differed among armies, regiments, and companies, and even from campfire to campfire.

Both Confederate and Union soldiers would surely have disagreed with today's axiom "You are what you eat." For if this had been true in their case, they would have been abysmal soldiers and—more often than not—simply not around.

Yet there is some truth at the core of the adage as it applies to the Civil War. For if people are defined by what they look like, how they behave, their political views, their choice of friends, and other facets of their personality, they are

During the winter months, the men built log huts—the lucky ones next to the company kitchen.

certainly also defined by what they do. While the young men who enlisted in the Army of the Potomac or the Army of Northern Virginia did so in order to become warriors, they spent substantially more time trying to feed themselves than fighting. And while simple subsistence was often the order of the day, there was also a constant effort on the part of the men to improve the quality of what they ate. In this most optimistic of gestures, set against the backdrop of the squalid and despairing universe of war, the soldiers on both sides defiantly asserted their humanity and worth as individuals.

It had not been expected to be this way. This most fundamental responsibility of an army—feeding its soldiers well enough so they could fight—had not been expected to be such an overwhelming problem. The armies of Abraham Lincoln and Jefferson Davis both anticipated a swift victory. The Union leaders believed they could extinguish the secessionists' rebellion quickly, and the Confederates assumed that they could force the Union to accept a negotiated peace before the year was out. Accordingly, the North was confident it could feed its armies on battlefields that were close to home and within easy reach of its extensive railroad system. While the South had a less developed transportation infrastructure, its leaders concluded that it, as a primarily agricultural society, could grow enough food to feed its men in the short run.

Government bakeries slowly rose upon the landscapes of war like bread.

Unfortunately for the troops, the war was not over by New Year's 1862, and neither side would ever be able to produce a reliable supply system for the men in the field.

At the outset of hostilities, however, both the United States of America and the Confederate States of America implemented ambitious plans to feed their armies. A camp staple, as it has been for soldiers through the centuries, was fresh bread. Inexpensive, filling, portable, popular, and relatively good for the men, bread was intended to be a foundation of their diet. In what was then known as Washington City, in the Capitol building, which was still being constructed, underground rooms were transformed into bakeries that produced 16,000 loaves of bread every day. Impressive as that sounds, the Confederacy, which usually lost to the Union in regard to mass production, outproduced its protoindustrial neighbor to the north. In Petersburg, Virginia, rebel bakers built a facility that produced 123,000 loaves of bread in a twenty-four-hour period.

Come and Get It

In the early months of the war, plans called for a centrally organized commissary system. Camps had kitchens or mess tents, where regimental cooks would prepare meals that were served at specified hours. The soldiers would arrive at the kitchen with mess kits in hand, stand in long lines, and wait to be served.

While it is a time-honored tradition for soldiers to complain about their food—and plenty did during the Civil War—it was not unheard of for new recruits to be pleasantly surprised by the quality of Union cooking:

> Sunday. June 31, 1861.
> We are having a rain today. . . . [O]ur Sibley tents are very comfortable and we feel quite at home. We march to our meals up to the camp of the First Rhode Island where the food is cooked. We have excellent food and not at all as I thought it would be. If we take the field I guess there will be a change of diet. Plum pudding, gingerbread, and milk and other good things are served daily.[1]

As in everyday life, the rules did not apply to everyone, and there were privileged men who did not have to stand in line. Since many officers represented the elite of their hometowns—as it was considered the responsibility of these community leaders to organize local companies in the first place—some were not yet prepared to relinquish the finer points of life. C. W. Wills, who served in the Seventh Illinois Cavalry, noted in his diary that not only was he eating well but the presentation of his meals was more than satisfactory:

> Headquarters 7th Ill. Cav.
> The major, Seavy, Billy Resor and myself mess together. We have the wife of one of the men cooking for us and are living as well as I want to in regular home style. White table cloth, white ware and a fork and spoon for every man. Warm biscuits and excellent coffee every meal.[2]

But the presentation of meals was not a concern of most soldiers; their needs were more prosaic. Ominous signs appeared almost immediately, within the first weeks of war, of a breakdown of the supply system. The magnitude of the problems to come was intimated by the failure to feed troops in places inside Union borders—and even in the capital itself—that should never have posed a problem:

> Philadelphia
> Honorable Simon Cameron [Secretary of War under Lincoln]
> My dear sir:
> The great discomforts of the troops which I have witnessed in Washington caused me much reflection as to how it could be properly remedied. Here, too, we have constant and well founded complaints about the suffering and almost starvation of the troops. Many of them are literally

COMMISSARY DEPARTMENT, STONEMAN'S SWITCH.

The railroad system enabled the commissary to transport food in a timely manner to men who wondered sometimes when and where and how they were ever going to taste another meal.

beggars. At Harrisburg the soldiers, I hear, have been at times treated more like brutes than men, and this, too, when an abundance of army rations are at command. The great difficulty seems to be in distributing and serving the food properly.

John Tucker[3]

While failures in the distribution system were corrected to some degree in areas close to home, the changing nature of the war altered the commissary's protocol. As the armies of the South and North began to move across contested territories, it became less practical to rely on central mess tents. With men sometimes in camp, sometimes scattered across the landscape at posts they could not leave, it was more practical for soldiers to carry their own rations. Certainly, company kitchens were used throughout the war, but the majority of soldiers soon became responsible for much of their own cooking.

Often, this suited them just fine. Once the armies began to be mobile, the quality of the central mess tents' cooking declined and the men preferred to be responsible for their own victuals. The administrative officers found this to be an acceptable solution for they were now accountable only for the delivery of food, not for its preparation.

Every few days or so, various rations would be distributed to individuals. Small groups of men would take responsibility for their own meals and form their own "mess," often consisting of six to eight soldiers who had rotating responsibilities around the campfire.

Well into the war, however, there was a fundamental disconnection between the promised supply of food and what was actually delivered. The utopian ambitions did not even come close to the desperate reality. In 1862, the Commissary of Subsistence Volunteers published a cookbook by Captain James M. Sanderson that was distributed to the Union soldiers, offering "Culinary Hints for the Soldier." It included an introduction:

> No Army in the world is so well provided for in the shape of food, either as to quantity or quality, as the army of the United States and very little attention on the part of the cook will enable him to lay up a liberal amount weekly. To the credit of the company [indecipherable] no one man can consume his daily ration although many waste it.[4]

In a conversational tone not dissimilar to that of a modern cookbook writer, Captain Sanderson provided instructions for the preparation of "Beef Soup with Desiccated Mixed Vegetables":

Civil War troops
enjoy a lunch that
probably does not
include "salt horse."

The Americans, as a rule, are not fond of soups, unless of the thicker kind: but in no form can meat and vegetables be served together more profitably and more nourishingly. As a matter of economy, it admits of no argument, because every portion is useful, both bone and flesh; and, when properly made, it is wholesome and palatable. On fresh-beef day, if among the rations there are some choice bits—such as sirloin, tenderloin, or rump steaks—cut them into neat slices, and use for breakfast, broiling them if it can be done: if not, fry them. Save all the bones, if large cut them in pieces and distribute equally among the kettles ... [after placing the beef in the pots] ... as soon as the water begins to boil, and the scum begins to rise, deaden the fire, and skim, carefully and faithfully, every ten minutes, and be very sure that the water does not again come to a boil—it should only simmer; for when the meat is boiling hard the pores of the flesh are immediately closed, the essence of the meat, and all its impurities, are retained within, no scum arises, the meat becomes hard and tough, and the soup thin and watery. If it is only permitted to simmer, the pores are kept open, the blood is drawn out, the juices are extracted, the meat is rendered tender and wholesome, and the soup rich, nutritious, and palatable. In one hour and a half, carefully skimming all the while, the meat should be done; but if it has only simmered, two hours will be better. Then take the meat out, leaving only the bones. An hour previous to this, however, break up a tablet of disiccated [*sic*] vegetables [see page 137] as small as possible, and divide into as many portions as there are kettles of soup. Place each portion in a separate pan, and fill with fresh clean water. When the meat is taken out, put the vegetables in, and let them boil gently two hours longer, during that time carefully skimming off all the fat which rises to the surface. Then season with pepper and salt, and a tablespoon of vinegar, and serve out.[5]

Overly confident of the supply department's ability to provide rations, Captain Sanderson also offered recipes for Brazilian Stew, Pork Soup with Vegetables, Pea Soup, and Corned Beef with Cabbage. In his optimism he even recommended dishes that could be made from leftovers, such as Bubble and Squeak:

> This is an old and favorite mode of getting rid of bits of corned beef among good housewives at home, and can be advantageously introduced into camps. Any pieces of cold corned or salt beef that may be on hand should be cut into slices and sprinkled with pepper; then put them in a pan, with a little grease or fat, and fry them slightly. Boil some cabbage, and squeeze it quite dry; then cut it up very fine, and serve a piece of beef with a spoonful of cabbage, first seasoning it with pepper, salt, and vinegar.[6]

Truth Versus Wishful Thinking

The reality of what a soldier received to eat was, however, very different. Initially, a Union soldier from New Hampshire or Connecticut could expect to receive twelve ounces of beef, pork, or bacon every day. Sometimes when it arrived, it was incredibly fresh. Armies traveled with butchers, and the meat would be delivered, "still quivering," to the troops, as it had been slaughtered only a few hours before.

Beef was the preferred ration, and how it was prepared often depended on its quality. The easiest and most common way was boiled in a pot over the campfire. When the troops were feeling more ambitious and were well supplied, they would fry it in a pan greased with pork fat. Other times they might salt and pepper pieces of beef and skewer them on a stick to barbecue—or simply roast the meat by placing it directly on the coals of a fire.

Confederate soldiers had similar preferences. Soldier James Hall described a Southern recipe in a letter from October 1863:

> We take some bacon and fry the grease out, then we cut some cold beef in small pieces and put it in the grease, then pour in water and stew it like hash. Then we crumble corn bread or biscuit in it and stew it again till all the water is out. Then we have . . . real Confederate Cush.[7]

When there was no meat or enough flour for biscuits, hungry rebels could whip up some "slosh":

> The bacon is fried out till the pan is half full of boiling grease. The flour is mixed with water until it flows like milk [and then] poured into the grease and rapidly stirred till the whole is a dirty brown mixture. It is now ready to be served.[8]

Obtaining fresh, healthy beef or pork was, however, often difficult. Transporting meat in a prerefrigeration era and before the awareness of bacteria was a questionable process at best. More often than not, troops on the move, and those encamped a distance from towns or railway junctions, had to contend with meat that was older, rotting, infested with maggots—or all three. In such cases the key to making a meal edible was to kill both the overly ripe flavors and the living creatures. A practical solution was to use rancid beef in a "lobscouse," a name applied to a variety of potluck stews made with whatever the soldiers had available or could find: potatoes, wild mushrooms, onions, wild garlic.

When even fetid beef was not available, the armies could turn to preserved meat such as salt beef, which, in its lack of popularity, was also called "salt horse." While the men may not have understood why salt beef or salt pork was less of a threat to their health (heavy salting killed bacteria), they knew enough to realize that it would keep them alive in a pinch. In order to cure the beef or pork, however, the food producers were required to use so much salt as to render the meat hard and inedible. Salt beef was

> thoroughly penetrated with salt petre and was often yellow green with rust from having lain out of brine and stunk hugely. Men would hold mock funerals for salt beef complete with a volley of shots.[9]

A Union railway engine, the quickest way to haul food to the troops. Confederates relied on the service of private rail companies and wagon haulers to get food to the front. But the Yankees constructed their own line to insure speedy delivery: the U.S.M.R.R., or U.S. Military Rail Road.

But hunger would usually overwhelm the satirical urge, and something would have to be done to the salt beef to make it palatable. A common method, when a company was camped near a river or lake, was to leave it soaking overnight in the water, secured by a rock or tree branch.

Even so, sufficient quantities of salted foods were not always available, and the troops had to rely on other products to sustain them. The soldiers were supposed to be rationed one peck of beans every hundred days or so, and the bean proved a more appealing source of protein (than rotten, spoiled supplies, especially meat). Beans of all varieties were a camp staple, and while they could become infested with insects, a little cooking fixed the problem.

Baking beans in kettles was a common recipe. More appetizing, however, was a slightly more complex approach. Soldiers would dig a pit and build a slowly burning fire at the bottom. Just above the flames would sit a kettle of beans mixed with pork chunks or pork fat and maybe even some molasses if it were available. A lid would be placed over the concoction, and the pot would be covered with dirt. The hot coals of the fire would simmer the beans and pork overnight. In the morning, the troops would dig out their breakfast and enjoy one of the better meals they could hope for.

Over time, the troops realized that beans were the most reliably decent part of their highly dubious diet. In fact, beans were so popular that the troops even wrote and sang a song in their honor:

THE ARMY BEAN

There's a spot that the soldiers all love
The mess tent's the place that we mean
And the dish we best like to see there
Is the old fashioned, white Army Bean.

'Tis the bean that we mean
And we'll eat as we ne'er ate before;
The Army Bean, nice and clean,
We'll stick to our beans ever more.

Now the bean, in its primitive state
Is a plant we have all often met
And when cooked in the old army style
It has charms we can never forget.

'Tis the bean that we mean
And we'll eat as we ne'er ate before;
The Army Bean, nice and clean,
We'll stick to our beans ever more.

The German is fond of sauer-kraut
The potato is loved by the mick
But the soldiers have long since found out
That through life to our beans we should stick!

Chorus: Reprise.[10]

Eat Your Greens!

Although in the 1860s the science of nutrition was still essentially unknown, soldiers were aware enough to know that beans contributed to their health. People were also aware, even if they did not know why, that green vegetables were an essential part of their diet. Absent the nutrients provided by greens, a real danger of scurvy existed. Unfortunately, the devastated areas surrounding battlefields and the worn-down lands near army camps were hardly suitable for gardening.

Efforts were made to ship perishable vegetables to the troops, but the result was often imperfect. The Union armies took advantage of their vast railroad network to ship goods from Northern farms to stations near the troops and used horse-drawn wagons to finish the job. The Confederates relied on horse- or cattle-drawn wagons and, more often, upon the troops' taking what they could find as they passed through farming communities.

To meet the enormous needs of the hundreds of thousands of soldiers, army provisioners experimented with a dehydration process and eventually offered the soldiers what would become a universally despised product: "desiccated vegetables." These consisted of turnips, cabbage leaves, parsnips, onions, and stems and other parts of a vegetable that were usually disposed of, mixed together and dried in two- or three-inch blocks weighing approximately one ounce each. When soaked in water, the dried vegetables would expand to several times their original size. While the soldiers knew that the vegetables were important to their health, they were still considered inedible. Before long they were rechristened "desecrated vegetables," and the soldiers suggested that they be "put before Southern swine [rather] than Northern soldiers."[11]

Confederate soldiers also struggled to keep vegetables a part of their regular diet. Robert Ames Jarman remembered a dish "made of Irish potatoes and green apples, boiled together, mashed and seasoned with salt, pepper, onions, or garlic."[12]

"Hard Crackers, Come Again No More"

The combination of beef, salt beef, beans, desiccated vegetables, and the occasional local produce was not enough to ease the hunger of men who drilled for hours each day, stood guard at all hours of the night, and endured extremes of weather. Both armies needed food that was both filling and inexpensive. Though bread fulfilled that role in established camps and in towns, it was difficult to supply men with it while on the march—nor could it survive the hazards of a mobile life lived mostly outdoors.

In its place the men were provided with an essential item known all too well to soldiers and sailors: the ubiquitous, despised "hardtack." Used primarily by the Union armies, hardtack was a rectangular flour-and-water cracker, often around three by three inches in size and half an inch thick. Its purpose was varied; it acted as a bread substitute, as a gruel or stew thickener, and as a cure, when prepared in certain ways, for "weak bowels." At its best, hardtack was a durable food that could literally go through a battle, perhaps deflect a bullet or two, and still be edible afterward.

Practical as it may have been, however, its advantages were often lost on the soldiers. At its best, it was solid indeed. Often it was so hard that it could not be bitten into and could be broken only by a strong punch or after being dashed against something harder—a rock, perhaps. The approved method of softening hardtack was by soaking it in water, but this too led to problems because it often took on a tough consistency that made it difficult to chew.

Further contributing to the unappealing disposition of hardtack were the food distribution problems. Soldiers wrote home telling their families of spotting sixty-pound boxes of hardtack sitting unprotected at railway sidings for long periods of time during inclement weather.

As a result, when the hardtack finally made its way to the soldiers' mess tents, it would often be moldy. Moldy hardtack was usually thrown away and replaced. But there were other threats to the integrity of the soldiers' hardtack. Often it would be crawling with maggots or weevils. One Union soldier recalled that weevils were the more common nuisance and that usually such hardtack would not be replaced unless it were too seriously infested. Soldiers became inured to the sight of weevils swimming in their cups or bowls if they had broken infested hardtack into their coffee.

Cooking with Hardtack

Still, the soldiers had to make do, and they soon devised dishes that worked around hardtack's liabilities. When the troops had only desiccated vegetables and perhaps some pork fat for a thin stew, the hardtack could be broken up and dropped into the pot to act as a thickening agent. Wealthier soldiers might make milk toast at the additional price of seventy-five cents a can for condensed milk. But soldiers who were earning around twenty dollars a month—when they were paid at all—could not afford such a delicacy very often. A slightly more ambitious soldier/cook would smash a piece of hardtack, soak it in cold water, and then fry the crumbs in a pan with animal fat. This was known as "skillygalee."

If "the old-fashioned white army bean" inspired songs of affection, hardtack aroused an opposite emotion among military lyricists:

THE HARDTACK SONG

Let us close this game of poker,
Take our tin cups in our hand,
While we gather round the cook's tent door,

Where dry mummies of hard cracker
Are given to each man.
O hard crackers, come again no more!

   'Tis the song and sigh of the hungry
   "Hard crackers, hard crackers, come again no more!"
   Many days have you lingered upon our stomach sore,
   O hard crackers, come again no more!

There's a hungry thirsty soldier,
Who wears his life away,
With torn clothes, whose better days are o'er,
He is sighing now for whiskey,
And with throat dry as hay,
Sings, "Hard crackers, come again no more!"

   'Tis the song that is uttered,
   In camp by night and day,
   'Tis the wail that is mingled with each snore,
   'Tis the sighing of the soul
   For spring chickens far away,
   "O hard crackers, come again no more!" [13]

Similarly, Confederate forces relied upon cornmeal for the basic building blocks of their rations. Cornmeal was flexible and could be used for a variety of recipes, including biscuits, stews, cush, and skillygalee. Because it was served so often and was vulnerable to many of the same faults as hardtack—insect infestation and a propensity to become rock solid when cooked—it was equally unpopular with the troops:

   These biscuits made a lot of boys sick. They were so hard, we saw several of the boys gouge holes in the biscuits, fill them with powder, and blow them open, as they said, so they could eat them.[14]

Unpopular as these basic rations were, they were the staple of massive armies and filled the haversacks of Confederate and Union soldiers for up to five days at a time when they were moving. Often, of course, mobile troops would run out of rations in an area where resupply was not possible, and they would then either go hungry or live off the land.

The Dark Elixir

As unappealing as hardtack, desiccated vegetables, and rancid beef may have been, there were a few bright spots in the soldier's regular diet. Held in the highest esteem and considered an absolute necessity by all soldiers on both sides was coffee. In his irregularly distributed rations, a Union soldier was issued ten pounds of green coffee beans or eight pounds of ground roasted beans. While veterans later recalled having left important tools and provisions behind in order to lessen the loads they carried on a march, it was rare indeed for the men to abandon their coffee beans. When one considers that the beans could add pounds of weight to their haversacks, one can understand just how much the men valued their brew.

One veteran recalled that soldiers made coffee at every possible opportunity: after drills, marches, camp chores, guard duty, meals, and even fighting.

When lucky enough to have raw beans, soldiers would roast them in the ground overnight and crush them with the stock of a musket prior to brewing. Coffee not only provided a strong flavor in contrast to their normally insipid diet but also gave a necessary lift to war-weary soldiers and warmth to those who were cold. Coffee was considered so important that when it became scarce the men were not shy about making their feelings known. German immigrants, like Samuel Saltus, who enlisted in the Union's Washington Light Infantry marched with torches into their camp early in 1862:

> 1st an illumination on one side a coffee pot pierced with an arrow, words "no more grounds for complaint." Other side—coffee mill—words "the last grind." Pall bearers followed, then priest. . . . They marched through the camp, halted; a sort of funeral ceremony was performed, preaching and singing, in German, and a bonfire made and the last grounds burnt.[15]

When coffee was unavailable, grumbling troops might be offered tea. Tea may have been better than nothing but never won as devoted a following.

The men of the Confederacy also cherished coffee, but their supply essentially vanished early in the war with the Union blockade of Southern ports. Accordingly, soldiers and citizens alike brewed ersatz coffee from items such as bark, sweet potatoes, grains, nuts, corn, and other vegetables that imitated the color of the drink more than its flavor.

Side Dishes

In addition to the fundamentals of meat, vegetables, and coffee, the army provisioners supplied items that filled out the balance of the soldiers' cuisine. While the men were in camp, these included fifteen pounds of sugar, ten pounds of rice or hominy, cornmeal, two quarts of salt, four quarts of vinegar, four ounces of pepper, and a half bushel of potatoes. With these basics troops could bake bread or fry up johnnycake, a kind of pancake, or simply mask the flavor of substandard meat.

Fluctuations in this spartan bill of fare existed, but they were not the norm and usually occurred around holidays. Here the Union troops enjoyed a decided advantage over their Southern counterparts, for they were the recipients of the altruistic and exceedingly well funded U.S. Sanitary Commission.

The sanitary commission was established in 1861 by influential men and women of the North, including the internationally renowned landscape architect Frederick Law Olmsted, who had designed New York's Central Park and Boston's Emerald Necklace park system. Its purpose was to monitor soldiers' living conditions, and it was a precursor of the American Red Cross.

The Southern soldiers had no organization that could compete with the sanitary commission in terms of finances or the extent of its accomplishments. As a result, they regarded the do-gooders with scorn. The feelings of the Union soldiers were quite different and the wealthy activists soon earned a place in their hearts for doing more to improve their living conditions than their own generals.

After months of a monotonously dreary diet, the Union troops were thrilled to be offered an Independence Day meal that the commission supplied, including stewed hen, hoecake, farina pudding, strawberry preserves, and whiskey punch.[16]

Water, Water, Everywhere, but Not a Drop to Drink

There were, however, vitally important things that even the sanitary commission's money could not buy. At the top of that list was clean, pure water. The acquisition of potable water was, perhaps, the greatest challenge to both the Confederate and Union armies. In its absence diseased water caused deadly epidemics and may have well killed more soldiers than actual combat did.

While the places where camps were established and troops marched were often rural, agricultural, and seemingly unpolluted, the arrival of regiments immediately altered the landscape. Instant cities were created, and none of the inhabitants was aware of the existence of bacteria or the threat they posed. Accordingly, basic rules of sanitation were often not followed. Soldiers would relieve themselves directly into waterways upriver from camps, and soon men drinking the river water became sick. Henry T. Johns of the Forty-ninth Massachusetts Volunteers remembered:

> I used to be an ultra temperance man but since driven to decide between going without fluid or drinking something called water obtained from the nearest bayou below where horses and mules drink and wash. . . . [O]ur drinking water is horrid and obtained from the dirtiest places. . . . [W]e have never yet pushed away dead mules to fill our canteen but we have drunk water that your farmers would hardly wash their hogs in. . . . [H]ere in the city the water is cleaner but very unwholesome. The colonel will not allow us to drink it so all our drinking water is carted from the river. . . . The water being so poor and warm having no snap to it we use coffee to excess hence diarrhoea. O! For one glass of Berkshire water I long for nothing so much . . . sickness is increasing rapidly among us.[17]

Other than some common sense regarding the disposal of waste, human and otherwise, there were no obvious answers to the question of how to find good water for the troops. Water could not be shipped in, and once the soldiers arrived in a place and made camp, the problem soon became intractable.

Pop-Skull, Old Red Eye, and Oh, Be Joyful

Some men dealt with the predicament by avoiding water as much as they could. Liquor was a favorite substitute, and as the high alcohol content of much of the homemade variety killed the germs in the local water, it probably saved some lives. There were many other reasons for imbibing, of course, but evading illness was a worthy justification.

In lieu of clean water, Thomas Wentworth Higginson indulged in local Southern concoctions while marching north:

> For beverage we had . . . the delicious sugar cane syrup, which we had brought from Florida and which we drank at all hours. Old Floridians say that no one is justified in drinking whiskey while he can get cane-juice: it

is sweet and spirited, without cloying, foams like ale, and there were little spots on the ceiling of the dining room where our lively beverage had popped out its cork.[18]

Another improvised beverage that had limited appeal but quenched the thirst of those who had strong stomachs was called "blackstrap." It was recalled as a drink that

is made of syrup unskillfully made from frost bitten sugar cane. It resembles a mixture of coal tar blucose [sic] and stale soda water. Sometimes it was mixed with whiskey.[19]

Although in many regiments alcohol was usually officially allowed only to officers, both Yankee and rebel grunts occupied themselves with fermenting whatever they could get their hands on to create home-brewed hooch. All varieties of fruits and grains were used, and even meat was known to have been added for flavoring. Nicknames for the hooch included "pop-skull," "old red eye," "oh, be joyful," "rifle knock knee," and "bust head."[20] Some soldiers made a type of beer from Indian meal that they let sit in water and called "sour beer." Still other soldiers managed to slip bona fide beer into their camps. C. W. Wills noted, "We have lots of beer sent us from Peoria, and drink a half barrel a day while it lasts."[21]

The soldiers who risked their lives for their nation resented the prohibition on alcohol, particularly since officers were allowed to indulge. Accordingly, they went to great lengths to hide their liquor from the officers who tried to enforce the law. One man is said to have walked right by an officer, carrying alcohol hidden in the barrel of his rifle as he held it up on his shoulder. Another is said to have poured whiskey into a watermelon and carried it into camp, hidden it in the floor of his tent, and drunk the contents with his friends by using straws.[22]

The jovial tone of these stories—which may or may not be tall tales—belies the serious problems brought about by a constant state of drunkenness in an army. Nineteen-year-old E. F. Palmer wrote home about a lapse of discipline brought about by too much drinking:

So occasionally one gets so much that he is noisy, and somewhat irregular in his action. This morning one is drunk and in for fighting. He speaks contemptuously to his lieutenant, strikes the corporal of the guard; pays no attention to the officer of the day; it takes 4 or 5 to manage him and get him to the guard house, and he bites one of them quite badly. But he is not abused. He strikes them but they do not return it, only hold him as well as they can. As soon as his hands are tied behind him, he gives up in despair and the poor fellow cries like a child. The guard house is a wall tent, and no fire in it; and being quite cold, when he comes to himself, so as to misuse no one, he is let out and nothing more was done to him.[23]

In itself Palmer's story is remarkable only for the gentle treatment of the drunken soldier. Alcohol proved to be a formidable enemy. In the South, drunken Confederate soldiers were known to destroy the very property they were supposed to be defending. In Georgia and Tennessee, hotels were ripped apart by drunken mobs. Officers, many of whom were resented by the men serving beneath them, were sometimes beaten up by enlisted men on a binge.[24]

Unfortunately, the abuse of alcohol sometimes had life-and-death consequences. While drinking can lead to brawls and murder in any environment or era, the Civil War offered peculiar opportunities for the bottle to kill. A fundamental part of being a soldier is obeying superiors' orders, and when a commanding officer was drunk, the results could be deadly.

Union soldier H. H. Penniman recognized the danger in his regiment's lack of discipline:

> Drinking is abundant in the army though this is a luxury denied at these situations except to officers. By liquor—time is killed, spirits supported, care dismissed, and thought drowned. . . . [E]very other man will get drunk if he can and every officer is frequently drunk. . . . General John A. L. ——— [sic] is stupidly drunk—report says every night—and officers follow suit.[25]

Officers who were drunk in the field sometimes made terrible decisions that cost the lives of their men. One inebriated Confederate officer is said to have mistaken Union troops for his own men and led them in killing the troops who were actually under his command.[26] As a result, Confederate General Braxton Bragg wrote, "We have lost more valuable lives at the hands of whiskey sellers than by the balls of our enemies."[27]

Perhaps it was the prohibition of alcohol consumption that created such havoc. For in some regiments alcohol was allowed to the men, and the behavior of the soldiers in those regiments was considered exemplary. Evaluating the camp conditions of the Thirty-second Indiana Regiment for the U.S. Sanitary Commission, Dr. J. S. Newberry reported:

> [T]he men are well disciplined and cleanly. . . . [T]he men drink moderately of lager beer, and draw one pint of whiskey each morning for every twelve men.[28]

Eating on the Run

For all the difficulties of securing good-quality rations while in camp, the soldiers could usually rely on a fairly steady supply of food. Much of a soldier's time, however, was spent away from camps, marching across the country to seek out the enemy. From the breakup of winter camp in the spring to the onset of the next season's cold weather and snows, the troops of both armies were confronted with brutally different challenges—and sometimes, surprisingly enough, rewards.

More often than not, the separation from cities and supply lines resulted in a significant decline in the quality of the men's diet. If, at the beginning of the war, women on both sides set up tables of food for soldiers in train stations as they passed through, such generosity could not last. As the two militaries pursued each other across an increasingly bleak American landscape, they were weakened by combat, the rigors of constant movement, and, perhaps most of all, by their empty stomachs.

Union trooper Elisha Rhodes noted in his diaries that "On the march salt pork toasted on a stick with hard bread and coffee is our principal diet."[29] An occasional treat for footsore soldiers might be boiled rice mixed with molasses or dried apples stewed over a fire and then spread as a sauce over hardtack. Dried peas also traveled well. After being soaked in water, they could be stewed with pork fat to make what passed for a soup and was known as "peas on a trencher."

Before a march, soldiers would be ordered to prepare enough food for the duration of the trip. By doing so they would not have to take the time to cook while moving or in combat. The weight of food was an important consideration for soldiers in transit: the bulkier and heavier the rations, the more difficult and debilitating their journey would be. Accordingly, they often made poor decisions about how to apportion their rations. Confederate enlisted man Carlton McCarthy recalled:

After hardtack only on the march, soldiers approaching the camp kitchen areas must have had a sense of home.

If, as was sometimes the case, three days' rations were issued at one time and the troops ordered to cook them, and be prepared to march, they did cook them, and eat them if possible so as to avoid the labor of carrying them.[30]

The effects of such a decision were predictable, noted McCarthy:

To be one day without anything to eat was common. Two days fasting, marching and fighting was not uncommon and there were times when no rations were issued for three or four days.[31]

Though General Robert E. Lee was brilliant at planning military strategy, he was not able to crack the problem of feeding his men. Aware that even the best tactics relied upon soldiers who were fit enough to carry out their orders, he worried during the battle of Chancellorsville in 1863 that his men were being provided with only eighteen ounces of flour and four ounces of bacon a day, with sporadic supplementary rations of sugar, molasses, and rice.[32]

Another Southern officer, C. Irvine Walker, noted that he

> frequently saw the hungry Confederate gather up the dirt and corn where a horse had been fed, so that when he reached his bivouac he could wash out the dirt and gather the few grains of corn to satisfy in part at least the cravings of hunger.[33]

It was difficult enough for men to perform their daily chores or march on such a meager diet, to say nothing of fighting. Ultimately, hunger and malnutrition took their toll on Yankees and rebels alike. Men became ill with diseases associated with dietary deficiencies. Scurvy affected both armies. It swept through one Union regiment after a period of six months during which "not a single full ration of fresh vegetables had been issued."[34]

Furthermore, chronic hunger weakened soldiers already pushed to the limits by the demands of combat, endless marching, and inadequate shelter during terrible weather. Thus enfeebled, the men were susceptible to a myriad of other, nondietary diseases that swept through the regiments with great loss of life.

A transport boat to Chattanooga, Tennessee, one of the vessels that brought rations to the hungry Yankee troops who were besieged there in autumn 1863.

As a coup de grâce, near starvation had a devastating effect on the morale of the men, and tens of thousands deserted, frustrated with the armies that could not provide them with the basics of survival. Eventually, the lack of decent provisions influenced the course of the war. With their manpower depleted by disease and desertion, the generals of both nations had to alter their strategies as they planned their campaigns.

While the Union men suffered greatly from privation, they were better off than the Confederates. Even though the Union transportation networks might be imperfect, the soldiers could depend on at least some provisions arriving at their campfires by locomotive, mule train, or boat. And as the United States could call upon a larger group of men to serve in the military, it was harmed less by the loss of soldiers to starvation and its accompanying sicknesses.

The South, on the other hand, could not afford to lose a single man, but, unable to feed or keep its troops healthy, it lost thousands.

At its heart, the Confederate cause was inextricably linked to the Confederacy's identity as an agricultural nation. Indeed, the dispute over slave owning that had led to secession had had its roots in an agricultural economy that required cost-free manpower for its survival. How ironic, then, that the nail in the coffin of the Confederacy was its failure to physically sustain the men who were defending its soil.

Living off the Land

As bad as conditions often were on the march, however, leaving camp did not always mean suffering. If traveling great distances under poor conditions could be debilitating, abandoning dirty, disease-ridden camps in pleasant spring weather could be liberating. While the supply of rations in camp was reasonably predictable if monotonous, the soldiers sometimes enjoyed moments of serendipity while trekking across the contested regions.

Most wartime landscapes were gray, ruined areas, but there were times when troops arrived at a new locale that had not yet been ravaged. In some cases the locals were delighted to share their plenty and the soldiers would eat far better meals than they would have in camp. Sam Watkins remembered the generous citizens of Huntersville:

> They had plenty of honey and buckwheat cakes, and they called buttermilk "sour-mil" and sour-mil weren't fit for pigs; they couldn't see how folks drank sour-milk. But sour-kraut was good . . . and occasionally we

would come across a small sized distillery which we would at once start to doing duty.[35]

Farmers also provided apples, peaches, huckleberry pie, grape pie, and plum and other preserves when they could, and these added much-needed fruit to the soldier's diet.[36] Expeditions through less settled areas and into wilderness regions offered the unsurpassed benefit of hunting:

> Everything seemed to grow in the mountains (near Huntersville)....
> [D]eer, bear and foxes, as well as wild turkey, and rabbits and squirrels
> abounded everywhere.[37]

In addition, fish could be caught in rivers and lakes. Birds of all kinds could be shot out of the sky. Armadillos could be trapped and barbecued. Possum was also served up at campfires, and one ambitious Confederate soldier was known to have baked one in an improvised oven, "chained with potatoes."[38]

The woods were a good source for finding wild game, and they also provided other means of nourishment. Many soldiers indulged in wild berries, which sometimes had to stand in for a main course when no animals could be caught.

Infantryman Sam Watkins from the landlocked state of Tennessee experimented—not always successfully—with new foods he stumbled across for the first time while serving in coastal regions:

> We were camped right on the bank of the Duck River, and one day
> Fred Dornin, Ed Voss, Andy Wilson and I went in the river mussel hunt-
> ing ... we soon filled our sacks with mussels in their shells. ... [W]e tried
> frying them, but the longer they fried the tougher they got. They were a
> little too large to swallow whole. Then we stewed them, and after a while
> we boiled them, and then we baked them, but every flank movement we
> would make on those mussels the more invulnerable they would get. We
> tried cutting them up with a hatchet, but they were so slick and tough
> the hatchet would not cut them. Well, we cooked them, and buttered
> them, and salted them, and peppered them, and battered them. They
> looked good, and smelt good, and tasted good, at least the fixings we put
> on them did.[39]

Similarly, Cambridge, Massachusetts, resident Thomas Wentworth Higginson came across regional foods that were unlikely to have been found at his home near the Charles River. While seemingly oblivious to the desperate nature of most soldiers' hunger, he was at least appreciative of new tastes:

> As for food, we found it impossible to get chickens save in the immature shape of eggs; fresh pork was prohibited by the surgeon and other fresh meat came rarely. We could, indeed, hunt for wild turkeys, and even deer, but such hunting was found only to increase the appetite without corresponding supply. Still, we had our luxuries,—large delicious drum fish, and alligator steaks, like a more substantial fried halibut.[40]

Elisha Rhodes also discovered delicacies as he marched near Downsville, Maryland, in September 1862. But his presented a unique challenge:

> Today we found a beet tree in a grove near camp. The tree was found to be well stored with honey. What a treat it was for us. The bees charged on the regiment and accomplished what the Rebels neve done, put us to flight.[41]

Union officers, who had the privilege of wealth and enjoyed superior dining facilities in camp, could sometimes mimic those facilities even while on the march. If the men were not satisfied with their mess, they would make arrangements to take their board at local plantation houses, where the families desperately needed Northern currency as their own grew increasingly worthless. Thomas Wentworth Higginson admired the ingenuity of a former slave who cooked for him, even if the appointments of the dining room and the ingredients of his suppers were not up to the standards of his hometown:

> Thrice a day we go to the plantation houses for our meals, camp arrangements being yet very imperfect. . . . [T]he adjutant and I still [are] clinging to the household of William Washington,—William the quiet and the courteous, the pattern of house-servants, William the noiseless, the observing, the discriminating, who knows everything that can be got, and how to cook it. . . . [Their table is] set in their one room, halfway between an unglassed window and a large woodfire. . . .
> . . . Thanks to the adjutant, we are provided with the social magnificence of napkins; while (lest pride take too high a flight) our tablecloth consists of two "New York Tribunes" and a "Leslie's Pictorial. Every steamer brings us a new table cloth. Here are we forever supplied with pork and oysters and sweet potatoes and hominy and corn bread and

milk; also mysterious griddle cakes of corn and pumpkin; also preserves made of pumpkin chips and other fanciful productions of Ethiop art. . . . [O]nce William produced with some palpitation something fricasseed, which he boldly termed chicken; it was very small, and seemed in some undeveloped condition of ante-natal toughness. After the meal he frankly avowed it for squirrel."[42]

Sutters, or Traveling Salesmen

Sometimes, however, officers could not find needy families to cook for them and enlisted men were not in territory that provided opportunities for hunting. At times such as these, soldiers had no choice but to turn to an officially authorized but unpopular camp follower called a "sutler."

Sutlers were traveling salesmen who provided whatever the army did not—food and nonedible supplies—at high prices. Considered a necessary evil, one sutler was sanctioned per regiment and followed the soldiers on their travels and sometimes even into battle. The stocks of the sutlers' wagons included everything that might appeal to a hungry, bored, cold, lonesome trooper: pies, baked goods, ginger cakes, half-moon pies, tobacco, candy, nuts, cheese, mending materials for clothing and boots, magazines, newspapers, writing materials, envelopes, stamps, playing cards, racy postcards, regulation army hats, cavalry boots, flannels, gloves, socks, suspenders, pineapples, oranges, lemons, sardines, and medications. Although alcohol was illegal, sutlers often sold it, albeit at the risk of losing their concession if caught by the military authorities.

The sutlers had a difficult and often hazardous job as they traveled with their goods alongside active armies. They cited these risks as justification for their steep prices. Butter cost a dollar a pound and was often of dubious quality. In the 1860s, butter held a more important position on a dinner table than today. (Women took such pride in the quality of the butter they made that it was considered quite rude not to compliment a hostess on the butter she served.) Meat pies were twenty-five cents apiece, cheese was fifty cents a pound, condensed milk seventy-five cents a can; navy tobacco could be bought for a dollar twenty-five cents a plug, and molasses cakes and cookies were a quarter for a half dozen.

Henry T. Johns bought from sutlers, as most everyone did, but resented the cost: "They are well patronized. There is neither time nor place for economy."[43]

The soldiers did not appreciate the "risks" taken by men who were getting rich at their disadvantage, who did not conform to military rules, and who were exposed to enemy fire only by accident, and they accused the sutlers of price gouging and profiteering. In the highly charged atmosphere of a military camp, such indignation could grow into violence. Soldiers were poorly paid—when they were paid at all—and they became infuriated when they became indebted to salesmen. Some sutlers would provide change only in tickets good exclusively in their own stores, a procedure that further diminished the value of the soldiers' dollars.

Repeatedly, sutlers were subjected to reprisals. Rampaging troops would pillage their supply tents, sometimes stealing, sometimes simply destroying—and often a sutler would be chased out of a camp at the risk of his life should he return. Rarely were soldiers prosecuted for such behavior.

Foraging for Food

Despite the presence of sutlers and the military's best efforts to supply its men, soldiers in the field often found themselves without enough food or drink to sustain themselves. Neither side could rely upon the kind of good luck enjoyed by a rebel cavalry regiment that raided a Union cattle corral in September 1864—and made off with twenty-five hundred cows.

The demands of a mobile fighting army made up of tens of thousands of men were huge. Even if the high command in Washington or Richmond had been able to factor in the ineptitude of its transportation services and ship enough goods to compensate for the shortfalls, there were too many times when both armies were simply unreachable. Something had to be done. A system had to be devised to prevent the soldiers from starving and keep them strong enough to keep fighting.

The solution was foraging. Both Confederate and Union soldiers relied heavily on the provisions they could take from the population of whatever territory they were passing through. In some instances, the food was provided voluntarily. Other times, locals would sell their animals or produce, preferably for U.S. dollars. C. W. Wills described the process in his diary while camped at Rienzi, Mississippi, in the spring of 1862:

> [T]hey charge outrageous prices for eatables throughout the country. Half grown chickens 25 cents each, eggs 25 cents per dozen, buttermilk 20 cents per quart . . . and we have six hens that lay as many eggs every day, and my colored boy plays sharp and buys new potatoes, peas, beans,

etc for half of what I can on the strength of his chumming it with colored folks of the farm.[44]

But more often than not, armies took what they needed without compensation. Technically, the law required them to give receipts to the people from whom they took supplies. The plan called for the aggrieved farmers, families, and storekeepers to exchange these chits for currency at a later date. The reality was, however, that thousands of men and horses would sweep through an area and strip it clean of the things that were necessary to life:

Headquarters 3rd Sub Dist. Dist. of Jackson
Grand Junction, Tenn.
July 7th 1862
Commandant of Foraging Expedition
Sir;
    You will proceed on the road leading to Sansburg [possible misspelling; writing is partially indecipherable], using your cavalry as scouts, both for protection against surprises, & hunting up forage. In taking forage you will use your discretion, & best judgement, as to the amount you should take from any one so as not to leave him without a sufficient supply to last until the new crop comes in.
    You will also give to each & every one from whomever you obtain forage, a memorandum re=script= of the amt taken, instructing them to present the same as soon as practicable to the post GM [name indecipherable] at these headquarters—you will also return a memorandum of the amt taken from each and every one to the same.
    M. D. Legget
    Col. 78th OVP Cavalry Post[45]

Perhaps some diligent soldiers filled out their "memorandums," and maybe some Southern farmers even tried to exchange them for cash. It was much more common, however, for horses, cattle, chickens, and other foodstuffs to be stolen outright from families who themselves desperately needed them to survive:

Camp Montgomery Aug. 17, 1862
    . . . Orders was rec in camp to take some men & go on a foraging expedition. I got permission to go with them. We started at 9 o'clock with 20 men and 24 horse teams. Went about 10 miles got considerable plunder:

1 cow, 5 sheep, 1 load of dry & green corn, hens, turkeys, peaches & apples. All we could eat and carry. Well, we had a fine time of it generaly [sic]. magine [sic] for yourself to see 20 great stout fellows among a flock of hens with bagonets [sic] stones clubs & all sorts of weapons coursing putting a lot of hens around a sesesh house. . . . We don't ask any questions but wade in take anything we can use. the [sic] Orders but it is divided equally among us in eatibles but if the Natives can prove that they are true Union men they get pay for all if not oooooooo I like the fun much beter for us all then laying in camp doing nothing I would like to go out every day.

Onley[46]

Foraging was an endless cause of discord between Union soldiers and Southern citizens. Sometimes, this friction would erupt into violence. Yankee pillagers who traveled alone or in small groups were found murdered and stripped of their clothing as a final insult. Still, Southern citizens who were robbed typically could do little to vent their frustration.

And surely the attitude of the Union foragers did not ease any tensions. C. W. Wills, who only two months previously had been "living on mush and the other messes, makeable from cornmeal . . . without coffee or anything else,"[47] clearly gloated about the spoils of occupation:

What do you think we'll have to eat to-morrow? Answer: lamb, roast goose, and liver (beef), blackberry pies, plum pudding, new peas, string beans, onions, beats [sic], apple sauce, etc. That's a fact, and we have a cow that furnishes us milk, too, and a coop full of chicken, maccaroni [sic] for our soup, and we get all the beef brains.[48]

As the Union armies satiated their tremendous hunger, there was precious little left for the natives of the Confederate States. E. F. Palmer of the Vermont Volunteers was confronted by an infuriated Southerner whose Union sympathies had not protected him:

About this time I called at a citizen's house to get a meal of victuals . . . as I approached and make it known my errand I soon observed that the owner is not in the best humor for some reason, when he turns his red face and stares at me with blood shot eyes: "Buy," he mutters, "soldiers buy? They've stole all I've got that they could carry away. . . . I never had any niggers, don't want them; but if soldiers should come into your country and steal your goods wouldn't you fight? . . . I still love the Union; but I reckon it will be a long time before things are settled. . . . [W]e can hardly live between the two armies.[49]

The irate Southerner made an impression on the young New Englander by making the point that the local populations were being taken advantage of by both sides. Even men who were defending their Georgian or Virginian soil stole from their fellow citizens:

One day a party of "us privates" concluded we would go across the Conasauga river on a raid. . . . [A]fter traveling for some time we saw a neat looking farm house and sent one of the party forward to reconnoiter. He returned in a few minutes and announced that he found a fine fat sow in a pen near the house. Now, the plan we formed was for two of us to go into the house and keep the inmates interested and the other was to toll and drive off the hog. I was one of the party that went into the house. There was no one there but an old lady and her sick and widowed daughter. They invited us in very pleasantly and kindly and soon prepared us a very nice and good dinner. The old lady told us all her troubles and trial. Her husband had died before the war and she had three sons in the army two of whom had been killed and the youngest who had been conscripted was taken from the camp with fever and died in the hospital at Atlanta, and she had nothing to subsist upon, after eating up what they then had.
I soon went out having made up my mind to have nothing to do with the hog affair. I did not know how to act. I was in a bad fix. I had heard the gun fire and knew its portent. I knew the hog was dead and went up on the road and soon overtook my two comrades with the hog, which had been skinned and cut up and was being carried on a pole between them. I did not know what to do. On looking back I saw the old lady coming and screaming at the top of her voice, "You got my hog! You got my hog!" It was now too late to back out. We had the hog and had to make the most of it even if we did ruin a needy and destitute family.[50]

Soldier V. S. Rabb turned down what he considered unsatisfactory rations because there was plenty of better food to be taken from the people he was supposed to be defending:

The government tries to feed us Texains [sic] on Poor Beef, but there is too Dam many hogs here for that, these Arkansas hoosiers ask from 25 to

30 cents a pound for there [sic] pork, but the Boys generally get it a little cheaper than that I reckon you understand how they get it.[51]

In an effort to curtail this practice, some generals instituted extreme punitive measures. Confederate Braxton Bragg let it be known that he approved of locals killing any of his soldiers if they were caught pillaging. Even so, the soldiers' hunger overwhelmed their fear of the law, and the practice of foraging continued until there was nothing left to steal. Spencer Welch noted how the hunger of his regiment affected the population of Orange County, Virginia, as they passed through:

> The crops of corn are magnificent and are almost matured, but wherever our army goes, roasting ears and green apples suffer. I have often read of how armies are disposed to pillage and plunder, but could never conceive of it before. Whenever we stop for 24 hours every cornfield and orchard within two or three miles is completely stripped. The troops not only rob the fields but they go to the houses and insist on being fed, until they eat up everything about a man's premises which can be eaten.[52]

When they could, some citizens protested. John R. Richards of Calhoun County, Florida, wrote to the governor to describe the desperate condition of his neighbors after pillaging:

> Right Hon. John Milton
> Governor of Florida:
> My Dear Friend: After my best respects to you as my friend and chief justice of the State of Florida, I avail myself of this opportunity of writing to you a few lines to ascertain if it is law for these "pressmen" to take the cows from the soldiers' families and leave them [the families] to starve. Colonel Coker has just left my house with a drove for Marianna of about 200 or 300 head. Some of my neighbors went after him and begged him to give them their milch cows, which he, Mr. Coker, refused to do, and took them on. And now, my dear Governor, I assure you, on the honor of a gentleman, that to my knowledge there are soldiers' families in my neighborhood that the last head of cattle have been taken from them and drove off, and unless this pressing of cows is stopped speedily there won't be a cow left in Calhoun County. I know of several soldiers' families in this county that haven't had one grain of corn in the last three weeks, nor any likelihood of their getting in the next three months; their few

cows taken away and they left to starve; their husbands slain on the battlefield at Chattanooga. This is a true state of things in my county; I vouch for them as an honest man. Now, if this is law I should be glad to know it, so I could know how to act by the law for I have had a different notion of the law; and as a sound man, I think this pressing of all the cattle will have a bad end, in my judgment, and I am not all that think so. I think if it could be stopped it would have a good effect on the part of the community. I should be obliged to you if you feel a freedom to write me on this subject soon, as I look upon procrastination as the great thief of time.

I remain your obedient servant,
John R. Richards.[53]

Eventually, there were no more farm animals or crops to "forage." And when the hungry troops finished off the last of the horses, mules, and dogs, there was literally almost nothing for them to eat. Men marched across the country and fought energy-sapping battles on rations that were pathetically small. Confederate soldiers at Vicksburg received "one small biscuit and one or two mouthfuls of bacon per day."[54] At one point besieged Confederate soldiers were subsisting on an unpopular bread substitute made of "pulverized peas." "Soups" would be made of bad water, roots, tree buds, weeds, and grass. Men would strip bark from trees and chew it, hoping to ease their chronic hunger.[55]

In January 1864, Confederate General Joseph Johnston introduced a novel approach to dealing with his hungry soldiers. As there was little in the way of food of any kind, he suggested issuing the soldiers enough whiskey to fill their stomachs or at least to ease their hunger pangs:

Office of the Chief District Commissary
Atlanta, GA.
His Excellency Joseph E. Brown
Milledgeville, GA.

Sir: I have just returned from the front, where I have held a consultation with General Johnston about feeding the army. In the frequent want of animal food he has determined to issue rations of whisky, and to do this it is necessary for me to make contracts for the same in large quantities. I have already made several, and in all cases require contractors to furnish me the entire product of the grain turned over to them. My object in addressing you is to ascertain if, under the statutes of the State, any other steps are necessary to enable my contractors to carry out their agreement. Please answer at your earliest, as the demands for whisky are urgent and beyond present means of supply.

Very respectfully,
your obedient servant, J.F. Cummings
Major & Commissary of Subsistence[56]

At the end of the war, Robert E. Lee's once proud Army of Northern Virginia was equally battered. As they marched to Appomattox, the enlisted men were forced to eat food that had been designated for their animals, as their officers had already eaten their rations:

When application was made for rations, it was found that the last morsel belonging to the division had been issued to the command and the battalion was again thrown on its own resources, to wit: corn on the cob intended for the horses. Two ears were issued to each man. It was parched in the coals, mixed with salt, stored in the pockets, and eaten on the road. Chewing the corn was hard work. It made the jaws ache and the gums and teeth so sore as to cause unendurable pain.[57]

In lands made barren by war, soldiers took desperate actions to feed themselves:

While . . . at Chattanooga, rations were very scarce and hard to get. . . . [A]bout this time we learned that Pemberton's army . . . were subsisting entirely on rats. . . . [W]e at once acted upon the information and started out rat hunting; but we couldn't find any rats. Presently we came to an old outhouse that seemed to be a natural harbor for this kind of vermin. The house was quickly torn down and out jumped an old residenter [sic], who was old and gray. I supposed he had been chased before. But we had jumped him and were determined to catch him or "burst a boiler." After chasing him backwards and forwards the rat finally got tired of this foolishness and started for his hole. But a rat's tail is the last that goes in the hole and as he went in we made a grab for his tail. Well, tail hold broke, and we held the skin of his tail in our hands.

After hard work we caught him. We skinned him, washed and salted him, buttered and peppered him, and fried him. He actually looked nice. The delicate aroma of frying rat came to our hungry nostrils. We were keen to eat a piece of rat, our teeth were on edge; yea; even our mouth watered to eat a piece of rat. Well, after a while he was said to be done. I got a piece of cold corn dodger, laid my piece of the rat on it, eat a little piece of bread, and raised the piece of rat to my mouth, when I happened to think of how that rat's tail did slip. I had lost my appetite for dead rat. I did not eat any rat. It was my first and last effort to eat rat.[58]

Still, there were times when necessity caused Union and Confederate soldiers to perform even more gruesome tasks. For men who had grown up in a youthful, prosperous nation—a land of bounty, family farms, thriving cities and towns—it must have been the most profound shock to descend to such a low rung on the ladder of deprivation and desperation:

> The most melancholy eating a soldier was ever forced to do, was, when pinched with hunger, cold, wet, and dejected, he wandered over the deserted field of battle and satisfied his cravings with the content of the haversacks of the dead. . . . Impelled by [hunger,] men of high principle and tenderest humanity became for the time void of sensibility, and condescend to that which, though justified by their extremity, seem afterwards, even to the doers, too shameless to mention.[59]

In this battle for the identity of a nation, the war's destructive influence upon the soldiers could, perhaps, be best seen through this degradation of the most fundamental of human actions: feeding oneself.

Today, people reflect upon the dehumanization of men and women caused by an industrialized society, which in the 1860s was in its infancy. In fact, this revolutionary change in society had a significant impact on the war, making it the first war of the mechanized era. Not only did industrialization affect the scale of destruction and tragedy by contributing new and more terrible weapons to the battlefield, but it was the manufacturing strength of the Union that allowed it to continue a war and outlast an enemy that enjoyed early success but could not maintain its momentum.

It was, however, a failure on the part of the country's immature manufacturing and distribution capability that redefined what it meant to be a soldier of the Union or the Confederacy. If Johnny Rebel or Billy Yank marched off to war expecting to find glory and to be transformed into great men under fire, they usually found something different indeed—for glory was hard to come by while sifting for food through the pockets and haversacks of the dead. If a hunger for a sense of national identity had started the war, it was not enough to sustain the men who fought it. In a contest that fed upon definitions of political and cultural identity, the greatest casualty may have been more personal: the soldier's own humanity. For when men are forced to take food from corpses, it is surely a low point in the long and troubled history of humanity.

Of course, many aspects of the human spirit were displayed during the American Civil War: bravery, altruism, patriotism, fear, homesickness, regret, pride, just to name a few. But hunger was ultimately the engine of both Confederate and Union soldiers' experience.

CHAPTER FIVE

Socializing with the Enemy

*L*iving in an army camp, surrounded by thousands of men, a soldier is nevertheless astonishingly alone—alone with his hunger, alone with his fear of dying, disturbed by his separation from his loved ones. It was only natural, then, that men sought out interactions with whatever friendly people they happened to meet. One of the more unusual phenomena of the Civil War was the relationship that developed between the soldiers of the Confederacy and the Union when they were not in combat. As savage as the fighting was during battle, in the periods between overt warfare there were numerous occasions of curiously affable socializing between the soldiers of opposing forces. This was mostly true at what should have been flash points of violence: the armies' forward positions, which were called the "picket lines."

Set several miles ahead of the military encampments, the picket lines were established at the points of confrontation with the enemy. E. F. Palmer, a native of Montpelier, Vermont, and a member of the Thirteenth Vermont Volunteers, recalled:

> The picket line is 3 miles south of the camp. . . . [T]here are 3 reliefs; each on duty eight hours. The beats are ten to fifteen rods apart; 2 soldiers are left at each, one watching at a time.[1]

A Confederate soldier fighting in Centerville, Virginia, wrote a detailed description of the picket and the dangers of patrol to his family in September 1861:

> Imagine a field about 300 yards in width covered with a growth of buckwheat. On each side of this field within twenty or thirty steps of each other, as the nature of ground will admit, are dug rifle pits about

three feet wide, three feet deep and eight or ten feet long. In front of each of these pits is erected a barricade of rails covered with earth. In each of these pits is stationed from two to six men who sit behind these barricades and fire at each other whenever they can either see or imagine they can see the "inemy." . . . The picket lines are so near that bold, daring scouts sometimes creep up from either side and shoot down pickets at night. For this reason no picket can sleep as it might be the sleep of death.[2]

Often separated by a distance measured in only yards, the picket lines served as an alarm system for the main army camps. If an enemy began to shift its position or even advance, the soldiers manning the pickets might fight, but their real function was to get off a few shots to allow time for the soldiers in the rear to prepare their defenses. Henry T. Johns of the Forty-ninth Massachusetts Volunteers remembered that pickets were commonly set up

forming a semicircle 5–6 miles [at the front of a camp]. Three men occupy a post. . . . In daytime one stands guard and the others rest but at night only one rests at a time. In case of an attack they fire two signal guns to prepare their camps for action and then fall back on the reserve pickets. If practical resistance is here made to the advancing enemy if not practical they retreat to the camp firing their guns.[3]

Picket duty was vitally important to the security of an army. It was often dangerous and unpleasant, but most soldiers coped as best they could. Despite the hardships, the authorities did not look kindly upon those who did not fulfill their responsibility, as Sam Watkins recalled:

One morning, about daybreak, the new guard was relieving the old guard. It was a bitter cold morning and on coming to our extreme outpost, I saw a soldier—he was but a mere boy—either dead or asleep at his post. The sergeant commanding the relief went up to him and shook him. He immediately woke up and seemed very much frightened. He was fast asleep at his post. . . . Two days afterwards I received notice to appear before a court martial at nine. I was summoned to appear as a witness against him for being asleep at his post in the enemy's country. An example had to be made of some one. He had to be tried for his life. . . . I trembled in my boots, for on several occasions I knew I had taken a short nap even on the very outpost.[4]

Perhaps because the men who guarded the front lines were in such a vulnerable position, such duty engendered a different set of rules to live by than when in camp. In their proximity to the enemy and possible sudden death, the men on the opposing armies' picket line shared a unique experience that may have encouraged a bond to grow between them that transcended national loyalties. It is also probably true that while the commanders tried to demonize the enemy, familiarity did not breed contempt among those standing picket. At such close quarters they may have realized that they were more alike than different. At the very least, the nearness of the adversary must have provoked profound curiosity. Communication with the opposing army, however, was not officially sanctioned, and in many places it was forbidden, as described by Elisha Rhodes of the Second Rhode Island Volunteers.

> Camp Near Falmouth, VA.
> We have returned from our three days of picket duty and I am glad to get back. We were posted on the banks of the Rappahannock. . . . [A]s firing at pickets is forbidden by each side the men were allowed to go down to the river banks. We did not allow our men to talk to the rebels, but they kept up a stream of questions. They were anxious to know where the 9th Corps had gone. It seemed queer to see them only a few yards away in their gray clothes. One of their bands played every day and we enjoyed the music with them. They were very anxious to procure New York papers and coffee but we obeyed orders and did not give them any.[5]

Rhodes was puzzled by his encounter with the Confederate pickets across the Rappahannock River and continued to resist their persistent entreaties and civil offerings of trade:

> We are on picket again. . . . [A]cross the river and only a few yards distant I can see fifty Rebels gazing at the Yankees. Just beyond them is a large fort with long lines of rifle pits on each side. The Rebels are very anxious to get northern papers. A few minutes ago I saw one of their little boats made of a board with a paper sail and a tin can nailed upon the board come sailing across the river. I received the boat and took out of the can a late Richmond paper. The Rebel called out: "Send me a New York paper" but I declined as it was against orders. In accordance with orders I broke that boat in pieces although Rebel shouted that he would shoot me if I did not stop. But I broke the board notwithstanding and he did not shoot.[6]

Rhodes's uncompromising behavior was not emulated by everyone, however. Even though policy prohibited fraternization with the enemy, the rules would sometimes be broken by men who were good soldiers but who shared a mutual experience that linked them more strongly to each other than to the command structure. Dr. Spencer Welch, for instance, visited the Confederate pickets along the Rappahannock River in Virginia at the end of 1862. It may have been the greetings of men such as Welch that Elisha Rhodes so studiously ignored. In letters home to his family, however, Welch noted that not all the Union soldiers were as dedicated to regulations as the young Rhode Island infantryman:

> Our regiment was on picket at the river a few days ago and the Yankee pickets were on the opposite bank. There is no firing between pickets now. It is forbidden in both armies. The men do not even have their guns loaded. The two sides talk familiarly with each other, and the Yankees say they are very anxious to have peace and get home.[7]

Five months later, Welch wrote to his wife, describing an increasing level of interaction with the Union soldiers manning the pickets near Hamilton's Crossing, Virginia:

Troops in the trenches at Petersburg, Virginia. For months Confederate and Union troops faced each other there. Especially out on the ends of the combat lines, troops shouted messages to one another and sometimes warned if an attack was coming. Union troops hated to hear, "Look out, Yank! We're comin'!"

Our corps is lying in line of battle in the trenches and has been for six days. The Yankees are still on this side of the river. The picket lines are within speaking distance of each other and we exchange newspapers with them every day. . . . I saw the New York Illustrated News and will try to get a copy to send to you.[8]

In the war that killed more American soldiers than any other, the civility sometimes became surrealistic. At one point the revered Confederate General Stonewall Jackson visited the front lines and was observed from across a river by Union troops:

[He] came down to the river banks today with a party of ladies and of-ficers. We raised our hats to the party and strange to say the ladies waved their handkerchiefs in reply. Several Rebel sentinels told us that it was Gen. Jackson. He took his field glasses and cooly surveyed our party. We could have shot him with a revolver but we have an agreement that nei-ther side will fire as it does no good and is simply murder.[9]

It was not long before the soldiers of the opposing armies began spending time in enemy territory and dealing with each other in a supportive manner, particularly when it came to treating the injured. Even in the aftermath of a battle, Confederate and Union soldiers would ignore the fact that only hours previously they had been killing each other. Once the fighting itself was over, the hostilities could be put aside:

The next morning [after battle] we did nothing. Several handsome young Yankee surgeons in fine uniforms came over with a white flag and I went to where they were attending their wounded. While there I talked with a wounded man from Ohio, and saw one of our soldiers cut a forked limb from a tree and make a crutch for a Yankee who was wounded in the foot.[10]

Ultimately, such noncombative behavior evolved into a relationship that would be hard to distinguish from actual friendship. Petty trade of news-papers, coffee, tobacco, and peanuts between Confederate and Union soldiers matured into card playing and drinking bouts. *The Richmond Daily Dis-patch* noted that alleged enemies had been seen swimming together, and stories were told of officers checking picket lines and finding the "posts deserted" as the guards had run off to spend time with their new friends.[11] One Georgian soldier described the increasingly cordial relations in a letter to his family:

> Sometimes the scene changes. The pickets seem by mutual understanding to cease firing for a while and show white handkerchiefs on each side, when they come out of their pits and stop fighting to begin cursing as an old fellow told me. They then begin a conversation in about this wise:
>
> YANKEE: "Got any whiskey over your way?"
> SOUTHERNER: "No. Have you got any?"
> YANKEE: "Yes. Don't you want some?"
> SOUTHERNER: "Yes. Come and meet me halfway and bring your canteen!"
>
> They meet in the center of the field, each without arms, and no one fires on them. They often talk for fifteen minutes, take drinks, swap canteens and drink toasts to the "Sweetheart they've left behind us." The Yankee always wants to make a trade of some sort, swap knives &c.[12]

Occasionally, the interaction between enemy troops was more than just a quick visit across a picket. One story tells of a Union soldier being invited to a rebel party, being provided with acceptable clothing, dancing the night away among Confederate women, and then being returned to the picket in the morning.[13]

For all the instances of goodwill exhibited by enemy soldiers toward each other, however, the picket was still an extremely dangerous place to be and a lonely spot to die:

THE PICKET ON THE POTOMAC—A SONG OF THE CIVIL WAR

> All quiet on the Potomac; they say
> Except now and then a stray picket
> Is shot, as he walks on his beat to and fro
> By a rifleman hid in thicket
> 'Tis nothing, a private or two now and then
> Will not count in the tale of the battle:
> Not an officer lost—only one of the men
> Breathing out all alone the death rattle.

Larger raft of blanket boats ferrying infantry across the Potomac River

All quiet along the Potomac tonight
Where the soldiers lie peacefully dreaming:
Their tents in the ray of the clean autumn moon
And the light of the watch fires gleaming
A tremendous sigh from the gentle night wind.
Through the forest leaves slowly is creeping
While the stars up above with their glittering eyes
Keep watch while the army is sleeping
Theirs [sic] only the sound of the lone sentry's tread
As he tramps from rock to the fountain
And thinks of the two in the low trundle bed
Far away in the hut, on the mountain.
His musket falls slack; his face dark and grim
Grows gentle with memories tender
As he mutters a prayer for the children asleep
For their mother may heaven defend her!

The moon seems to shine as serenely as then,
He dashes the tears that are willing
And gathers his gun closer up to its place
As if to keep down the heart swelling.
He passes the fountain, the blasted pine tree
The footstep is lagging and weary;
Yet onward he glides through the broad hell of light
Towards the shade of a forest so dreary
Hark! Was it the night wind that rustled the leaves?
Is't the moonlight so suddenly flashing?
It looked like a rifle—Ha! Mary, goodnight!
His life blood is ebbing and dashing.

All quiet along the Potomac tonight
No sound save the rush of the river;
But the dew falls unseen on the face of the dead
The picket off duty—forever.[14]

Soldiers and Civilians

Sometimes, the locations where the two armies confronted each other were in or nearby towns, and ordinary citizens lived close by the picket lines. In such cases, the soldiers were often exposed to local people—with varying results. Technically speaking, the soldiers were dealing with "the enemy"—but the common ties between them were, in many cases, too strong for real hostility to ensue. Elisha Rhodes, who would not speak to enemy soldiers across a picket line, was more willing to deal with civilians:

> Winchester, VA.
>   We posted our pickets about the outskirts and then cooked our dinner in the street. We found plenty of milk, peaches, and grapes which the people gladly sold to us. One lady invited me into her house and gave me a good lunch. Two young ladies present turned their chairs and sat facing the wall but this did not take my appetite away. . . . [O]ne young girl told me that when the Union and Rebel troops were fighting in front of her house she ran out in excitement.[15]

Spencer Welch, marching with the Confederate army toward the battle of Gettysburg, was also treated kindly by the "enemy" and was welcome at the dinner table of a Union family in U.S. territory:

Our stopping place was in a basin of mountains which was very fertile and contained a few very excellent and highly cultivated farms. Awhile after we stopped I started off to one of these farmhouses for the purpose of getting my dinner. . . . On going to the house a very nice, smiling young girl met me at the door, and, upon making known my wishes, she very pleasantly said she "guessed" so; but said they already agreed to accommodate a good many, and they would do the best they could by us all if I would return at four o'clock. This I did. . . . It seemed that there was no end to everything that was good. We had nice fried ham, stewed chicken, excellent biscuit, lightbread, butter, buckwheat cakes that were most delicious, molasses, four or five different kinds of preserves and several other dishes. We also had plenty of coffee and cold, rich milk to drink. None but a soldier who has experienced a hard campaign can conceive of how a gang of hungry men could appreciate such a meal. I must say this late dinner was a perfect Godsend.[16]

Local people were not, however, always so welcoming to the occupying troops. Often soldiers who were marching through enemy territory would be met with polite defiance, as John Perry discovered as he passed through a Confederate town in June 1862:

In the afternoon I walked through some of the principal streets with several officers. . . . It was the hour when the houses were thrown open to the cool evening breeze, and as we looked through the grass grown streets people were sitting on every piazza and doorstep. When they saw us coming there was much shifting of chairs and rearranging of skirts; some ran into the house and closed the doors in our faces, then flew to the window to peep through the blinds, while others remained and turned their backs upon us. The children of one family were placed in a row and told to sing "Dixie" as we passed, which they did vociferously. I did not blame them; under similar circumstances, between all members of the human family there is a strong likeness. The same thing might occur anywhere.[17]

Henry T. Johns of western Massachusetts strolled through occupied Baton Rouge with a superior attitude regarding the Southern way of life. These walks were not simply an exercise in snobbery, however. During his foray through the Louisiana city, Johns learned a great deal about Southern social structures and how slavery, the institution he was fighting to end, fit in:

As the doors are generally open in the middle of the day we can see how southern houses are furnished which is in a style very inferior to corresponding houses in the north. Carpets are few in number and the walls are seldom papered. It is not unusual to see pianos in rooms thus destitute. Coolness and cleanliness are at least secured. Green shutters are attached to doors and windows to keep out the heat. . . . [F]ew who can afford plantations live in cities save doctors, lawyers, ministers, and merchants. The wealth is in the country. . . . [L]andowning and consequent slave owning is the criterion of respectability. . . . [T]he feudal south can only be republicanized by impoverishing the great landlord. . . . [T]he war is doing that.[18]

For some Union men, meetings with the adversary were less studied and more of an adventure or flirtation. C. W. Wills vowed to move to the Confederate states once they were defeated:

I fell in love in Paducah while I was there, and I think I will settle there when the war is over. I never saw so many pretty women in my life. All fat, smooth-skinned small boned, highbred looking women. They hollered "Hurrah for Jeff" at us, some of them, but that's all right.[19]

Some time later, however, Wills rethought his plans. Perhaps the attractiveness of what had previously been exotic was now less so after becoming more familiar. Too, some Southern women amazed and appalled him with their conduct:

You have no idea to what an extent the habit of dipping is carried here. I have, while talking to women who really had in every way the appearance of being ladies, seen them spit tobacco juice, and chew their dipping sticks, perfectly at ease. I don't think it common to do so openly, but I have seen two ladies, and any number of common women, engaged in the delightful pastime.[20]

Overstaying Their Welcome

Although relations between the opposing sides could often be surprisingly collegial, there were, in the end, more instances of open belligerence. Union troops in Southern territory were, after all, an invading force, and the local people often defied them. The same was true in the North, particularly at the beginning of the war, when the Confederate armies entered and threatened U.S. territory. In both cases the military authorities authorized the destruction of property, despite official proclamations to the contrary, as a method of preventing the enemy from being fed or sheltered or earning money to pay for supplies:

> Moscow July 13, 1862
> To Genrl. Hurlburlt
> No rebels should be allowed to remain an hour at Davis Mills. . . . [A]mbush them, or attack with a superior number but don't let any party stay at Davis Mills one night. . . .
> If the people want to burn their cotton or other property let them—if burned by the soldiers. And if the people can muster up the courage to resist their help then but make it a condition that the people take part in resisting—if the owner of cotton consents to its being burned let him know he may burn his cotton, his house, himself and family, but not his corn. We want that.
> W. T. Sherman[21]

Neither group of citizens was kindly disposed to the soldiers who stole their food, burned their property, and menaced their sovereignty. The result was armed resistance, usually in the form of guerrilla tactics and the destruction of supplies that the enemy might want:

> Today I took the 2nd Rhode Island Vols. and the 5th Wisconsin Vols. and went into the country to search the houses for arms. The people are honest farmers during the day, but at night they arm themselves and mounting their horses are guerrillas and fire upon our pickets and destroy our wagon trains if they overpower the guards. The work was not pleasant but we had to perform our duty. The people were often wild with rage but we found that those who professed their innocence the loudest had the most contraband arms.[22]

The harshness of the orders directing soldiers to destroy property and harass citizens created great doubt in the minds of some. While they acknowledged the need to counter attacks upon their regiments, men such as C. W. Wills tried to distinguish between guerrillas and local citizens who were simply trying to defend themselves:

Orders have been given to put every woman and child (imprison the men) across the line that speaks or acts secesh, and to burn their property, and to destroy all their crops, cut down corn growing, and burn all the cribs. That is something like war. Tis devilish hard for one like me to assist in such work, but believe it is necessary to our course. . . .

People here treat us the very best kind, although they are as strong as Rebels live. Bring us peaches and vegetables every day. I can't hardly think the generals will carry out the orders as above, for it will have a very demoralizing effect upon the men. I'd hate like the deuce to burn the houses of some secesh I know here, but at the same time don't doubt the justice of the thing. One of them has lent us his cook, or rather his wife did; and they don't talk their secessionism to you unless you ask them to.[23]

Equally confusing were situations that arose when young soldiers had to make instant judgments about the behavior of locals who may have treated them kindly but at a later date proved themselves to be on the wrong side. James Sawyer of the Eighteenth Connecticut Volunteers wrote home to his father about such a confrontation that occurred while he was on picket duty:

Old Campbell, who lent us guns to go hunting, has turned out to be a negro hunter. The other day we heard a terrible shouting and swearing in the vicinity of his house, and pretty soon a negro crossed the railroad between the pickets and bridge keepers house, running for his life with Old Campbell, his two sons and two or three dogs after him. The two boys had guns and the old man was shouting to them to shoot the negro. The nig. ran around through the lots to the bridge puffing and blowing with his pursuers close upon him. The guard stopped Campbell, but let the darkey cross over and thus escape. . . .

Campbell's story is this. He said he was going through the pines near his house when he met the darkey who attacked him with a club (when the nig. came up to our guard he had a heavy club in his hand). He said he called his boys who care [sic] runs and drove the darkey off. The darkey tells a different story he said he was crossing through the pines when he met Campbell who attacked him with a club because he was crossing his land. . . . He had a scuffle with Campbell and got the club away from him, when Campbell called his boys and set his dogs upon him. The nig. thought it best to run and did so, with the whole gang after him. These are the stories of both and that of the darkey is believed by us. Campbell around here is considered an old secesh and pro slavery man.[24]

Acts of Mercy

The natural sense of justice in a young man like James Sawyer when confronted by a situation that was both confusing and intimidating is remarkable. Equally so was the recurring demonstration of compassion among enemies in the aftermath of battle. If the relationship between the soldiers was ripe with ambiguity—they were political adversaries but cultural cousins—the ability to see past narrow factional loyalties was strongest when put to its greatest test: in life-or-death situations:

> May 7, 1864—Wilderness
> On the 5th we marched all day on the plank road from Orange Court House to this place. We got into a hard fight on the left of the road rather late in the afternoon. The fighting was desperate for two or three hours. . . . After night Major Hammond rode up to where we doctors were and told us that about two miles to the rear there was a poor Yankee who was badly wounded. He insisted that someone of us go back to help him. I went, and found him paralyzed from a shot in the back. I gave him water and morphine, and made him comfortable as best I could. The poor fellow seemed very grateful.[25]

If it is true, as written by some scholars, that the Civil War forged the sense of a single national identity for Americans—whereas previously they had had regional loyalties—the greatest contribution to this development may well have been the merciful actions of men toward their enemies as they died. For if these men killed one another because they were enemies, the outstanding demonstrations of compassion that occurred proved that they were members of the same family after all:

> Virginia: May 10. 1864
> Dear Sisters:
> While lying here under the shade of these pines, I am having this man write a few lines to you to let you know that on last Friday I had the great misfortune to get a very severe wound in the battle of that day by a minie ball. It passed through my left hip very high up and smashed it very badly, and it is so high up that the doctor says he can't do anything for me. After I was shot I was taken by the enemy and am now at their hospital among their wounded and some few of ours are here. The surgeon told

me today that there was no hopes of my living. But where there is life there is still hope.

Lorrie and Sarah, as that is what this gentleman tells me is his sister's names, I would just say to you your Brother is pretty badly wounded, and I think life with him is quite uncertain although we can't tell. We are all in the hands of God. I am a Northerner but I always sympathize with affliction. I am sitting by him, have been trying to do what little I can for him. He seems quite resigned and composed. . . . Unless I am moved again from here you can hear from me. . . . .[F]or my part this is a strange place to me, and there is none here that know the name of the place. All I know is that we are in Virginia. Now he don't tell me anything more to write, so I must close by saying farewell for him to you.

Written by James E. Smith for Harmon Robinson to his sisters Sarah and Lorrie Robinson.[26]

CHAPTER SIX

Their Brothers' Jailers

Despite the abundant number of uplifting stories describing soldiers reaching across enemy lines to be friendly, such behavior was not always the case. One of the most profound and saddest ironies of the American Civil War is that the displays of greatest cruelty did not occur during the panic-inducing heat of battle, as might have been expected. Rather, the war's most extreme demonstrations of inhumanity took place after the adrenaline rush of combat had worn off and soldiers had a chance to consider their actions. As unsettling as the truth may be, both Confederate and Union soldiers behaved unforgivably upon thinking matters through and arriving at considered decisions.

If people may be judged by the way they administer those over whom they have control, the treatment of Civil War prisoners of war stands as a scathing indictment of both sides. When the history of Civil War prisoner-of-war camps is considered, it is a compelling reminder that while the war may have forged a national identity, this occurred only after the most horrible crimes were committed against those who should have been considered part of the same human family.

Captured

Along with other members of the House of Representatives and Washington socialites, Congressman Alfred Ely of New York ventured out of the nation's capital on Saturday, July 20, 1861, to watch what was expected to be the first great battle of the Civil War:

> We left Washington at five o'clock a.m. in a double carriage drawn by fine horses with our provisions for the day laid in and our company in fine spirits.[1]

Little did Congressman Ely expect that he would soon become a participant in the war he had come to watch while lunching. As the picnickers passed Centreville, Virginia, they were surprised to find that the battle of Bull Run had already begun and that they were caught in the middle of it. Approached by Confederate troops, Ely was asked if he had any connection to the federal government. When he admitted he was a member of Congress, Ely was arrested courteously and taken to a Confederate army camp, where he was treated less well:

> [A Captain] took me to the Colonel sitting on horseback and introduced me in these words: "Colonel, this is Mr. Ely Representative in Congress from New York" to which the Colonel in a most angry tone replied, drawing his pistol and pointing it directly at my head, "G—d d—n you white livered soul! I'll blow your brains out on the spot." The Captain and another officer . . . prevented him from carrying out his threat. . . . [T]he Colonel immediately rode away, when the Captain stated to me that he was ashamed of his Colonel that he was very much excited and had been drinking.[2]

Whatever fear Ely may have felt at this time, his subsequent handling was relatively benign. Others were not so fortunate, and throughout the war prisoners were subjected to a wide range of treatment. A variety of circumstances surrounding prisoners' capture had an effect on how they were treated. Perhaps the two factors that most influenced how a given captive would fare were the state of readiness of his captors to handle large numbers of prisoners and the captors' own physical condition and access to supplies.

At the beginning of the war, neither side was prepared to house many prisoners, and soldiers found themselves being held in buildings converted from their original purposes into jails. Congressman Ely, although technically held under different auspices than a fighting man would be, nevertheless found himself quartered with other imprisoned soldiers:

> Late this afternoon we were removed into our new quarters—an adjoining building which is also a tobacco factory and the lower floor about 70 feet long by 30 feet wide is our apartment. It is divided midway by a row of tobacco presses the space on one side being exclusively our quarters, while the other half is occupied by the guards especially to sleep in at night and is constantly resounding with a great noise from the stacking of guns, and the tramps of soldiery. The two stories above us are occupied

Being a prisoner under guard in a setting like this one, which resembles camp, would be bitter irony for prisoners, who craved the camp life as free men.

by Union soldiers but they have no access to our apartment. The building fronts on Main Street. All the windows both in front and rear of the first and second stories are secured by seven round iron bars reaching from the lower to the upper sills. The rear half of the floor is occupied by us and overlooks the James River which is directly in view except as the prospect is interrupted by buildings or trees. The room is not supplied by even a chair or bench to sit upon and is destitute of every article of furniture. We are all to sleep upon the floor without any exception.[3]

Other prisoners were exposed to harsher conditions. One of the first humiliations of life in the prisoner-of-war camp was the removal of personal items—called "skinning"—as experienced by one Union prisoner:

The skinning process resorted to was sufficient to satisfy any one that there was not much left in our possession. Each prisoner was called up singly and ordered to strip, which was done to the last stitch. Clothing was turned wrong side out and thoroughly searched in the pockets and between the linings, plugs of tobacco were cut open, daguerreotypes taken out of their cases, fingers were run through the hair, the mouth ordered to be opened, arms raised and every imaginable means employed to thwart Yankee ingenuity in secreting valuables. . . . Many of the old soldiers understand a disease known as the "Green piles." The rebels had heard of it and no prisoner was permitted to pass without a careful examination on this point. Knives, rings, papers, envelopes, extra clothing of all kinds was confiscated, pictures of friends were torn up or stamped under feet, for no other purpose than lest they might prove a comfort to the prisoners.[4]

Once the initial search of the prisoners' possessions was finished, the men were shown into their new living quarters. The world of a prisoner was intimidating in its unpredictable cruelty:

We were taken up to the second floor in a large room where were confined a number of other prisoners. The windows of the room were secured by iron bars, such as adorn prison cells. The building was surrounded by sentinels, whose beats were on the pavement below. No one was allowed to put his head close enough to the bars to look down on the street under penalty of being shot. In the afternoon, this being the third day after our capture, we drew our first rations from the Confederacy, consisting of four or five ounces of corn bread, two spoonfuls of cooked rice, and two ounces of boiled bacon. This, once a day, constituted our rations while in Libby Prison.[5]

Prison Fare

Conditions varied widely among prison camps and even among different sections of a single jail. In no aspect of the prisoners' lives was this more true than in the food they subsisted on. Some men ate well and in style, while others suffered terribly. Congressman Alfred Ely enjoyed having meals prepared for him by a manservant:

Our mess, consisting of eight persons in all, sit down to breakfast, prepared mostly by our servant who is a private in one of the New York regiments; the food is . . . beef, bread, and coffee, as the only rations furnished by the government; but our own private funds supply us with vegetables, milk, tea, and such other delicacies as we choose to purchase. Our table consists of a rough bench, about 12 feet long, made of oak boards, no table cloth, and seats made of boards, supported by blocks of wood at either end.

Each person is supplied with a tin cup and plate, but no knives, forks, or spoons excepting such as are supplied by ourselves.[6]

Union prisoner Warren Lee Goss could not have cared less about manservants and table settings. A prisoner in an enlisted men's jail at Belle Island in Richmond, Virginia, Goss would have been happy with a steady supply of food:

There were three stages of hunger in my experience; first, the common hungry craving one experiences after missing his dinner and supper; second, this passes away, and was succeeded by headache and a gnawing at the stomach; then came weakness, trembling of the limbs, which, if not relieved by food, was followed by death. Ordinarily we received just enough food to keep us hungry.[7]

Prison Life

At the beginning of the war, the relations between prisoners and captors were often reasonable and not unnecessarily harsh. This would change, but at the time one of the prisoners' greatest challenges was how to while away the long hours of the day. Removed from normal regimental life, which, with its drilling, camp policing, cooking, and other activities took up most of their time, the prisoners found themselves with nothing to do. For Cuban native F. F. Cavada, the empty days at Libby Prison, situated in the middle of Richmond, provided too much time to reflect upon his predicament. Overcrowded with more than one thousand other prisoners in the cramped four floors of what had previously been the warehouse of Libby & Son—Ship Chandlers & Grocers, Cavada was taunted by his proximity to free citizens:

It is difficult for one who has never before been compelled to look out upon the world from behind the bars of a prison, to convince himself of the fact that he is really deprived of his liberty. There is a merry group of children, romping and playing near the river; I listen to their joyous laughter, and, somehow, it has a very mournful sound. . . . The passers-by on the pave below, with what indifference they glance up at the pale faces that peer out between the bars![8]

Cavada was also troubled by other, more physical problems of his imprisonment. Although not especially dire in themselves, they were uncomfortable and dehumanizing, and in some cases could have led to disease, which would have been dangerous. After the war he recalled

> being absolutely soaked on "scrubbing day." A dozen black men enter with buckets & broom, people, rations, clothing, bedding soaked, everything pretty much, that you possess, your bed, your baggage, and your dinner are on the floor and that floor, will be in a few moments a tempestuous ocean of splashing, filthy water. You may baffle the foe, perhaps, for a short time, by rapid and well conducted retreats to little islands of dry floor here and there, where you stand on tip toe, your blanket over your shoulders, your day's rations in one hand, and your coffee pot in the other; but you will, finally, be compelled to surrender, and resigning yourself to your watery fate.[9]

Although Libby Prison was infamous for its grossly overcrowded conditions, abundant vermin, and volatile guards who would open fire on men leaning out of windows, it was also a place where, apparently, a basic level of decency could be maintained. Though confined inside the jail itself for months at a time, the prisoners were in good enough condition to imitate some of the normal pleasures of life. One Union prisoner recalled:

> It is curious to see with what earnestness and alacrity every branch of learning is undertaken. There have been at different times in the prison, classes of French, German, Spanish, Italian, Latin, and Greek, English Grammer, Phonography, Fencing, Dancing, Military Tactics and a bible class.[10]

Imprisoned in the tobacco warehouse, Congressman Alfred Ely petitioned President Lincoln to arrange his liberation by trading him for a Confederate prisoner. During the early part of the war, the president resisted making such formal trades because he felt that doing so would acknowledge the legitimacy of the Confederacy. Stuck for an indeterminate amount of time, Ely and his fellow prisoners found numerous ways of entertaining themselves:

> After breakfast, the officers employ themselves in a variety of ways— some playing whist; others gamble upon a small scale, pitching cents, boxing with stuffed buckskin gloves, promenading the long range of our quarters, talking, singing, so that the time may hang less heavily. . . . Dinner is announced, and sometimes the wonder is what has become of the

morning. . . . [T]he ceremony of "taking tea" has much the same routine and the day has lapsed into the evening hour, which is altogether the most lively and cheerful portion of the 24. Conversation is more brisk, wit more brilliant, and repartee keener by far.[11]

Aware that a semblance of structure in their days combined with distracting entertainment would help them maintain their sanity, the Union soldiers at Libby Prison also organized musical entertainments, as recorded by F. F. Cavada:

> The passion for music is quite general in the prison; a tolerable orchestra has been organized, consisting of a violin, banjo, guitar, tambourine, and the bones. They have done much to enliven the gloom of the prison, and invariably attract a large crowd of listeners. They have given several performances imitative of the Ethiopian Minstrels, in the cook room. These performances are quite creditable . . . and are attended by large and enthusiastic audiences.[12]

Imprisoned on Johnson's Island in the middle of Lake Erie, a group of Confederate men not only sought diversion by organizing a debate society but, in an attempt to gain some control over their lives, also elected a House of Representatives.

At holiday times, the prisoners would mark a special day by imitating the celebrations they would have enjoyed at home with their families. The prisoners would buy extra provisions when they were available, and when that was not possible, they would embellish their meals with the power of their imaginations:

> I am invited out today to a Christmas dinner. . . . [W]hen I say I am invited out I mean over there in the north east corner of the room: I shaved my face, and combed my hair this morning, for the occasion. I am promised a white china plate to eat from! . . . When I arrive at the north east corner, I enquire after my host, who is not present. I am informed that he is down in the kitchen, stewing the mutton (!) . . . there he comes, in a violent perspiration, with a skillet in one hand and a tea pot in the other. . . . There are four of us,—the dinner is excellent,—I have never tasted a better, even at the Maison Doree: the wine, not very choice, of course,—it is put down on the bill of fare as "Eau de James, couleur de boue."[13]

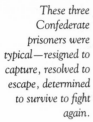

These three Confederate prisoners were typical—resigned to capture, resolved to escape, determined to survive to fight again.

Some holiday pleasures, however, could not be authentically re-created, and one New Year's Eve the prisoners had their inventiveness put to the test:

> In the evening there is a "Grand Ball" in the kitchen. The musicians are mounted on a table placed against the wall; they discourse tolerable music from a tambourine, violin, banjo, and bones; there is a great crowd; with one exception, all are men—that one is a man also, but disguised into a ludicrous representation of a negro woman—well blacked up, and with a wreath of flowers on her (his) head. . . . What a sight!—to see several hundred men dancing together at this inhuman unnatural Ball, in the gloomy cook room of a prison! . . . Oh, what base uses we may come to! To think of placing one's arm around and gracefully seizing the hand of some rough, hairy Hoosier, or some porpoisine "gun boat," and whirling them through that exhilarating maze, reserved only for delicious contact with slender waists and soft, white hands.[14]

A few prisoners enjoyed other, more unique opportunities for diversion as well. As a captured U.S. congressman, Alfred Ely attracted the attention of many citizens of Richmond. His presence in the Confederate capital ensured that he would not suffer the isolation of so many other prisoners later in the war:

The public journals have made me so conspicuous that every stranger coming to Richmond seems to seek an interview with the "Yankee Prisoner." Indeed, if fond of such notoriety I might almost be a "lion" in this renowned city. The commissary this morning remarked that he could make one hundred dollars per day from admission fees to see me by citizens and strangers. A Yankee Congressman, how attractive! Barring the music this cage of American citizens reminds me of Barnum's museum . . . yesterday a gentleman from uptown offered five dollars for a sight. Our outside doors and sidewalks are so constantly crowded with visitors that it is with difficulty the guard can keep them at a distance.[15]

Not every prisoner who sat down with people from the outside was on display, however. In the days before the attitudes of the opposing armies to each other hardened, prisoners were allowed visits by friends bearing gifts. Confederate soldier J. Harleston was captured and imprisoned in the "Tombs" of New York City. In early July 1861, he wrote that despite the discomfort of "close confinement" he had recently been called on by people he knew:

> Friends send me plenty of cigars and books. Yesterday Miss Sabina W———— came to see me and brought some raspberries. She comes regularly every week. Doctor Thomas also came to see me yesterday. E. C. ————y comes regularly every week, sometimes twice. Mr. A. and many others. All treat me with the utmost kindness, so I have everything to keep me in good spirits.[16]

For young men such as Connecticut infantryman James Sawyer, guarding the prisoners provided an insight into the character of the "enemy" that was surprising. Stationed at Fort McHenry in Baltimore, Sawyer discovered a respect for his wards that exceeded his feelings for his fellow Yankees:

> Dearest Father, Mother, and Sisters:
> . . . [T]here is a great deal of guard duty to do here. . . . [W]e stand every other day. 24 hours on; being on two hours and off four. . . . [T]here are about 200 prisoners. 130 Union prisoners, such as deserters and thieves, and the others are rebel prisoners. They are confined in a large brick building. The Union prisoners are the hardest, meanest, set of men I ever saw. . . . [T]he rebel prisoners are a very different set of men. They are quiet and gentlemanly. . . . [T]hey do not make half so much trouble as the deserters.[17]

Paroles and Exchanges

During the early stages of the war, before the last vestiges of goodwill between the two nations evaporated, it was informally agreed that an exchange-and-parole arrangement would be honored. Confederate prisoners of war could be exchanged for Union prisoners and vice versa. Later, in the summer of 1862, President Lincoln's original objection to negotiating with the Confederacy was put aside and the agreement was formalized. In some cases, prisoners were paroled without an exchange but agreed not to fight again until the other side received a prisoner in return.

To work out the terms for the exchange of prisoners, a system was established that set the worth of a soldier in comparison to those he might be traded for. A commanding general was worth the exchange of sixty privates. A major general was worth forty privates. A brigadier general would be traded for twenty privates. A colonel was worth fifteen privates. A lieutenant colonel would be exchanged for ten privates. A major was worth eight. A captain was worth six. A lieutenant would bring four privates. A noncommissioned officer was equal to two privates.

The exchanges were not always ruled by mathematics, however. Sometimes the procedures and motivations for arranging certain trades could be quite personal:

> US. Flag-ship Minnesota
> Hampton Roads, October 10, 1861
> Brigadier General Huger
> Commanding Forces, Norfolk, VA.
>
> Sir: By a letter from Lieutenant Sharp (now as you are doubtless aware a prisoner at New York) to his wife, forwarded to Norfolk today by a flag of truce, I perceive that he is very anxious to be exchanged. Without any specific authority on the subject of exchanging prisoners I venture nevertheless to say to you that I think he may be exchanged for Lieutenant Worden, of our Navy, who I understand is still confined at Montgomery. Lieutenant Worden sailed with me some years ago and I am on terms of intimacy with his family. Hence the reason of my feeling deeply interested in his behalf. Will you be good enough to inform me whether this suggestion be acceptable to yourselves or otherwise?
>
> Respectfully, your obedient servant
> L. M. Goldsborough
> Flag-Officer, Commanding Atlantic Blockading Squadron[18]

The response to a request for an exchange would list the names of the prisoners being returned and include the terms of parole for prisoners whose counterparts were desired back:

Headquarters Department of Virginia
Fort Monroe, Va., January 18, 1862
Maj. Gen. B. Huger, Commanding at Norfolk, Va.
General: By the flag of truce this day you will receive the following named persons:

1. Lieutenant Tattnall, prisoner of war, who is unconditionally released from his parole, being sent in exchange for William Dickinson who is also by you unconditionally released from his parole.
2. Lieut. G. W. Grimes Seventh (Seventeenth) North Carolina Volunteers, who is also unconditionally released from his parole in exchange for Lieut. Issac W. Hart, Twentieth Indiana Regiment, who is by you released from his parole.
3. Lieut. Julian G. Moore, Seventh (Seventeenth) North Carolina Volunteers, who is on parole for thirty days unless within that time Second Liet. William Booth, Second Wisconsin Volunteers, be unconditionally released and put at liberty at Fort Monroe.

Very Respectfully, your obedient servant John E. Wool Major General.[19]

Upon receiving their parole, prisoners of war would have to sign an affidavit, sometimes in their own handwriting, describing the terms of their release:

Grand Junction Tenn July 4 [illegible, possibly 7] 1862
I, R. G. Duke of Co "K" 31st Reg Tennessee Volunteers in the service of the so called Confederate States do hereby most solemnly swear and affirm not to give aid and comfort in any manner whatsoever to the enemies of the United States of America be they domestic or foreign that I shall consider myself a prisoner of war on *parole* until regularly exchanged.
Signed R. G. Duke[20]

Directly beneath the parolee's oath would be handwritten a description of the soldier so that on the man's journey home he could be properly identified by any authorities who might challenge him:

The bearer R. G. Duke heretofore belonging to Co. K 31st Tenn Volunteers. A private 24 years of age, grey eyes, black hair, dark complexion, six feet high, by profession a farmer born in Wrackly [indecipherable] state of Tenesee [*sic*]

[indecipherable] Jacobs
Provost Marshall[21]

At times prisoners' requests for exchange were remarkable in their obliviousness to the war raging around them—almost to the extent of being funny:

Columbia Jail, S.C., January 20, 1862
General Huger
Commanding General Confederate Forces, Norfolk, VA.

Dear Sir: I have just received a note from my wife which greatly increases my anxiety for an immediate exchange. I have received an appointment to the presidency of a college in Oregon which I propose to accept. I wish to make arrangements for as early removal thither as possible. Can you do anything toward obtaining my release? If you are unable to do anything yourself will you please communicate the facts to the authorities at Richmond and likewise at Washington? Captain Shriver will add a note to this upon the same subject.

Hoping for a favorable and speedy issue of the matter,
I am, sir, very respectfully, your obedient servant,
Geo. W. Dodge
Chaplain Eleventh Regiment New York Volunteers[22]

Prisoners freed from war camps were often subjected to further incarceration prior to returning home. Some prisoners were released from one form of incarceration, only to be transferred to parole camps, where they would wait for an exchange:

It is located on a kind of sandy plain and covers an area of about 20 acres. There is no trees inside the lines under which to get shelter from the hot rays of the sun in summer, no green grass to lay on nothing but the hot schorching [*sic*] sand which on the slightest breeze raises in little cloud, almost penetrating through one's clothes. . . . [A] single tall wooden pump supplies warm water for the whole camp and as there was about 6000 prisoners depending upon it for water the old pump was kept moving all the time. You could look to it any minute of the day and see a crowd around it, each waiting their turn, and could wake up at any time of night and hear the creak of the old handle.[23]

Surviving the Prisoner-of-War Camps

The majority of prisoners, however, never got the chance to be exchanged, and other arrangements were made, under flag of truce, to lessen their suffering. Hungry, cold prisoners benefited greatly from shipments of food and clothing from their families. Acceptance of such supplies was not always motivated by humanitarian instincts but because the supplies lessened their own obligations:

> Richmond, VA. December 4, 1861
> Hon. B. F. Granger
>   Dear Sir: I take the liberty of addressing you, the Representative of the First Congressional District, in behalf of 72 sons of Michigan, 40 of whom are from your immediate district. . . . They are prisoners of war. Most of them have been in close confinement under very unfavorable circumstances over four months. . . . I have just read a note from an educated young man of a Northern city who left a situation as a bank clerk and enlisted as a private to serve his country. He was wounded and taken prisoner at Manassas. He says; "I have no shirt or socks and suffer much from cold and damp and at every breath it seems as if a knife were plunged into me: I cannot stand it much longer. . . ."
>   We have frequently heard that clothing was to be sent to us but winter has come and no clothing, but sickness has. It has been said that the Confederates send the most destitute to the far South from motives of humanity. However that may be I saw some go without shirts and many without shoes or socks, and even some with drawers and no pants. . . . Clothing can be sent safely. The Massachusetts men having been here but about six weeks have already been supplied with full outfits from their friends at home. Cannot our Government send as well as they? The Confederates have recently furnished quilts as substitutes for blankets, which could not be obtained, and straw sacks, which is some improvement, but we still need blankets, and clothing, especially pants, shirts, drawers, socks, and shoes.[24]

In response, state governments or local charitable organizations would endeavor to put together supplies that were necessary to make imprisoned brothers, husbands, and sons more comfortable. A cover letter would often accompany the gifts and explain precisely what was included:

> Headquarters Department of Virginia
> Fort Montor, VA., December 5, 1861
> Maj. Gen. B. Huger, Commanding at Norfolk, Va.
> General: I forward to you by flag of truce six boxes addressed to Lieut. I. W. Hart Twentieth Regiment Indiana Volunteers, at Norfolk, containing the following articles of clothing for prisoners of war: 53 woolen blouses, 53 caps, 53 shirts, 53 blankets, 53 pairs of trousers, 53 pairs of drawers, 53 pairs of shoes, 53 pairs of socks, and 37 greatcoats. Also nineteen cases addressed to First Lieut. Charles L. Peirson, Twentieth Regiment Massachusetts Volunteers, a prisoner of war in Richmond, containing the following articles for distribution to Massachusetts troops, prisoners of war: 350 blankets, 350 overcoats, 700 flannel shirts, 700 pairs of socks, 700 pairs of drawers, 350 pairs of trousers, 350 pairs of shoes, 301 towels, 170 handkerchiefs.
> Very respectfully, your obedient servant
> John E. Wool Major General[25]

Even more extraordinary than the shipment of supplies across hostile borders was the civility with which both nations permitted family members of prisoners of war to visit their loved ones:

> Hdqrs. First Division, Western Department
> Columbus, Ky. February 23, 1862
> To the Commanding Officer, U.S. Forces, Cairo, Ill.:
> Presuming you would be willing to reciprocate the courtesy shown to the families of officers of the U.S. Army after the battle of Belmont in allowing them to visit those officers who were prisoners within my lines, I take the liberty of sending up under a flag of truce the families of several of our officers who were captured at Donelson. These are the families of General Buckner, Colonels Hanson and Madeira. They are accompanied by Colonel Russell, Mr. Vance and [Mr.] Stockdale as escorts; also by Mr. Mass.
> Hoping you will find it convenient to send these ladies forward to their husbands I have the honor to remain, respectfully, your obedient servant, L. Polk. Major-General Commanding.[26]

In Northern prison camps, civility was allowed to an absurd degree. Rushed prematurely into operation, Camp Douglas in Springfield, Illinois, had an insufficient staff, practically no weapons for its few guards, and no fences. When Confederate officers who were supposed to be prisoners of war were seen enjoying dinners in the best hotel dining rooms in Chicago, action was demanded:

> Chicago, February 24, 1862
> Major General Halleck:
>   There are about 7,000 prisoners here at Camp Douglas. There is not even a fence about the barracks. The troops there are all skeleton regiments and artillery companies, with most of their men absent. . . . There is not sufficient force under the present discipline to properly guard the prisoners. . . . I have seen two men guarding 300 feet with no other arms than a stick. . . . The secession officers are not kept separate from the men, and our best citizens are in great alarm for fear that the prisoners will break through and burn the city. . . .
>   Julian S. Rumsey
>   Mayor of the City of Chicago[27]

The World's First Concentration Camps

While some prisoners of war feasted in restaurants, attended New Year's Eve balls, or were exchanged in a cordial manner, prison life for most men was full of hardship. For all the stories of lenient treatment toward captured soldiers, anytime a man's liberty was taken away he suffered. Still, during the first years of the war there existed a fundamental decency in the prisons that allowed the men to survive and at times actually to enjoy themselves.

In 1862, however, this began to change. Captors began to treat their prisoners more severely, and the potential for truly despicable actions became apparent. The cause of these changes was the building pressures and consequences of war, which altered the relationship between the two countries, their prisoners of war, and those prisoners' captors. Months of suffering, destruction of property, fears of losing the war, and the deaths of thousands of soldiers hardened the attitudes of the men toward their captured enemies. As supplies diminished, soldiers and citizens were less interested in how prisoners of war were fed, clothed, or sheltered. Any pretense of a "gentleman's war" vanished, and those who were most vulnerable to the evolution of hatred were the prisoners.

When Union soldier Warren Lee Goss was captured after the battle of Savage's Station, he was immediately introduced to a barbaric world in which the struggle to stay alive was fought daily:

> On the 5th of July we were packed into filthy cattle cars, the sick and wounded crowded together and sent into Richmond. About twenty of our wounded are said to have died during the passage of little over one hour. Arriving at the depot in Richmond we were formed in order around the canal, preparatory to marching to prison. We were a hard looking crowd, made greatly so through suffering. The heat of the day was such as to make the thinnest garment intolerable. Many cast away their shirts and coats, and others their pantaloons and shoes. "So many wounded and sick men in the streets of the rebel capital, pale, bleeding, and in some cases nearly naked. . . ."[28]

Unlike early in the war, by the middle of 1862 prisoners were required to spend more of their time struggling for survival instead of organizing musical groups or preparing Christmas dinners. Sent to Belle Island prison, Warren Lee Goss received rations that were deficient in quantity and abysmal in quality:

> Our rations at this time consisted of one half loaf to each man per day, and beans, cooked in water in which bacon had been boiled for the guard,—usually containing about twenty percent of maggots, owing to the scarcity of salt, thirty percent of beans, and the remainder of water. . . . It was issued sometimes twice a week and sometimes not at all. . . . [T]he insufficiency of the food was aggravated by neglect of the prison authorities to issue regularly; sometimes we got no rations from Saturday morning until Monday night. The excuse usually given was that the bakers in the city were on a drunk.[29]

As a result, Goss and his fellow prisoners were required to spend much of their time and energy organizing food to supplement their meager rations:

> As soon as I obtained sufficient strength to walk round, I entered into a competition with others and after trading away my shoes and coat for food set up as kind of commission merchant for dealing in boots and any other article of clothing of trading value. By this means, with perseverance I managed occasionally to obtain an extra johnny cake, a potato, or an onion.[30]

Further contributing to the decline in the prisoners' treatment was a developing attitude that captives should be dealt with just as harshly as the enemy was handling "our own" soldiers:

> Our government might benefit us a little I think by taking the same number of prisoners as we are, sending them to Charleston and locking them up in cells as we are, making them in fact answerable for us in every way. Let their treatment be governed by ours.[31]

Soldiers and citizens on both sides of the conflict agreed with this sentiment, and their anger was stirred when they witnessed the condition of exchanged soldiers—even when the former prisoners defended the actions of their captors:

> July 21st, 1862
>
> Four hundred released prisoners arrived today under flag of truce, and I assure you it was a most distressing sight. All of them were captured during the seven days' fight and had been prisoners but three weeks; yet they were starved, ragged, and filthy beyond description. Some had on only shirts, others drawers without shirts; and one wore simply a rough blanket over his naked body, they all were either wounded or ill. Their wounds had been dressed only by what each could do for the other, and by making use of the water given them to drink. These men were released because the Confederates could not feed them. They never complain, talking with reluctance of their suffering while in prison and always saying, "It was the best the enemy could do for us."[32]

The following year saw the breakdown of parole and exchange agreements as both sides argued over real and perceived violations of the terms and conditions. Quickly both the Confederacy and Union prisoner-of-war camps were overwhelmed as populations mushroomed because the apparatus that had previously existed to reduce their numbers no longer existed.

The deteriorating atmosphere led to the sanctioning of other forms of abuse. Punishments that were irrational and unconscionable were perpetrated by both sides, as the trial transcript of Private Clarence Wicks of Company E, Nineteenth Wisconsin Volunteers, indicates:

> Q: How old are you?
> A: About seventeen years.

Q: Are you a soldier in this regiment?
A: I am, a private in Company E.

Q: Were you on duty as sentinel in this camp yesterday morning?
A: I was.

Q: Do you know of a prisoner having been shot in camp yesterday morning?
A: Yes, sir.

Q: Do you know who shot him?
A: Yes, sir; I did.

Q: Relate the circumstances attending to it.
A: There was a sink hole being dug right by the side of my beat. It was unfinished and I had special orders not to allow the prisoners to use it under any circumstances.

Q: Who gave you the orders?
A: The sentinel who I had relieved. Somewhere about 7 o'clock in the morning a man came out from the prisoners' barracks to this sink, and removing his pants sat or squatted down apparently for the purpose of moving his bowels. I told him that place was not to be used for that purpose and twice or three times ordered him away and told him to go to one of the sinks. He did not move and I picked up a small stone and threw it at him, hitting him on the side of the face.

Q: What then happened?
A: Six or seven of the rebels came running toward me from their barracks and one of them, said to be his brother, said to me, "You damned son of a bitch! I will report you." I had orders to shoot rebels insulting me and did shoot him.

Q: Did he fall?
A: Yes, sir; he fell dead.[33]

Private Wicks was acquitted of murder.

If the circumstances at Camp Randall, where Private Wicks was stationed, were harsh, there was worse to come. As the prison camps filled up and supplies ran out, both nations sent their overflow prisoners farther away from the urban centers where the original jails had been located. The prison camps established in remote areas were more distant from the supply lines that provided

Andersonville Prison, an uncovered pen near Plains, Georgia. Conditions there horrified Confederate civilians as well as Union troops.

food, clothing, tents, and medicines—and were correspondingly more brutal. When Camp Sumter was established in rural Andersonville, Georgia, it was far from the provisions it needed and perhaps, more important, out of view of those who might have objected to the gruesome events that would occur there. Still, when the prison camp opened the propaganda directed to the prisoners being sent there painted a bucolic picture more reminiscent of a holiday camp than the deadliest penitentiary in North America:

> So liable are men to deceive themselves with false hopes and expecta-
> tions, that when the rebel guard informed them that their destination
> was Andersonville, a beautifully laid out camp, with luxuriant shade trees
> filled with birds, and a running stream in which fish sported, they swal-
> lowed the whole story undoubtingly.[34]

The truth was different, as Warren Lee Goss discovered in what was among the world's first concentration camps:

> As we waited the great gates of the prison swung on their ponderous
> oaken hinges, and we were ushered into what seemed to us Hades itself.
> Strange skeleton men, in tattered, faded blue,—and not much blue either,

so obscured with dirt were their habiliments,—gathered and crowded around us; their faces were so begrimed with pitch-pine smoke and dirt, that for a while we could not discern whether they were negroes or white men. . . . [T]he air of the prison was putrid; offal and filth covered the ground; and the hearts buoyed with expectation of good quarters sank within them when they knew that no shelter was furnished beyond what could be constructed of blankets or garments.[35]

Andersonville was established on a sixteen-acre parcel in a wooded area with the insignificant Stockade Creek running across its property. Originally intended for ten thousand prisoners, the camp saw its population balloon to thirty-three thousand within six months. At its most crowded, Andersonville earned the dubious distinction of being between the fourth and fifth largest population center or "city" in the entire Confederacy. Later expanded to twenty-seven acres, the camp was still far too small to house properly the number of men behind its stockade fence, and its vital natural resources, such as water and wood, were pitifully inadequate. The trees that should have provided wood for fires, heat, and shelter disappeared to those purposes almost immediately. The creek and boglike areas were befouled by the prisoners' and guards' excrement, as they were used for toilets: "The stream was not strong enough to carry away the filth and the swampy lowland became indescribably foul."[36] The stream, which was also known as the Sweetwater Creek, was the source of many deaths from typhoid fever, dysentery, and other fatal diseases:

> Originally the interior of the prison had been densely wooded with pitchpine, in which that country abounds, but at the time of our arrival it had been, with the exception of two trees, entirely cut to supply the want of fuel demanded by the prisoners. The camp at the time was dependent upon the roots and stumps of the trees which had been cut down for fuel. A limited number of those who were among the first arrivals had constructed rude shelters of the branches of trees, thatched with pitch pines to shed the rain.[37]

But for the prisoners who were sent to Andersonville after the initial arrivals, there would be no shelters. Men who would be nearly starved to death by their daily ration of one teaspoon of salt, half a pint of unsifted cornmeal, and three tablespoons of beans also had to survive extreme weather conditions without any real protection. John England of New York's Company E, Second Cavalry, wrote:

During the time in the stockade [Andersonville] I had no shelter from the sun by day, the dew by night, or the terrible rains that so often visit the state; but indeed I was not alone in this for thousands of others were in the same sad predicament. The only shelter if such it could be called which many had was either in the shape of holes dug in the ground and roofed over with mud and rags, and would-be tents made out of old clothes, pieces of old blankets and now and then some brush the best of which was unable to keep out the rain. Men died at the rate of three hundred a week![38]

Weakened by the camp conditions, the sick had to make do without a proper, sheltered hospital. Exposed to the sun and heat or to the cold and rain, they simply lay on the ground to either die or heal themselves. Doctor Joseph Jones, who visited the prison camp in October 1864, noted that the camp and its inhabitants were in a general state of degeneration:

> From the crowded condition, filthy habits, bad diet, and dejected, depressed condition of the prisoners, their systems became so disordered that the smallest abrasion of the skin, from the rubbing of a shoe, or from the effects of the hot sun, or from the prick of a splinter, or from scratching a mosquito bite, in some cases took on rapid and frightening ulceration and gangrene.[39]

A third of Andersonville's prisoners died in its one year of operation. Part of the prison camp's daily ritual was the removal of the dead in horse-drawn carts to be buried in shallow mass graves little more than a mile from the stockade.

Among all the horrors of the American Civil War, it is likely that Andersonville represented the nadir of the soldiers' experience, and perhaps even of the "American experience" itself:

> [The] northern section of camp is swamp used as [our] toilet. Horrible stench at night better during the day: Men reduced by starvation and disease would drag themselves to this locality to lie down and die uncared for almost unnoticed. I have counted fifteen dead bodies in one morning near this sink, where they had died during the night. I have seen forty or fifty men in a dying condition, who, with their little remaining strength, had dragged themselves to this place for its conveniences, and, unable to get back again, were exposed in the sun, often without food, until death relieved them of the burden of life. Frequently, on passing them, some

were found reduced to idiocy, and many, unable to articulate, would stretch forth their wasted hands in piteous supplication for food or water, or point to their lips, their glazed eyes presenting that staring fixedness which immediately precedes death. . . . [D]uring one week there were said to have died 1,308 men.[40]

Though Goss's estimate may be high, the truth is no less horrible. Other appraisals calculate that on the single worst day at Andersonville 127 men died—or one every eleven minutes or so.[41] Eventually, thirteen thousand Union prisoners of war would die at Andersonville.

While the sanitary and health conditions at Andersonville were a form of barbarity, the camp commanders' lethal intent was not always so passive. Another harsh reality in the world of the Civil War could be found in the so-called dead line that surrounded the perimeter of the prison camp:

One of the great instruments of death in the prison was the dead line. This line consisted of a row of stakes driven into the ground, with narrow board strips nailed down upon the top at the distance of about fifteen feet from the stockade, on the interior side. This line was closely guarded by sentinels stationed above the stockade and any person who approached it, as many unconsciously did, and as in the crowd was often unavoidable, was shot dead, with no warning whatever to admonish him that death was near . . . frequently the guard fired indiscriminately into the crowd. . . . [A] key to this murderous inhuman practice was . . . a standing order at rebel headquarters that "any sentinel killing a federal soldier approaching the dead line shall receive a furlough of sixty days; while for wounding one he shall receive a furlough for thirty days." . . . [M]en becoming tired of life committed suicide in this manner. They had but to get under the dead line or lean upon it, and their fate was sealed in death.[42]

Death was literally in the air, as a stench that was "beyond imagination, seeming to solidify the atmosphere" hovered over the prison camp.[43] Starved, diseased, and with little hope of ever leaving Andersonville alive, the prisoners of war were reduced to something less than completely human, and their will to live seeped away:

Within the inclosure we found 23,000 poor creatures, some of whom had scarce a trace of manhood left in their appearance, some feeble and emaciated from starvation, and disease, clothing worn to tatters, filthy

rags. . . . [T]hree of our squad, in utter despair at such a prospect of existence, stepped over the "dead line" and received their call for another
world, satisfied that death, with all its uncertainties, would not produce a
worse place than this.[44]

Soul killing as the conditions in the Civil War prison camps were, some prisoners refused to give up. The greatest breakout of the war occurred at Libby
Prison, from which 109 Union officers escaped through a tunnel dug with improvised tools. But Andersonville was a more difficult, possibly impossible challenge, and only a few had the strength and initiative even to try:

> Our only chance of escape was in tunneling under the stockade, which
> was slow work, and very uncertain. Many attempts were made in this di-
> rection only a few of which ever proved successful. The distance from the
> dead line to the stockade was about sixteen feet, and it certainly was not
> safe to emerge from the ground nearer than the same distance from the
> other side. The ground was loose and sandy on top and a tunnel necessar-
> ily had to be deep in the center and narrow all the way through to pre-
> vent the earth from caving in. In addition to the great labor of the
> undertaking was the constant danger of detection. The Confederate offi-
> cer of the guard patrolled the camp outside the stockade every morning
> with a pack of bloodhounds; besides which, spies were in our midst all the
> time. . . .
>
> Three of us at one time started a tunnel . . . we carefully hid it from
> view by putting up an old piece of shelter tent. . . . [U]nder this tent, one
> of us was ostensibly sick, and lay during the daytime directly over the
> hole on a board. . . . [A]t night we dug out the dirt with a piece of tin
> taken from an old canteen, and carried it off in our clothes, first tying our
> pant legs tight around our ankles and coat sleeves around our wrists, then
> filling these with dirt as well as our pockets. After being thus loaded we
> started for the swamp, where we buried the fresh dirt. . . .
>
> In this slow way we worked for over two weeks and calculated we had
> got about under the stockade. . . . [O]ur disappointment can possibly be
> better imagined than described when, one afternoon, a rebel sergeant
> and four guards with shovels came to camp, and marched directly to our
> tent, took off the board and commenced to fill in our tunnel. Our "sick"
> comrade had by merest chance crawled out after a drink of water and the
> other two of us were spending the time with a acquaintance. . . . [S]ome
> treacherous prisoner or rebel spy had . . . betrayed us.[45]

Although Andersonville was most likely the worst of all prison camps, the Union camps had their share of debased behavior. The death tolls were tragically high among the prison populations of both sides. At the Rock Island prison camp in Illinois, more than 75 percent of the prisoners, or just under two thousand men, died when smallpox swept through the camp. The smallpox epidemic, however, was not the result of any particularly cruel behavior or unusual negligence on the part of the Union captors; it could have just as easily occurred in the prisoners' home regimental camps.

On the other hand, captors knew all too well what would happen to their prisoners if they were forced into grossly crowded conditions and not provided with the means of taking care of themselves:

> Fort Columbus, Ny Harbor October 8 1861
> Col. G. Loomis, U.S. Army, Commanding
> Colonel: I have the honor to report that the condition of the sick prisoners has not improved. Death occurs daily and there continues to be a large number of cases of measles, pneumonia, typhoid fever, &c. I have taken as many cases into the hospitals as can be accommodated. The sickness will continue and increase so long as so large a body of men is crowded together in Castle William. If 100 are removed to Bedloe's Island as contemplated and including a large proportion of the sick there will be better facilities for improving the condition of those remaining.
> Very respectfully, yours, &c., Wm J. Sloan
> Surgeon, U.S. Army[46]

Despite a statistically lower mortality rate than Rock Island's, the most notorious of the Union camps was opened in the spring of 1864. Located in Elmira, New York, the prison was called "Hellmira" by its inhabitants. Intended to house five thousand men, Elmira was woefully unprepared for the twelve thousand prisoners who would eventually live there. Many inmates would die from exposure or the diseases that are caused by living without appropriate shelter. Once the underheated barracks were full, prisoners were lodged in flimsy tents, and when those ran out, they slept outside. The dangers posed by the weather in Elmira were quite different from those in the South. Snow, sleet, ice, and terrible cold caused the freezing deaths of men who had no adequate protection from the elements or decent clothing. Although Elmira was in operation for slightly less than a year, almost three thousand of its population were buried on its grounds.

For all the horrors of life in the prison camps, however, there were those for whom the hope of survival could not be extinguished. Even after years of debilitating, humiliating treatment, there were men who maintained their dignity and found ways to survive with their humanity intact. One man actually used the callous treatment of the prisoners, living and dead, to his advantage:

> March 20.
> A great joy has come to me this day, an unlooked for and inexpressible joy! A card was brought to me, and I took it with a sigh because so many cards are brought in and we have so little time for the rest. But the name upon that particular card made my heart thump and thump so fast I thought it would thump clean out of my body. It was my dear brother's name—the scout, who has been in prison two years. . . . I rushed into his presence and into his arms. He's the rowdiest, shabbiest, patchiest looking fellow you ever saw, but as handsome as ever. . . . It is a thrilling romance, the way he escaped from prison. In a dead man's shoes it was! The Man's name was Jesse Tredway, and he died in his bunk after his name had been entered on the list of exchange. My brother put his dead comrade in his own bunk and said nothing. He answered to his name in the roll call and quietly took his place in the ranks of outgoing prisoners.
> Malvina S. Waring Columbia SC[47]

The excuses offered by those involved, as well as by apologists, for the excessively cruel behavior toward prisoners have a trace of validity. It cannot be denied that supplies of building materials, food, medicine, clothing, and other items necessary for prisoners' survival were in desperately short supply. It is also correct that in many cases, particularly as far as the Confederacy was concerned, each side's own fighting men were themselves deprived of the basics required to remain healthy.

The truth was, however, that the commanders who made decisions regarding the prisoners were not without choices. Undesirable as it may have been from some perspectives, the military leaders could have sent prisoners back to their homes once the scale of the impending catastrophe became clear. Doing so would not have been unprecedented. Early in the war, instances of Confederate captors releasing prisoners when they were no longer able to feed them were known to have occurred. The Union had done the same, most notably with General Grant's release of more than thirty thousand rebel prisoners in 1863.

Ultimately, the manner in which the Confederacy and Union dealt with the men they captured was unfathomable. In a war where the enemy was fellow countrymen, neighbors, and sometimes cousins, brothers, fathers, and sons, it is difficult to imagine how the treatment of the prisoners was ever allowed to devolve to such an inhuman level. Theories that suggest that the two nations were impoverished, that the rations of the prisoners of one side were linked to the amount of those provided to its prisoners by the other, or that people did not really know what was going on do not stand up to scrutiny.

The sad fact is that both nations allowed their prisoners to be abused in the cruelest fashion and murdered in cold blood. These crimes did not occur spontaneously or because there was no specific strategy for handling the prisoners. Andersonville and Elmira did not arise simply because no one was paying attention. Instead, these tragedies were the direct result of policy decisions that money was not to be spent on captives, regardless of the consequences. A certain attitude was established toward the captive soldiers, and the men who ran the camps, as well as those who guarded them, acted accordingly. In some cases supplies that were available and could have saved prisoners' lives were simply not distributed. The motivations behind such decisions could only be vengeance and a desire to kill.

What is most striking about the prisoner-of-war camps is that they serve to remind those of us in the twentieth century about the viciousness of the American Civil War. Almost 140 years after the surrender of General Lee at Appomattox, there is a tendency to romanticize the war, to remark on how well the enemy soldiers got along when they were not fighting, and to emphasize what ensued in the decades following the war as a nation of independent states grew together into a single national identity. While those are valid topics of discussion, it must not be forgotten that when given the opportunity to abuse and destroy vulnerable people, Americans on both sides did so with gusto. While the American Civil War was influenced, to some extent, by complex and noble purposes, it was also one of biblical simplicity: the conscienceless slaughter of brother murdering brother—Cain murdering Abel.

CHAPTER SEVEN

Military Crimes and Punishments

*B*rutality and less serious wrongdoing were rarely the exclusive province of prisons and battlefields. By their nature, military encampments were volatile places, where men from all walks of life were forced into cramped quarters during the periods between grueling marches and desperate fighting. The great majority of Civil War soldiers came to the army from ordinary civilian lives in which they had never been subjected to such extremes of discipline. The juxtaposition of unrestrained savagery in battle and enforced obedience to strict rules in camp often created a confused moral atmosphere for the soldiers. The result was a nearly constant challenging of superiors and regulations by men who were expected to engage in the frenzy of violence but who, when they returned to their tents, were not allowed to drink alcohol and were required to obey their officers' commands.

Minor Infractions and Punishments

The most frequent minor infractions of the law were drunkenness, talking back to an officer, not saluting a superior, missing roll call, causing "turbulence after taps," not standing up while on guard duty, and gambling.

For these violations a soldier could expect to be sent to the regimental guard tent for a period of hours to days. While some considered the deprivation of liberty to be a sobering punishment, for others incarceration alleviated the fatiguing responsibilities of camp life. Either way, men who frequently risked their lives on the battlefield were not going to be intimidated by such discipline. Soldiers who disrespected officers were not going to change their ways because of a slap on the wrist. Nor would gamblers give up their passion or swearing men suddenly speak like preachers. The world of a soldier was a rough one, the command recognized the fact, and when troops behaved crudely or broke less significant regulations, there was not much that could—or should—be done about it.

Digging Ditches, Thievery, and Corporal Punishment

Other transgressions that warranted mild discipline often involved a soldier not fulfilling his responsibilities in a manner that could potentially have threatened the safety of his regiment. Often this meant a soldier not returning from a visit into a nearby town by a prearranged time at night, temporarily slipping out of camp without permission, or leaving sentry duty before the arrival of a replacement.

A wide range of punishments was meted out, depending on the attitude of the commanding officer. Moderate discipline usually required the transgressing soldier to participate in the least desirable of camp activities, such as maintaining the open-trench toilets, mucking out stables, and disposing of dead horses.

Some offenses, however, were more serious in nature and required more profound forms of punishment. For example, petty thievery, a frequently occurring crime, was dealt with harshly.

For those living in military camps, life was reduced to its elements: eating, drinking, performing duties, and living with a minimum of physical comforts. Soldiers had few personal possessions, and when they were stolen by men with whom the victims were to risk their lives in battle, the theft was not easily forgiven. The magnitude of the crime was increased if it involved food or clothing, particularly in times when rations were scarce or the weather was bad. In such cases, theft could literally make the difference between life and death.

Soldiers needed to know what kind of men their compatriots were, and thieves were dealt with accordingly. As punishment they were often forced to march through camp bearing a sign describing their crime and then subjected to various forms of corporal punishment.

The dispensers of justice in the military camps were quite creative in the invention of suitable forms of behavior modification and seemed to take perverse delight in their diversity. They ranged the gamut from the merely humiliating to the physically cruel.

Meeting both criteria was a punishment called "bucking and gagging," in which a soldier's wrists and ankles were bound tightly, and a wooden gag was inserted into his mouth for hours. One unfortunate Confederate soldier was bucked and gagged for eight hours a day for thirty successive days, given seven days off, then bucked and gagged for another month.

Less brutal sentences included "standing on the chines," in which a soldier was forced to balance himself on the staves of a barrel whose top had been removed. Some wore wooden "jackets" made from ordinary barrels suspended from prisoners' shoulders with holes in the side for their arms. Dressed this way, they were forced to march through camp to be ridiculed by their fellow soldiers. Mounting a "wooden horse" was an uncomfortable punishment during which the miscreant was forced to sit on a crossbar ten feet above the ground for long periods of time. Other disciplinary actions included forcing a man to march for hours while carrying a knapsack filled with bricks, making him stand for long periods on a raised platform without protection from the elements, strapping him to the spare wheel of a moving cannon, making him carry a loaded saddle or shoulder a heavy wooden beam, extending his guard duty, docking his salary, attaching him to a heavy ball and chain for hours or days, and sealing him inside a "sweat box" that resembled a coffin.

More serious transgressions, such as self-mutilation to avoid duty or striking an officer, led to long sentences at hard labor in desolate places such as the Dry Tortugas off the coast of Florida. Solitary confinement for long periods of time with only bread and water for rations was another typical punishment.

One of the more draconian penalties for criminals was being hung by their thumbs, with their toes just touching the ground, for hours at a time. If an offense were serious enough, on the order of a serious assault of an officer, a court-martial, prison term, and dishonorable discharge might follow.

Provost Marshals

Military discipline involved risk for the soldiers responsible for law enforcement, who were known as provost marshals. Outnumbered and outgunned by troops who resented their authority and the prosecution of their friends, provost marshals were sometimes threatened and insurrections were known to occur. Union soldier William H. Sallada witnessed one such response to a punishment that was considered particularly cruel by the rank and file:

> It happened one day that a recruit . . . was found guilty of some misdemeanor, and the thumb punishment was applied. While the poor fellow was suffering the tortures of the inquisition a sympathizing soldier . . . clandestinely cut him down and hurried him off in the direction of his

regiment, which was encamped on the other side of the bluffs. An immediate excitement in the camp was the result. Hundreds of enlisted men, whose sympathies were actively with the victim, and against the abuses of tyranny, followed the two in a tumultuous throng.[1]

As the enlisted men got rowdier, protesting the treatment of the recruit, one officer was beaten. Not until a group of officers opened fire on the men—albeit with blanks—was the "mutiny" put down. Sallada did not record the punishments of those involved, but an attack on the disciplinary arm of the military was a serious offense and could elicit a harsh response. Confederate soldier Richard Lewis witnessed the execution of two Louisiana Zouaves who were caught as they took a man out of the guard house by force.

Cowardice

The second most serious crime—after desertion—a soldier could commit was displaying cowardice while engaged with the enemy. According to the military code, a soldier could be executed for such behavior, but rarely was a death sentence carried out. Instead, the common penalty for cowardice was being expelled from the army with a dishonorable discharge and loss of pay. The convicted soldier would be stripped of his uniform, often his head was shaved, and he would be led out of camp by armed guards as the jeering regiment watched and the musicians played "The Rogue's March."

Punishments varied from regiment to regiment, however, and a crime that received negligible attention in one might be dealt with harshly in another. Fortunate soldiers convicted of leaving camp without leave might be given extra guard duty to perform. Unlucky soldiers who left their units at times when the military authorities wanted to make examples of those who were flouting the rules were treated quite differently, as Sam Watkins witnessed:

> To their minds [the rebel infantry] the South was a great tyrant, and the Confederacy a fraud. They were deserting in thousands. . . . And when some miserable wretch was to be whipped and branded for being absent ten days without leave, we had to see him kneel down and have his head shaved smooth and slick as a peeled onion, and then stripped to the naked skin. Then a strapping fellow with a big rawhide would make the blood flow and spurt at every lick, the wretch begging and howling like a hound, and then he was branded with a red hot iron with the letter

D on both hips, when he was marched through the army to the music of the "Rogue's March." It was enough.[2]

Capital Punishment

Desertion was the most serious crime a soldier could commit, and the punishments were accordingly severe. While amnesty was occasionally offered to encourage men to return to their units, it was generally ineffective as soldiers knew that the military had little chance of catching them once they returned home. The unfortunate deserters who were caught, however, were in serious trouble, as Dr. John Perry noted in a letter to his wife in 1863:

> I have a very disagreeable duty to perform this morning,—that of tattooing a man's breast for desertion. He is to have his head shaved and be drummed out of camp to-morrow. It would be better to shoot the man than to permanently disgrace him, but he does not seem to mind it much, and probably is so demoralized that he is past feeling shame.[3]

Brutal as this treatment sounds, John Perry's tattooed deserter most likely did not object to his treatment, for he realized he was lucky to be alive. Death by firing squad was the prescribed penalty for desertion. While not every deserter was executed, there were periods during the war when desertions were numerous and the authorities felt compelled to act. Deserters unlucky enough to be caught at times such as these were quickly made examples of.

To make the deepest impression on the soldiers, the execution of deserters was a staged spectacle that hundreds, perhaps thousands of men were forced to witness. Often the regiments would be organized into three sides of a rectangle in double ranks facing each other, creating a corridor through which the condemned soldier would proceed. The third side of the rectangle would be open. There, a grave would have been dug, and sometimes a coffin would be waiting for its future inhabitant.

The procession would begin at the mouth of the double ranks with the provost marshal in the lead. As the chief law enforcement officer of the regiment, he was commander of the proceedings. The regimental band would follow, playing appropriately mournful music. Twelve armed guards would then be followed by the prisoner himself—sometimes on foot with his coffin next to him, sometimes in a horse-drawn ambulance, sitting on his casket. Accompanied by a minister and two guards holding his arms, he was followed by the twelve members of the firing squad itself. Behind them was a backup firing squad in case the original members balked at their task.

After the condemned man made his way through the corridor created by the members of his regiment, he would be made to sit on his casket beside the waiting grave. After a prayer by the chaplain, the man's eyes would be covered, his hands would be tied behind his back, the order of execution would be announced, and the firing squad would do its duty. If the prisoner were not killed by the first volley of shots, the reserve team would apply the coup de grâce. Confederate doctor Spencer Welch witnessed such an execution at a camp near the Rappahannock River in Virginia on March 5, 1863:

> A man was shot near our regiment last Sunday for desertion. It was a very solemn scene. The condemned man was seated on his coffin with his hands tied across his breast. A file of twelve soldiers was brought up to within six feet of him, and at the command, a volley was fired right into his breast. He was hit by but one ball, because eleven of the guns were loaded with powder only. This was done so that no man can be certain that he killed him. If he was, the thought of it might always be painful to him.[4]

Several months later, in September, Welch had an opportunity to talk with a man who had known a condemned prisoner. Welch felt sympathy for the doomed man, who, he believed, had been encouraged to desert by men who had been guilty of the even more serious crime of incitement:

> We had nine more military executions in our division yesterday. . . . Colonel Hunt was a member of the court martial which sentenced them, and he tells me that one of the men from Lane's Brigade was a brother of your preacher, and that the two looked very much alike. He said that he was a very intelligent man, and gave as his reason for deserting that the editorials in the Raleigh Standard had convinced him that Jeff Davis was a tyrant and that the Confederate cause was wrong. I am surprised that the editor of that miserable little journal is allowed to go at large. It is most unfortunate that this thing of shooting men for desertion was not begun sooner. Many lives would have been saved by it because a great many men will now have to be shot before the trouble can be stopped.[5]

A number of enlisted men would have disagreed with Welch about the shooting of deserters. Sam Watkins, for instance, was particularly incensed by the punishment, as most of the deserting soldiers had fulfilled the twelve-month obligation they had volunteered for and resented the fact that the Confederacy had forcibly extended their term of service. Instead of encouraging soldiers to remain faithful to the cause or offering moral support to the men who did not desert, the spate of shootings left the rebels disheartened, furious with their commanders, and near rebellion:

Well, here we are again "reorganizing," and after our lax discipline on the road to and from Virginia, and after a big battle, which always disorganizes an army, what wonder it that some men had to be shot, merely for discipline's sake? And what wonder that General Bragg's name became a terror to deserters and evil doers? Men were shot by scores, and no wonder the army had to be reorganized. Soldiers had enlisted for twelve months only, and had faithfully complied with their volunteer obligations; the terms for which they had enlisted had expired, and they naturally looked upon it that they had a right to go home. They had done their duty faithfully and well. They wanted to see their families; in fact, wanted to go home anyhow. War had become a reality and they were tired of it. A law had been passed by the Confederate States Congress

Zouaves from Louisiana, "a wild set of men." These troops were led by Colonel Gaston Coppens. The Louisiana Tigers that Josiah Petterson wrote about were members of a Zouave regiment that was reputedly recruited off the New Orleans waterfront.

called the Conscript Act. . . . From this time on till the end of the war, a soldier was simply a machine, a conscript. It was mighty rough on rebels. We cursed the war, we cursed Bragg, we cursed the Southern Confederacy. All our pride and valor had gone, and we were sick of war and the Southern Confederacy.[6]

Although men such as Sam Watkins reported that firing squads could be heard performing their task on a daily basis, official records suggest that executions were more infrequent. Nevertheless, the witnessing of executions was a shared experience of many diaries and recollections. Confederate soldier Josiah Patterson even used them as a dire object lesson for his children while instructing them to behave "like a good little soldier":

My dear little sons. . . . I will tell you what they did a few days ago with two members of the Louisiana Tigers for insubordination. Well, these are a wild set of men and may well be called "tigers." These two would not behave themselves . . . so they were court martialed and taken [away] from camp, made to kneel down at stakes in the ground, their feet was tied to the kes [sic] below, their hands tied about the top, were blindfolded. A file of twenty men marched out in front of them about ———— paces. Ten of these men had muskets with balls. The other ten were loaded with powder alone. These men were ordered to take aim and fire, and these bad men that would not obey orders fell over dead. . . . May God bless and protect you, my dear little Sons. Be good little boys. Do not quarrel, kiss little Anna four times apiece for me. Your Father.[7]

As much as the execution of deserters may have demoralized the soldiers of both armies, there was, at least from a military perspective, some dignity in the ritual; men who had been condemned of crimes that were considered particularly heinous were not allowed the "privilege" of a firing squad and were sent to the gallows. Hanging was the province of spies, murderers, rapists, those guilty of treason—and often African Americans.

During the war, certain protective aspects of the American judicial system were circumvented, most notably the writ of habeas corpus signed by President Lincoln on July 2, 1861. In the explosive atmosphere of wartime America, military courts were sometimes given to issuing draconian judgments instead of following the rule of law. While military law is different from civil law, the sentences handed down by military judges were often flagrant violations of anyone's sense of justice, as the punishment could well far exceed the seriousness of the crime:

HDQRS. Department of the Gulf. New Orleans. June 5, 1862
Special Orders
No. 70.
  William B. Mumford, a citizen of New Orleans, having been convicted before the military commission of treason, and an overt act thereof, tearing down the United States flag from a public building of the United States for the purpose of inciting other evil minded persons to further resistance to the laws and arms of the United States, after said flag was placed there by Commodore Farragut, of the U.S. Navy:
  It is ordered that he be executed according to sentence of said military commission on Saturday, June 7, instant, between the hours of 8 a.m. and 12 m., under the directions of the provost marshall of the District of New Orleans, and for doing this shall be his sufficient warrant.
  By the command of Major General Butler, commanding department:
Wm. H. Wiegel
First Lieutenant and Acting Assistant, Adjutant General.[8]

Mumford was hanged for having torn down an American flag from in front of the U.S. Mint, having

dragged it through the streets, followed by an excited mob, tore it in shreds and distributed the pieces among the gamblers, assassins, and murderers, his comrades, and was tried, condemned, and executed on Saturday the 7th instant, on the spot where he committed his heinous crime.[9]

Most vulnerable to summary execution were freed slaves serving in the military. Although they often distinguished themselves in battle once they were allowed to fight in 1862, they were susceptible to conviction by a lesser burden of proof—even as, it could be argued, they still are today. Esther Hill Hawks was a doctor, which in itself was unique in this era, who attended to the medical needs of an African-American regiment, which was even more unusual. Doctor Hawks witnessed the recklessness of military justice:

This morning, seeing the Provo Marshall, Capt. Willoughby, standing near the guard house, I enquired if there was any trouble and he pointed to three boyish looking prisoners belonging to the 55th Mass. who were under guard.—They had been arrested about midnight, taken directly before acting Brig. General Littlefield, tried and condemned to suffer death by hanging on the afternoon of the same day.—They had committed an outrage on a white woman. At the appointed 3 pm our regiment and the 2s.c. [*sic*] were drawn up in line and the poor fellows launched into eternity. They showed no sign of emotion of any kind, but our soldiers sobbed aloud and were all greatly affected. General Seymore who had come from J.Ville to witness the execution, after it was over turned to the men and said loud enough for them all to hear "served them right, now let any other man try it if he dares." The bearing of the general and his manner of speaking left an impression of our offices of utter heartlessness. If the same measure had been meted out to white officers and men who have been guilty of the same offense towards black women, Gen. S. might have grown hoarse in repeating his remarks. The dreadful affair has spread a feeling of gloom over our camp.[10]

Although soldiers of the Civil War were punished for a variety of reasons and executed for crimes including murder, treason, and rape, ordinary soldiers paid most attention to those condemned for desertion. The death penalty, however, was carried out in only a fraction of these cases, and most of those who were captured were let off with lighter sentences.

While there was some support for killing deserters as a deterrent, the effect on the morale of the troops was often negative. But the sentences continued to be carried out in order to influence the majority of the soldiers to stay in camp. Otherwise, a desertion rate that was already high might have rendered both armies incapable of fighting. An unlucky minority of men were executed to make a point.

In that sense, the rule of law during the American Civil War mirrors that of our own era. While corporal punishment was more frequent and cruel and the recklessness with which capital punishment was applied more liberal, there existed then and exists now a fundamental unfairness in the selection of those who are delivered up to the ultimate punishment.

But most men do not march into enemy fire willingly, nor do they instinctively control their baser instincts and obey the law without the threat of sufficient retribution. President Abraham Lincoln appealed to "the better angels of our nature" in his first inaugural address during the opening days of the war. But Lincoln was also aware that the time for words was past: to deal with what he perceived as the lesser angels of the seceding citizens' natures, he would have to use force.

Perhaps what was most remarkable about the use of punishment during the Civil War was the reaction of the audience it was intended to influence. In a world in which common soldiers frequently saw friends killed or grievously wounded and were often themselves suffering to some extent, it is extraordinary that they still reacted with shock and sympathy when observing an execution. Men who should have been inured to death were appalled and perceived the ceremonial killing of a prisoner as something very different from a battlefield casualty.

Their reaction speaks of the tremendous reserve of compassion in these men, in that they could still feel this way after all they had been through. Tired, sick, wounded, sad, and afraid as they might have been, common Civil War soldiers never surrendered their decency.

Exceptions existed, of course, but as reluctant witnesses to these dark moments, these men demonstrated that their humane nature was stronger than their hatred.

CHAPTER EIGHT

Letters, Lovers, and Lifelines

The bizarre polarities in the lives of the Civil War soldiers, caught between fighting to survive and tedium, made them think constantly about being somewhere else and with different people. For the vast majority of the men, their thoughts were directed toward home. The soldiers' inability to overcome the loneliness they felt while separated from regular society and their inability to communicate with their loved ones at home was a tremendous challenge.

While many aspects of normal civilian life could be imitated in camp, the contentment provided by daily interaction with their wives, children, and parents could not be duplicated. As the war continued, the men missed their families profoundly and discovered how deeply they wished for the tenderness of the women they loved.

There were not many ways the soldiers could satisfy this need, and the armies recognized the problem. Accordingly, limited efforts were made to provide the soldiers of both armies with a connection to their families and women in general—even if they were not relatives—whenever and however possible.

Writing Home

In this era, prior to the mass communications revolution, the best solution was the intermittent and often one-sided dialogue provided by letters. As unsatisfying as letters were, in some ways the soldiers had to make do, and soon their lives began to revolve around the arrival of mail from home.

Their joy was great when they received a letter and their disappointment profound when they did not. As regimental movements were unpredictable and the endeavors of mail carriers often thwarted, the troops commonly did not receive the letters sent to them.

For the soldiers, many of whom had a limited education, the effort to write an informative letter was significant and time-intensive. Yet many men attempted to become regular correspondents, and the subject matter of their letters ranged from the recounting of ordinary events such as weather and descriptions of towns they passed through to matters of greater significance.

One unusual characteristic of Civil War correspondence could be seen by recipients even before they opened their letters. For soldiers who had only recently been civilians and were accustomed to many personal freedoms, including the right to express their opinions, serving in the military could be restrictive. Letter writing allowed them an outlet through which they could voice their feelings on world affairs in a very public way. For a number of soldiers, the envelopes that contained their personal communiqués were used as small "billboards" to espouse their political views.

Usually, these convictions were expressed in the form of elaborate graphic designs, which might take up as much of the soldier's free time as the letter within. One Union soldier printed the abbreviated names of all thirty-four states, drew a Federal eagle, and included the maxim "Love One Another." Another drew a picture of the United States as seen from an omniscient point of view, plus an eagle and the homily "What God Has Joined Let No Man Put Assunder." One envelope bore a drawing of George Washington accompanied by the words "A Southern Man with Union Principles." Drawings of a hanged Jefferson Davis graced some envelopes, and one showed a slave and the opinion that "Massa can't have dis chile, dat's what's de matter."

From the eastern theater to the western theater soldiers made time, when they could, to mend their clothes — and their lives, by writing letters.

Sometimes the soldiers' opinions were less controversial. At the beginning of the war, for example, soldiers were required, like everybody else, to use stamps to post their mail. Eventually this would change, but before it did one soldier turned to poetry on the outside of his envelope to ask the post office's grace:

> Soldier's letter, nary red
> Hardtack and no soft bread
> Postmaster, please put it through,
> I've nary a cent, but six months due.[1]

Care Packages

Once past the envelope, the recipient of a soldier's letter was more than likely to encounter requests for food, clothing, reading material, and other items. These solicitations were prosaic but of vital importance, as the men were often hungry, poorly dressed, and bored. Supplies from home often made the difference between men being healthy enough to fulfill their duty and being too weak or ill to do so. When the system worked, packages could be delivered to army camps quickly enough for wives, mothers, and daughters to include baked goods and fresh vegetables and have a reasonable hope that they would arrive unspoiled. Usually the men would share their supplies with friends, and then more letters would have to be written to acknowledge the receipt of packages. Especially at the beginning of the war, these thank-you notes reflected what was still a relatively optimistic attitude:

Cairo, September 9, 1861
. . . The refreshment and drygoods from home arrived Saturday. We were at Paducah then and . . . [when] we returned this morning and after acknowledging the excellence, profusion, variety, gorgeousness, and confiscarity of your benevolent appropriation to our temporal wants, I will particularize by saying that you needn't worry about your picture, as it is in my possession, that the cakes are both numerous and excellent, that the pickles are prodigious in quantity, beautiful quality and remarkably acceptable. That the butter and cheese are no ad com caloru. The tobacco and Hostetter, the boys say, are very fine.[2]

The items requested by soldiers were wide-ranging and included nails for mending boots, hatchets for chopping kindling, tent poles, pudding, turkey, onions, pepper, writing paper, envelopes, socks, potatoes, chocolate, condensed milk, sugar, broma (probably a digestive aid but also possibly "bromine," which was a solution used to clean wounds and gangrene, even though people were not yet aware of the value of antiseptics), butter, woolen shirts, towels, needles, thread, yarn, ham, tea, cheese, cakes, and preserves. John Billings recalled that pleas for alcohol—contraband for the troops—would be answered with ingenuity. To avoid losing a bottle to the men who inspected packages, "a favorite ruse was to have the bottle introduced into a well roasted turkey, a place that no one would for a moment suspect of containing such unique stuffing, or inserted into a cake."[3]

Sharing Their Burden, Living on News from Home

A large number of letters written home to loved ones, however, had a different purpose. A great many were intended to share the experiences of soldiers' new way of life. Families wanted to hear about the loved ones' great adventures. In response men would try to describe what a soldier's routine was like, the new places they were seeing, and how much home was in their thoughts. Soldier Henry Graves wrote to his family in an uncomplaining, informative tone:

> Dear Aunt Hattie,
> . . . the weather has been intolerably hot here. . . . [S]tanding with a spade in my hand on top of a big bank of red clay or with a mattock in a deep broach ditch, I would, in order to pass off time, imagine myself at home with my coat off, sitting out in the east end of the piazza at home, enjoying the cool breeze that almost always is blowing fresh through there, with a basket of peaches at my side and all the homefolk around. This is the way I employ myself when I get into an unpleasant place, and by this means, the time passes much more swiftly and pleasantly. I don't know what poor mortals and especially soldier mortals would do if they were not blessed with the gift of imagination and the pictures of hope.[4]

When the war did not end in quick victory, many letters home came to be more than just travelogues and began to serve a cathartic purpose. As the soldiers' isolation grew and the reality of war became more apparent and seemingly endless, the subject matter of their letters grew darker. They wrote about the people they missed most and the happiness they feared they would never experience again.

Henry Graves, for example, made an effort to remain lighthearted when writing to his Aunt Hattie, but his melancholy is palpable as he describes a girl he knew back home. In a world that combined terror, unrelieved boredom, hard living, and cold nights, the young soldier's loneliness is tangible:

> Night dreams for instance are as a general thing much more vivid than day dreams. The sweetest dream I have had for many a day past I had the other night. . . . My dream of course had a "goddess," a sweet little hazel eyed girl who lives away down in Georgia and for whom I feel a "Very tender feeling" was by my side, my arm was around her waist and her head on my shoulder, and her soft cheek laid lovingly against mine . . . when alas! alas! the cracking of a stick near by, by an approaching foot, caused me to spring from the embrace of my darling to grasp the cold steel of my gun barrel and from the gentle accents of love to cry out the rough challenge, "Who goes there?" and, instead of the warm breath of the little girl which I had felt on my cheek but a moment before, I wiped from my face the cold night dew and with half a groan I turned me to my rail again.[5]

Once the thrill of going off to war dissipated, the soldiers began to realize that the world at home was carrying on without them. For a newlywed such as Spencer Welch, the realization that he had spent almost an equal amount of time with his regimental companions as with his wife and son was dispiriting. Despite his cultivation of stoic attitude, Welch revealed his fears when he sought information about his young son, George. Requesting the details any father would know under normal circumstances, Welch was desperate to maintain a connection with his family:

> Feb 15 1863
> Two years ago from last Friday you and I were married and how changed is the scene since then! Little did we think that devastation and distress would so soon spread over the entire land. War seems to be a natural occurrence. It has been our misfortune to experience it, and there is nothing we can do but endure it philosophically and try to become resigned to it.
> When you write tell me all the little particulars about George. I dreamed last night of being at home, but thought he would have nothing to do with me and treated me like an entire stranger.[6]

Other young fathers sent letters home that delivered news of their whereabouts and also served as an attempt to fulfill their responsibilities as parents— even over a great distance. Georgian soldier Theodore Montfort may have been six months and several states removed from his family, but he asserts his authority as head of the family with a "Wait till your father gets home" admonition:

Meadow Bluff, Virginia November 3 1861
My dear children, David, Molley, and Tebo:
　　Your father is here in the mountains of northwestern Virginia, some 800 or 900 miles from you, encamped with several thousand soldiers in a low wet marsh at the foot of the mountains doing his duty as a soldier in serving his country. . . . I have requested your Mother to write if any of you fail to obey and attend to her kindly. I have no fear but what you will all do your duty and be kind and dutiful to her. . . .
　　I have plenty to eat, yet the life of a soldier is a hard one. The weather is now and has been for ten days very cold, and it rains every other day. On the day before yesterday I had to take 30 men and stand picket guard some three miles from camp for 24 hours a day and night without fire, and it raining and sleeting all the time . . . and when we are relieved from duty we have no comfortable rooms with a fireplace to go to and dry or put on dry clothes, but have either to go to our tent that is damp and wet and go to sleep in this fix or stand around a fire outdoors in the cold and rain. So while you are all at home where you can keep dry with a good room, fire and bed to sleep in, you should feel grateful. . . .
　　You must attend to everything but especially your Mother, as I should be deeply mortified for her to write me that either one of you was [not being] dutiful and kind. . . . I wish I was there with you all, if it was only to remain one hour. Yes, if it was only long enough to kiss you all. . . . I have written now until I am nearly frozen and must close this letter to go to the fire. Each one of you kiss your Mother for me and tell her to kiss you all for me. I hope some day to get back home to kiss you all, whom I dearly love.[7]

Children were not the only targets of reprimand. For a soldier such as Union trooper Onley Andrus, it was a matter of concern when other men received mail and he did not:

Head Quarters Gen Hamilton's Army Abbeville Miss
December 4th 1862
　　Mary it is now 4 weeks or one month since I left Camp Fuller. In that time I have written some 6 or 8 letters to you & have received 2. Why

dont get any more is somewhat strange to me. Others get letters almost every mail, but I am still sure that you havent entirely forgotten that you have a husband in the army. . . . I have asked you times enough to write. Now I am going to tell you to do as you like & see if you wont mind. You had better use your time now for I shall be back up there one of these days & take the reins of Govt in my own hands. Till then I remain your Obt humble Servt & poor miserable Husband, Sgt. O. L. Andrus! Take good care of Sissy & better of yourself & write as often as you can. On[8]

During the course of the war, Sergeant Andrus would continue to be displeased with the number of letters written to him by his wife, Mary. Occasionally, he would receive word from other members of his family—all of whom were, apparently, poor correspondents:

Nunda, Il.
    Dear son Onely [sic] I see by your letter you still remember the old folks. We se by your letter that you enjoy a degree of health of whictch we are thankful whilst there is so many that are calle a way. . . . We Received a lttr from you Brother John last night. He was well but complains that he gets no letters. Wel I shouldent wonder if that he complaines of father and myself for you no it is quite an act to write and I am such a poor pensman that I dont do much in that way. That you no. . . . Oh Onely [sic] we do count the Months yet that you must be in the service and our dailey prayer to god is that he will spare you & your brother. . . . I must close by asking you to over look all imperfections. Good by. I shall write to your Brother to Night. I remain as ever your affectionate Mother.[9]

Generally, although the men complained about not receiving word from home, they understood why letters did not come:

Grand Junction Tenn 10 of July 1862
My dear son,
    I suppose I have written "10th of July" over one hundred times today, and every time I have written it I have thought of you. I wish I could be whre I could make you a birthday present or give you a good birthday floggin. I would not care which.
    Except for the letters brought by Samson & Search we have not received word from home since the 8th of June,—so there must be a large mail somewhere for us. I suppose the reason we have not recd mail is that

An army telegraph wagon, a portable telegraph office. Troops could send or receive telegrams with important news only if they were away from camp on a pass. For soldiers, letters were still the quickest way to hear from home.

we move about so much it can't catch us . . . west of us there are no United States forces nearer than Memphis and East of us none nearer than Corrinth. The nearest troops North of us are at Bolivar—21 miles—and the enemy are in force in our front only six miles from where I write now. Our pickets are within talking distance of each other. . . .

I expect reinforcements tonight, for it will be hard work to hold the place with my present force—though under my present orders I shall "fight for the top," to the last. If I can't be reinforced in time, I presume I shall be ordered back to Bolivar—though I very much dislike to leave this point to the rebels again. I drove them out once. I had rather keep them out than be obliged to drive them again.[10]

Matters of Life and Death

While correspondence was intended to narrow the gap between soldiers and their families, the unpredictability of the mails underscored the tenuous nature of the connection between them. This was particularly true in regard to news of ailments suffered by loved ones, which in the nineteenth century could progress swiftly from minor illnesses to death. In exceptional cases men were allowed to go home when a family member was mortally ill, but more commonly communication and transportation limitations made this impossible.

Compounding the concern and guilt of soldiers when a family member became ill was the understanding that in some cases it was their very absence that had triggered the illness, as their enlistment often meant a substantially increased workload for those who remained at home. When a departed soldier had been the main income earner or the man who had done the most demanding chores on a farm, the effect on his loved ones could be debilitating. Union soldier Edward Boots's anxiety about the health of his mother is the focus of his letter from April 1863:

> Newbern N.C. Tuesday Evening April 28th
>   Dear Mother. . . . The last letter from home (from Emma), spoke of your being unwell. I hope that you are better now. I can endure the hardships of army life but I cannot endure the thought of your being sick. Dear Mother, I beg of you to take care of yourself. I know that you have made yourself sick by toiling too hard. You must rest yourself more. I know that you will answer, "I must work or things will be left undone." Well then let them be undone. Your health is more account than they are. If I should live to get home again I want to find you there & well, otherwise it will be no home to me.[11]

Edward Boots would never return home to be reunited with his mother and spare her the difficulties of hard labor. A year and a half after the writing of this letter, he died a prisoner of war at Andersonville.[12]

Spencer Welch not only was concerned about his family but wrote continuously to learn news of the son he did not know. His letters to his wife during the year 1863 are filled with questions about their son and hopeful assertions about what kind of child George was growing up to be—which he could only surmise from correspondence he received from his relatives: "I am anxious to see George. I know he is a charming little fellow." "I am glad that George is so bright and intelligent." "My father wrote me that George was the liveliest child he ever saw, and that it was a matter of rejoicing when you and George were seen coming." "I have George's picture yet. It is a wonder I did not lose it."[13]

The greatest fear of the soldier far from home was that a child would become gravely ill. Infant mortality was commonplace in the nineteenth century, and most families lost at least one child. In March 1861, having only just left home to serve as a mapmaker for Confederate General Stonewall Jackson, Jedediah Hotchkiss received word that every father dreaded: his child had scarlet fever:

> My afflicted wife: I read with streaming eyes, b [sic] the camp fire, where we stopped after a long advance the first news I have received from home. Sad, sad indeed. May God forgive me for the sorrows of last night and may He, in mercy, spare my child. But I am now resigned. May you be supported in your extreme sorrow. But I would that I could be with you, but it is forbidden me and it is now too late to reach you before the crisis is passed. I wait in painful solicitude the further news.[14]

At times like these, a soldier's need to receive news from home was desperate. But even for men whose loved ones were not so threatened, the connection to civilized life was paramount in their minds. The focus of their attention for days at a time was the next letter from home:

> December 7th, 1863 Stevensburg, VA.
> Last night about midnight news came that mail had arrived which was too large to be distributed until morning. Tired, even exhausted, as I was, the thought of a near letter which I knew was in that bag for me prevented the possibility of sleep. I soon found Macy was under the same restlessness as I, and we quickly agreed to saddle our horses, ride to the brigade headquarters, get the mail, and distribute it ourselves.
> Off we went, found the mail, of many days accumulation, threw it across the saddle and rode home in high glee. . . .
> . . . I sat on the floor, placed a candle between my feet, and with a freshly lighted pipe went happily to work. A whole hour passed; the last letter was in my hand, and not a single one for me. . . . I felt wicked, then distressed, and then really sick with disappointment, and so, finally, turned in. This morning I discovered that the whole mail had not arrived last night; that the rest was on its way; and before noon the best letter I had ever received was in my hand.[15]

The mails did not always bring bad news, however. For Jedediah Hotchkiss, who was resigned to the death of his daughter, a letter in early April 1861 offered relief and he responded joyfully:

Nelly's sweet littel [*sic*] voilet [*sic*] dropped out of my letter as I opened it and I was very happy to think that my little daughter was reviving and getting new life against just as the sweet flowers opening under the influence of the vernal sun. She must be very thankful . . . that her life is spared and we will join her in . . . [being grateful to] Him and hope she may live long to be a blessing to her parents and to her friends. The birds are singing very sweetly here and I suppose they are also singing at Loch Willow and papa would like to sit out on the porch with the little girls and mama and hear them sing rather than be here, where he has to see and hear so much of men killing and being killed, doing all the damage they can to one another, burning up bridges, etc. Oh, how I wish war would cease and that we might all have peace in the enjoyment of our rights and liberties, but those rights we [must] have, cost what it may.[16]

Although life at home was not as precarious as that in war, a relatively minor illness could quickly escalate into something more serious, as shown in this letter from Spencer Welch to his wife:

Camp Near Rappahannock River, Culpeper County, VA.
    . . . Your brother tells me you look better than you did before you were married. He says George is badly spoiled and that he will cry if you crook your finger at him. I am sorry to hear that he has been sick. In your letter you speak of his being pale and thin from teething.[17]

It was not long before Welch had to rush home to attend to his gravely ill son. Some time later, as he made his way back to his regiment, he wrote to his wife and tried to express his anguish at his son's death:

I was delayed about ten hours at Charlotte, N.C. and did not arrive in Richmond until seven o'clock this morning. . . . I ate but once out of my haversack the whole way here. My appetite was gone, for the death of our dear little George, together with parting from you in such deep grief, made me sadder than I ever felt before in my life. The heaviest pang of sorrow came upon me when I entered the train to leave. . . . I have no fear that there will be any trouble about my staying over my furlough. Had I remained at home a week longer not a word would be said.[18]

"I Will Never See You Again—Only in Dreams"

But for most soldiers, letters dealt with less tragic matters and were a chance to share the discomforts, fears, surprises, and pleasures of an experience that was totally new and unpredictable. For men who were shaken to the core by the brutality that existed all around them, a connection to the comparatively stable world of home served as a soothing support system. And the element of family life that they most desired to maintain in their letters was the continuation of a reassuring relationship with the women they loved:

> Dear wife . . . this is quite a wet morning, keeps us in our tents, but we are comfortable. . . . [W]hile in my tent listening to the pattering rain the greatest pleasure I enjoy is to imagine that you are with me. I can remember exactly how you looked when I kissed you goodbye. I can feel the pressure of your arms about me, your warm sweet breath on my cheek. I can see the tears in your eyes. I picture you to myself in smiles. You look lovingly & pleasantly into my eyes & encourage me with your cheerful conversation. I think your living breathing presence is here warming & cherring [sic] my lonely tent, but it is only a day dream. Yet I call it up each day & if the dream is so pleasant how much more pleasant the reality.[19]

But mail was not the only method of combating the demoralizing effects upon men living for long periods of time without women. When possible, women were allowed to visit their husbands. Sometimes wives and other family members joined a camp for a time, living in tents or nearby rooming houses. While living with the troops, women would often cook, although usually only for officers, and help with the chores that made life more livable such as sewing, mending, and cleaning. The wife of Colonel Mortimer D. Legget of the Seventh-eighth Ohio Volunteers visited camp during the summer of 1862, accompanied by several of their children. It would be wrong to assume that women and family members visited only camps that were far from harm's way. When the Leggets visited at Grand Junction, Tennessee, the Confederate forces were within six miles. Nor were women and family members hidden and protected in the rear of the camp. Instead, Colonel Legget and his family traveled to the front in a manner suggestive of a holiday outing, as Welles Legget noted in a letter to his brother Leverett, who was still at home:

I am confident they can't whip us although they may cut us to pieces pretty badly for father is fully prepared to meet 3 times his number in a attack. . . . Ma . . . & Bub went out with us on a scout last night. They rode in an ambulance, started about 5 o'clock and returned about 8 o'clock. We had a first rate time but saw none of the enemy we expected. . . . [Y]esterday pa made me a present of a horse that used to belong to the rebel Col Polk. It is not a very pretty horse *now* because he has been badly used, but he is very fast "Racer" and rides so easy that I can hold a cup of water in my hand and ride at "full gail."[20]

Luckier than most soldiers to have his family visit, if only for a few weeks, Legget was still extremely lonely when they left:

My dear wife. You don't know how I miss you—it was real wicked for you and Mortimer & Bub to go at once.[21]

And if his spirits were raised temporarily, his yearning to be reunited with his whole family was not assuaged. Shortly after his wife left for home, he wrote to his daughter Mary, who had stayed behind in Ohio that summer:

23 Aug 62
My dear Mary,
    I have just been looking at your picture and it almost makes me homesick. O how I want to see you! I have seen Ma and Bub and Welly, & Mortimer and expect to see Leverett but my darling Mary I don't know when I can see her. It seems now as if I wanted to see you more than all the rest put together. . . . [I]f you had been along it would have seemed almost like home. I suppose Ma will tell you that your Pa begins to look like an old man . . . but I don't feel very old after all. . . . I had a real good visit with Bub, the little tike learned to be quite a soldier. He always went to drill and got so he would say "guide right" & "guide left" etc. to the horses and everything else.[22]

When the daughters and wives of officers spent time in the military camps, it was not only their immediate relative who benefited. In most cases, the presence of women encouraged men to have more hope, dress better, and keep their quarters cleaner, and it generally improved their morale overall. In some unique cases, the relationship between the visiting women and the war-weary soldiers grew to be more significant. While visiting a Confederate regiment, a reporter for *The Cincinnati Times* reported the story of a young woman who had become one regiment's mascot and indispensable to the positive attitude of its fighting men:

> One of the features of the 1st Tennessee Regiment is the person of a brave and accomplished young lady of but eighteen summers, and of prepossessing appearance, named Sarah Taylor, of East Tennessee, who is the step daughter of Captain Dowden of the 1st Tennessee Regiment. . . . Miss Taylor has formed the determination to share with her late companions the dangers and fatigues of a military campaign. She has donned a neat blue chapeau, beneath which her long hair is fantastically arranged; bearing at her side a highly finished regulation sword, and silver mounted pistols in her belt. . . .
>
> . . . [S]he is quite the idol of the Tennessee boys. They look upon her as a second Joan of Arc, believing that victory and glory will perch upon the standards borne in the ranks favored by her loved presence. Having become adept in the sword exercise, and a sure shot with the pistol, she is determined to lead in the van of the march bearing her exiled and oppressed countrymen back to their homes, or, if failing, to offer her own life's blood in the sacrifice. . . . [W]hen the order was issued for the Tennesseeans to march to reinforce Colonel Garrad, . . . the wildest excitement pervaded the whole camp, and . . . the young lady . . . mounted her horse, and, cap in hand, galloped along the line like a spirit of flame, cheering on the men. . . . Miss Taylor is regarded by the troops as a guardian angel who is to lead them to victory.[23]

There were, however, other instances of women caught in battle who caused annoyance for the men responsible for their welfare. Elisha Rhodes noted one such visitor to his camp:

> Well, we have had a very queer experience today. Last night I received a letter . . . from Colonel Brown, the RI State Agent in Washington that he and Dr. Richard Browne of RI (a dentist) with a Miss Lena Lunt of Chicago would pay me a visit. . . . [W]e put everything in fine order, decorated my Headquarters and then a party of officers in full dress uniforms went over to the depot . . . to receive the party. . . . They came all right and we escorted them to our camp. Just as we entered my hut the Rebels attacked our pickets in front of my camp. I hastily told Col. Benedict to take the lady to a deep hollow in the rear of our camp and then started

for the Regiment. . . . The firing front was furious for a while and some of the bullets came over our works. Much to my surprise I soon found Miss Lunt behind the works with the men clapping her hands in great glee. I tried to send her away but she would not go. . . . It was all over in a few moments but the lady seemed to enjoy the novelty.[24]

On occasion women were also permitted to cross enemy lines to provide care for wounded prisoners. Not only was this considered good for the spirit of the captured men, but it also relieved the overburdened nursing staffs on both sides. Southerner Flora Darling, who found herself in England when war broke out, had to return to the United States instead of her home because of the Union blockade of Confederate ports. Her husband wrote to her in February 1863:

> My Own Darling: I wonder if you fancy the reason I do not write? Or have you heard I was wounded at Murfreesboro? It was supposed my wound would prove fatal when brought here, where I have lingered for days and weeks, suffering much that avails little to write of for now, for I must husband the little strength left me to tell you my most earnest wish.
> Flossy, will you come to me? God forgive me for complaining, but this separation is simply intolerable, and is more wearing upon me than wounds or sickness. I love my sweet little wife devotedly, and must have her with me again. . . . Your face is with me and constantly in my dreams, but I long for the "real presence." Will you come my darling? A strong conviction comes over me that I cannot dispel, that I will never see you again—only in dreams.
> I do not write this, Flossy, to alarm you, but to prepare you for a certainty, unless I soon receive something besides mechanical care and cold encouragement now given. Your presence will inspire hope, and renew a new lease of life. "If the thought of seeing you is so delicious, what will be the reality?" Still, darling, if you shrink from the journey; if your heart does not second my wish, do not come, and I will do the best I can without you; but I feel you will respond with your usual warmth and fervor to my request and soon be with me.
> Flags of truce are constantly exchanged between Washington and Richmond, via Fortress Monroe. Your father can procure a safe convoy for you, if your health is sufficiently assured to endure the fatigue and exposure of traveling at this inclement season. . . . Kiss my boy for his proud papa, and remember me in love to each member of your family, and believe me, my own dear Flossy, Yours always EID[25]

"Her Little Bosom Rested on Mine . . . Diable!"

Well aware of the importance of women to the men in the field, the military leaders made other efforts to ensure that their soldiers had opportunities to spend time with the opposite sex. If wives and daughters were too far from the battlefront to visit, other arrangements could be made with surrogates. The preferred choice of the military authorities was for respectable local women and girls to visit the troops in camp. Confederate soldier Carlton McCarthy recalled:

> But the lady visitors! The girls! Who could describe the effect of their appearance in camp! They produced conflict in the soldier's breast. They looked so clean, they were so gentle, they were so different from all around them. They were so attractive, they were so agreeable, and sweet, and fresh, and happy.[26]

Soldier Harry St. John described plans that were made for soldiers to attend social functions in the communities near their camps:

> [A]ttended a "storm" at Miss Cuny's last evening. . . . Took the "little humming bird"—the little thing was chattering & smelling camphor all evening—waltzed with Miss Annie Cozart till my right arm ached. What makes men so impure? Why cannot he have the manhood to resist temptation?—Her little bosom rested pantingly upon mine need I confess I squeezed a little—just a little bit—soft, convulsive! And something else—our knees—Diable![27]

The authorities were aware of the positive effect women had on the men, and they encouraged their interaction before battle. As Georgian regiments marched north toward Richmond, they were feted by Southern women the whole way. Not only did the women help the men maintain their morale, but they gave the soldiers a reminder of exactly what they were fighting for:

> In Savannah, Charleston, Petersburg and Richmond we were received with every demonstration of joy and affection. The ladies, God bless them, contributed no little to our pleasure and comfort. Immeasurable little delicacies found their way from mysterious packages and baskets carried by beautiful girls and spirited dames to the haversacks of the soldiers. Many a beautiful bouquet traced the hat or gun of some handsome

boy. The enthusiasm of the people is unbounded. Our encampment is in a beautiful grove on the suburbs of Richmond, and every evening our quarters are crowded with beautiful girls, who, when they come to the encampment, immediately come to our quarters. At afternoon drill dress parade you can hardly walk about for them they are so thick.[28]

At other times soldiers would seek out feminine companionship on their own initiative. At holiday times, homesick troops sought out local women to entertain and feed them:

> On Christmas day we were all at a loss what to do for the accustomed egg nog and trimmings, when, at the suggestion of some great genius, we determined to call upon one of the belles of the town, the youngest member of the staff, and the ladies man, promising to introduce us all. We went, and the young lady was quite charming. We had all the egg nog and plumcake we desired, and a pleasant time was had of it.[29]

Sometimes, soldiers' socializing with women was purely serendipitous. Sent on a foraging expedition by his superiors, Sam Watkins was invited by a local farmer to join his family for dinner:

> At the head of the table was the madam, having on a pair of golden spectacles, and at the foot the old gentleman. He said grace. And, to cap the climax, two handsome daughters. I know that I have never seen two more beautiful ladies. They had on little white aprons, trimmed with jaconet edging, and collars as clean and white as snow. They looked good enough to eat and I think at that time I would have given ten years of my life to have kissed one of them.[30]

It is doubtful that Sam Watkins suffered from loneliness more than any other man. He was, however, more willing than most to pursue what he desired, regardless of the consequences:

> On one occasion . . . Andy Wilson and I thought we would slip off and go down the river in a canoe. . . . [W]e had not gone far before the thing capsized and we swam ashore. But we were outside the lines now and without passes. So we put our sand paddles to work and landed in Columbia that night. I loved a maid, and so did Andy, and some poet has said that love laughs at grates, bars, locksmiths, etc. I do not know how true this is, but I do know that when I went to see my sweetheart that night I asked

her to pray for me. . . . [I]t took me one day to go to Columbia and one day to return, and I stayed at home only one day, and went back of my own accord. When I got back to Shelbyville, I was arrested and carried to the guardhouse, and when court-martialed was sentenced to thirty days' fatigue duty and to forfeit four months' pay at eleven dollars per month.[31]

Love for Sale

Wives, daughters, respectable ladies, and not so respectable ladies were allowed to spend time in the military camps of both nations. As armies always have, both the Union and Confederate soldiers had camp followers who provided a number of unique and necessary services. Israel Gibbons, a reporter for *The New Orleans Daily Crescent*, reported:

> It is really curious to observe how well and how strictly the three classes of women in camp keep aloof from each other. The wives and daughters of colonels, captains, and other officers constitute the first class. The rough cooks and washers who have their husbands along . . . form the second class. The third and last class is happily the smallest; here and there a female of elegant appearance and unexceptional manners; truly wife like in their tented seclusion, but lacking that great and only voucher of respectability for females in camp—the marriage tie.[32]

Women visiting their men at camp. These are "decent women," wives and sisters on approved visits. The lady seated on the porch holds an infant in her lap.

The appearance of prostitutes in the world of the soldier was hardly a new development. With a built-in clientele of young men, many of whom were sexually inexperienced and who faced dangers and hardships every day, business was good. In the Union army alone, there were a quarter-million reported cases of venereal diseases.[33]

> On a beautiful hill . . . surrounded by beautiful groves . . . we found a bevy of nymphs encamped enjoying soldierly life in real earnest. There were twelve or fifteen of them, of differing ages, all young, and more or less fair to look upon. They sat around the campfire, and cooked their breakfast, a little disheveled and rumpled, as might, perhaps, be expected, in remembrance of the scenes of excitement they had passed through, but yet as much composed, and as much at home, as though they had campaigned it all their lives. There was a stray lock of hair hanging here and there, an unlaced bodice granting chary glimpses of vast luxuriance of bust, a stocking down at heel, or a garter with visible downward tendencies—all of which was attributed to our early visit.
>
> There were all the marks of femininity about the place. The embowering trees were hung with hoop skirts and flaunting articles, which looked in the distance like abbreviated pantaloons. A glance at the interior of their tents showed magnificent disorder. . . . These feminine voyagers were real campaigners. The chivalry of the South, ever solicitous for the sex, could not resist the inclination for its society, and hence the camp of nymphs by the riverside. . . . I will not say much for their fair fame, or for the good fame of the Confederate officers, whose baggage was mingled in admirable confusion with the rumpled dimity and calico, whose boots and spurs hung among the hoop skirts and unmentionables, and whose old hats ornamented the tent poles or decked the heads of the fair adventuresses.[34]

The soldiers, writing in their own diaries or letters, were less delicate than the journalists in their description of their sexual exploits. One man wrote to his father of a "whole city of whores."[35] Harris Levin of the Virginia Reserves recalled:

> Several nights a week our lonely post is visited by two sisters who are rentable for riding. . . . Amanda is about 15 and my favorite. She has never asked for more of me than good poking, but does of the others, but her sister, Carrie, will ask pay for her accommodations to me, so you know which I choose.[36]

Prostitutes also did a thriving business away from the camps, setting up brothels in cities that were transportation hubs to take advantage of troops on leave and those moving on to new battlegrounds. Both national capitals, Washington and Richmond, supported a large community of prostitutes. Eli Veazie, who visited Washington, D.C., wrote:

> I had a gay old time I tell you. Lager beer and a horse and buggy and in the evening Horizontal Refreshments or in plainer language Riding Dutch Gal.[37]

Purer Pursuits with Man's Best Friend and Other Creatures

The man without a family to write home to had to find other outlets for the expression of love. Many companies had dogs as mascots; these traveled with them, camped with them, fought with them, and sometimes died with them. Henry Graves wrote to his aunt about a discovery he had made in the aftermath of a skirmish:

> While we were going over the battlefield of Gaines' Mill, one squad of our boys came across a dead Yankee, who, on being wounded, had dragged himself to a sort of shed where he had died. Folded in his arms was a beautiful littel [sic] tan-colored pointer about half grown, with large black wistful, sorrowful looking eyes. They tried to coax her to leave her dead master but without avail. She actually seemed to weep and, when they had at one time succeeded in getting her to follow them for as much as ten steps, she ran back whining, to the body and curled herself up in his arms. . . . One of the dead man's comrades told us afterwards that the little dog had been by its master's side in all of his battles, had shared his rations and his blanket for three months and had been with him in all his marches. I would have given anything almost for the little creatre [sic], but we were hurried away, so that I did not have time to go back after it.[38]

Other pets of the Civil War soldiers included cats, snakes, mice, and whatever else happened to scurry about. Confederate trooper John Casler developed a relationship with an animal that provided companionship and, in a pinch, even dinner:

Sam Nunally brought a pig along that he had caught in the road near some negro shanties, and gave it to me to raise. I told him I did not want to be bothered with it, but he insisted we should keep it, and as it was quite a pet we adopted it and called it "Susan Jane." It would run around the quarters and eat the scraps and find some corn at the stables and get plenty to eat. At night we would let it sleep in our shanty under the bunks; but when we got up every morning it would be lying in the fireplace in the ashes to keep warm. Every wash day we would wash it clean in the suds, and then make it stand on the bed until it got dry. It was a white pig, and improved rapidly, and was as tame as a dog and would follow any one who called it. I had to tie a clog to keep it from following some of the soldiers to their camps.[39]

As Susan Jane grew—along with the appetites of the rebel soldiers—Casler decided to slaughter her and give the men of his company a feast. Before he could do so, however, soldiers from a different company beat him to the punch, and Susan Jane disappeared onto the plates of strangers.

Roosters were also commonly kept as pets. They not only provided the troops with meals when necessary but were a popular form of entertainment:

The favorite pet of the camp, however, is the hero of the barnyard. There is not a regiment nor a company, not a teamster nor a Negro at headquarters, nor an orderly, but has a rooster of one kind or another. When the column is moving, these haughty game-cocks are seen mounted upon the breech of a cannon, tied to the packsaddle of a mule among pots and pans, or carried lovingly in the arms of a mounted orderly. . . . They must all fight, however, or be killed and eaten. . . . Cock-fighting is not, perhaps, one of the most refined or elevating of pastimes, but it furnishes food for a certain kind of fun in camp; and as it is not carried to the point of cruelty, the soldiers cannot be blamed for liking it.[40]

Union soldier C. W. Wills pursued another kind of animal companionship. While the creature of his choice could not provide the spirited interaction of a dog or pig, the animal did offer something that was rare indeed for the common soldier: a glimpse of natural beauty:

By the exercise of a little strategy, this morning I caught a chameleon who had ventured out of a hollow tree to gobble some flies for his breakfast. I enveloped him or rather lassoed him with a pocket handkerchief

Army pets. On the left, the dog that says he went through the war with the Twenty-fifth Iowa Regiment. On the right, "Old Abe" the war eagle, carried into battle on a perch by the men of a Wisconsin regiment. Abe became a newspaper celebrity in the war years.

and then slipped him into a bottle. He only showed two of his colors, changing from a very pretty snuff color to a beautiful light green.[41]

Amid the insanity of four years of war and the influence of its shattering terrors, it may have been Confederate soldier Theodore Montfort who earned the distinction of developing the strangest emotional attachment of the entire conflict:

My dear wife and children: . . . I have separate and distinct command of three large casement guns, one 64, one 42, and one 32 pounder. I have the naming of my own guns. The first 64 pounder I have dubbed "Elizabeth" after Ma, the second 42 pounder "Sarah" in honor of Mrs. Hall, the third 32 pounder "Louise" after yourself. The names are handsomely written on each piece with white paint in large letters. They are known in garrison as all the other guns are by their names. I really feel attached to my guns and so do the men. My guns feel to me a part of my family. You would be really amused to hear the endearing epithets and see the tender care and consideration that is paid to them. I love them on account of my frequent and hourly association with them. Second, I love them because they are willing and submissive instruments in my hands to protect myself and my country. Third, I love them because it is human and natural to love and pet something. They are my pets.[42]

Love as Life

In a chaotic world that introduced mass killing on a totally new scale during the first real war of the Industrial Revolution, Theodore Montfort's projection of warmth and affection onto machinery demonstrates how desperately the soldiers of the Civil War yearned for the stabilizing influence and life-sustaining qualities of love.

The letters the soldiers of the Union and Confederacy sent home to loved ones represented the desperate reaching out of men to "life preservers" as they drowned in a sea of dehumanizing events and barbarity. In a world where hundreds of men could die in an instant or a single man wounded in a manner so grotesque that it had previously been unimaginable, the significance of any one individual's life was diminished. The things that defined a person as an individual—his loves, ambitions, fears, and pleasures—were overwhelmed by the horrible events around him.

Letters from wives, children, parents, and friends reminded the soldiers of who they were, where they had come from, and what they were fighting for. Perhaps even more important, their ability to express love and receive it reminded them that in the face of incalculable brutality, suffering, and debilitating boredom, they were still alive and had a reason to go on.

And when words were not enough and they required the closeness that came from dancing with a local girl they had never met before and would never see again, they simulated the type of relationship that was an integral part of who they had once been. It was an attempt to reestablish their connection with the sanity of a civilized life they had once known.

Similarly, when they required the pleasure of physical intimacy, even if the only partners available to them were weak proxies for true lovers, they were participating in a basic human function that defied the nihilism of their surroundings. Even if the great majority of the soldiers' visits to prostitutes were simply for "a poke," as Harris Levin described it, they were still, at some unconscious level, imitating a more profound relationship.

In reaching out to women and loved ones across the immeasurable gulf between war and peace, the soldiers of the Civil War asserted that they were living, breathing men deserving of affection, with dignity and a future worth surviving for. Despite the best efforts of the enemy and the negligence of their own commanders, they refused to be devalued into numbers on a regimental ledger. Their defiance saved their souls and prevented their degeneration into little more than bodies waiting to become corpses.

❧ CHAPTER NINE ❧
The Invisible Enemy

When the recruits of the Confederate and Union armies set off to war, they accepted certain risks. Many men considered the possibility of dying for their country in battle to be a distinct possibility and a glorious end. Visions of spectacular regimental charges, brave hand-to-hand combat, and swift death in the course of a heroic fight were an integral part of their idea of what it meant to be a soldier. While few viewed the opportunity of self-sacrifice with the same eagerness, there was little doubt that grave dangers awaited them when the first shots were fired.

Indeed, fighting during the Civil War was fierce, and the number of battlefield casualties was unprecedented in the history of the American military.

For all of the profound horror and peril of combat, however, the greatest risk for the rebels and Yankees did not occur in armed confrontation with the enemy. Instead, they faced graver dangers every morning by simply waking up in their tents, drinking from a nearby river, frying up breakfast, and joining their company for roll call.

Despite the horrific bloodletting at Gettysburg, Antietam, Shiloh, and numerous other battlegrounds, twice as many men were killed by disease than were lost in actual combat. Some estimates are even more shocking, placing the ratio at six deaths from illness to every one from fighting.

What is indisputable, however, is that of the various reasons for this disastrous mortality rate, the core cause was an earnest but ignorant medical community.

Today doctors casually dispense medications that would have seemed miraculous to people of the 1860s. But medicine at the time of the Civil War was primitive and had made few advances over the previous thousand years. The most fundamental discovery, that of the existence of microorganisms that cause disease, was still several years in the future. Without this basic knowl-

Field hospitals were like limbo, between battle and genuine hospitals, and full of possibilities for death by infection or a slow, painful recovery within the nursing routine and among new friends and comrades.

edge, medical practitioners were capable of doing little more than playing doctor.

Elementary medical concepts were only just being considered. In England, Dr. Joseph Lister (of Listerine fame) began to use carbolic acid to sanitize wounds, although he had no idea that the cause of his successes was the elimination of disease-producing organisms. Even so, Lister's work did not occur until 1863—a full two years, and many lives, into the American Civil War. In fact, his influence would not be felt in America for some time after that, and even then his technique was met with skepticism. In France, Dr. Louis Pasteur was approaching the discovery of microorganisms as the agent of disease but had not yet had his breakthrough.

Unaware as nineteenth-century doctors were of the real origins of sickness, it followed that their treatments were spectacularly ineffective. Armed with a variety of ersatz patent medicines and debilitating techniques such as bleeding patients or offering strong purgatives to men dying of dysentery, the doctors' diligent but misguided efforts were swept away by a tidal wave of illnesses and death.

The result was that, along with hunger, incapacitating sickness was among the most common shared experiences that defined the soldiers' world.

Breeding Grounds of Disease

Although the people of the mid–nineteenth century were substantially more vulnerable to the ravages of disease than we are today, the concentration and ferocity of illness among Civil War soldiers was unprecedented. To be sure, in everyday society, people became ill and died, but there was not the constant state of near-epidemic conditions that existed in military camps. The cause of this was an amalgamation of factors that produced a uniquely lethal breeding ground for contagion.

To begin with, soldiers were affected by the radical increase of population that surrounded them in the military as compared to at home. Prior to enlistment, many of the soldiers had lived on farms or in small towns, where their exposure to contagion had been limited. They had spent their lives in contact with friends and families, but visitors from far away had been rare. Travel beyond short distances was uncommon in the mid–nineteenth century, and there were few opportunities for carriers to spread infectious microbes.

Upon arriving in a military camp, tens of thousands of men who had previously not been exposed to a variety of diseases, and therefore had no immunity to them, began living in close quarters. Conditions were ripe for the transmission of diseases; recruits slept shoulder to shoulder in crowded, often unventilated tents. Their natural resistance to infection was worn down by chronic exposure to poor weather conditions, fatigue, and malnutrition. Among the Massachusetts Forty-ninth Volunteers, half a dozen men died even before leaving their first camp in their hometown of Worcester. And while doctors knew that sick men should be separated from the general camp population, they had no idea of how easily some diseases could be passed along.

Common colds were widespread, but there was no way of distinguishing their symptoms from a disease that was immeasurably more serious: measles. In both cases a soldier would sneeze and have a runny nose, reddish eyes, and a slight fever. Initially he would stay among his company, in his tent, performing his duties; all the while spreading his disease. Infection with measles requires only a passing touch and is most contagious in the days before the appearance of the identifying rash.

As W. O. Gulick of Company M of the First Iowa Cavalry noted in a letter of November 24, 1861, the treatment for measles did little to alleviate the symptoms or the sickness:

> Dear Brother:
> I received your letters (In answer to Johns I suppose) some time ago. And I am sorry to say it found me just able to sit up in my Bunk and nibbling on a piece of Toast. I was quite unwell for two or three days before I received it, but did not know just what was the matter with me. I reported myself sick and the Doc said the symptoms of measles were quite strong but not enough to take me to the Hospital. In the course of two or three days they applied mustard to my brest [sic] but could not start the Measles and I could not go to the Hospital untill [sic] I knew. The next night they applied the mustard, and gave me some sweating powders, also about a galon [sic] of hot tea. You ought to have seen the measles start on me then. After so long a time they seemed to come out double Proportion.[1]

As high fever settled in, a sick man would be removed to an infirmary tent or hospital, having already created a legacy of dozens of other infections.

From a single case of measles, an outbreak could rapidly develop, sweep through the defenseless camp population, and devastate it. Other childhood diseases, such as mumps and chicken pox, also incapacitated many men. Other diseases that existed in normal society, such as pneumonia, also took many lives and did so in an exaggerated fashion because of the concentrated population.

What is difficult to comprehend from today's perspective, an era in which the diseases that were once the scourge of humanity have been largely vanquished, is that in the 1860s there were simply no cures of any kind for any of the maladies. When a man became ill, the only thing that could save him was his physical strength and perhaps luck. A visit to a doctor or hospital might make him more comfortable, but there were no panaceas. An illness that today is easily remedied with a course of antibiotics could often be fatal.

The early days of the war saw the worst effect of the epidemics in camp. In August 1861, Brigadier General J. Bankhead Magruder wrote from Yorktown, Virginia, to the adjutant general of the Confederacy in Richmond that in one of his regiments, which had 1,150 men serving in it, only 190 were healthy enough to perform their duties.[2]

Although the medical authorities did not understand the cause of the spreading sicknesses, they did recognize the relationship between new recruits and outbreaks. General Robert E. Lee suggested that "it would be better that

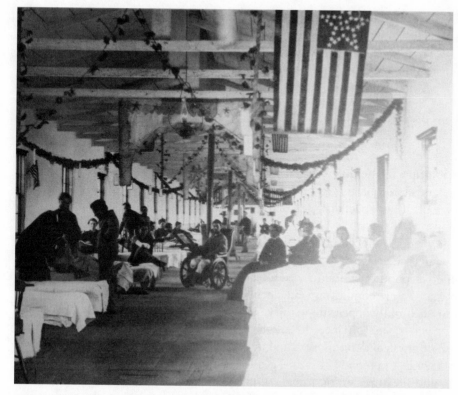

The very lucky few wounded who made it to hospitals such as this one made a life similar in many ways to camp life— invaded by the invisible enemy of disease all too often.

the conscripts be assembled in camps of instruction so that they may pass through these inevitable diseases and become a little inured to camp life."[3]

As the war progressed, soldiers either survived their diseases and, in some cases, became immune—or they died. Though the number of men unfit to fight because of illness grew smaller, it was still high. Disease actually influenced the strategy and outcome of numerous battles, as often neither army could muster up enough men to take the field.

It was abundantly clear to Confederate doctor Spencer Welch what the soldiers' greatest enemy was. Writing home to his wife, he remarked, "I trust we will be exposed to no greater danger in the future than the bullets, for they do not compare in destructiveness with disease."[4]

From the capital of the Confederacy in Richmond, Mary Chesnut wrote in July 1861 of seeing convalescing soldiers waiting to be transported on trains. Her sympathy for the men is matched by her surprise regarding the cause of their incapacity:

Yesterday as we left the cars we had a glimpse of war. It was the saddest sight. The memory of it is hard to shake off. Sick soldiers—not wounded. There were quite two hundred lying about as best they might on the platform. . . . [T]hese pale, ghastly faces. So there is one of the horrors of war we had not reckoned on.[5]

Camp Fever

In addition to the diseases that were common to the era and amplified by the soldiers' close quarters, there were also outbreaks of other diseases that were not typical but specifically caused by the appalling conditions of the military camps.

First and foremost among these diseases was typhoid fever, which was also known at the time as "camp fever." Caused by the *Salmonella typhi* bacterium, which is found in contaminated food or water, typhoid fever thrived in the unsanitary camp conditions and decimated both the Union and Confederate armies. Initially appearing with symptoms like those of influenza—headaches, body aches, loss of sleep, fever—typhoid took its victims down a two-week path of physical deterioration and mortal complications. Typhoid often caused septicemia and blood poisoning and led to cardiac failure, peritonitis, pneumonia, and life-threatening intestinal problems. Even if the doctors had known how to treat some of the ailments, they could not keep up with the patients' spiraling deterioration. The patients did not have a chance, and most of them died.

Typhoid fever was a terrifying disease, and while the various medical staffs labored bravely to save their patients, the threat of infection could bring out the worst in people. Katherine Prescott Wormeley of Newport, Rhode Island, worked aboard Union hospital ships, technically as a "housekeeper" but for all intents and purposes as a nurse. Although she understood how dangerous typhoid was, she cared for those who were infected and held those who avoided such duty with contempt:

> Colonel X was very ill with Typhoid Fever and was madly anxious to get home. He knew he must die and he craved to see his wife. The gentlemen of the excursion (visiting congressmen carrying roses held to their noses and "ladies in silks and perfumes and lilac kid gloves") were asked to take him back on their boat. They refused; alleging that they were a "select party" and "not prepared to incur infection" they made the ladies

the ground of their excuse. So Mrs. Griffin went at midnight to the ladies and begged them to consent to take him and of course they did so. I could enlarge upon this but the subject is hateful.[6]

Despite the best efforts of the nurses and doctors, typhoid fever and other camp diseases, such as dysentery and chronic diarrhea, would remain an intractable problem because the conditions that caused them were never thoroughly cured. While some in the command structure were aware of the importance of well-designed sanitation facilities, their understanding of the reasons for doing so were limited. Indeed, there were those who challenged even the most rudimentary advances in camp maintenance:

> One regimental surgeon thought the fecal odor that developed around every camp might be dangerous and proposed to get rid of it. His colonel claimed this was impossible as the odor was inseparable from an army and that it was a "patriotic odor."[7]

A number of the misconceptions were not the product of such stubborn ignorance. Doctors and soldiers grappled with the problem of health and improving the camp's sanitary conditions. But lacking an awareness of germs, they inevitably pursued the wrong course. Henry T. Johns shared the commonly held belief that disease was bred by certain topographies:

> Poison lurks in the smile of beauty. Throw yourself down on the ground though in full glare of the sun. Keep up this habit and you do not contract a cold as in the north but a fever. The ground damp is our enemy. It is hard to convince the tired soldier that there is danger, ay, death, in lying down on that sun heated dry ground. He believes it when he finds his last farewell to loved ones was final. Bad air, bad water, kill many, but the earth damp is one great scourge.[8]

Johns's conviction that the ground itself caused disease is incorrect but not far from the truth. Malaria incapacitated tens of thousands of soldiers and was identified with the odors emanating from the swamps and marshes where military camps were often established. No one suspected that the debilitating and sometimes fatal disease was transmitted by the bites of anopheles mosquitoes, which found the wetland conditions excellent for breeding. Within several days of the initial insect bite, the protozoans that caused malaria would attack the victim's red blood cells and begin a cycle of illness that infected as many as

Laborers picking up the bones of the dead in Cold Harbor, Virginia, a year after fighting passed through the area. Not only human bodies, but the corpses of horses and draft animals killed in battle poisoned streams and the groundwater in some areas for months.

a million Union soldiers during the war.[9] Over the course of eighteen months at the beginning of the war, nearly forty-two thousand Confederate troops suffered from malaria.[10]

The lives of malaria victims revolved around a forty-eight- or sometimes seventy-two-hour sequence that began with violent shaking followed by chills, high temperatures, and headaches and culminate in heavy sweating. Although quinine was an effective remedy—and perhaps the single useful medicine available to doctors of the era—it still treated only the symptoms of the disease. Inevitably, the *Plasmodium* parasite that caused the disease lingered in the victim's bloodstream for the duration of the war, and many veterans were afflicted by relapses in the decades following their service.

Try as they might, the Civil War medical officers' fundamental ignorance regarding the bacteriological causes of disease ensured that their best efforts to keep their soldiers healthy were almost completely futile. Even if, for example, the troops' latrines were constructed at a distance from their living quarters because some felt the odors caused sickness, they were often built upstream from the camp. Thus the source of drinking water became polluted and became a grave threat to the men. Other contaminants of the soldiers' drinking water included waste from horses and cattle, the by-products of washing clothing and mess utensils, offal from slaughtered cattle, and the decomposing corpses of soldiers and animals.

Often the result would be epidemics of intestinal diseases that would incapacitate the majority of a regiment and kill thousands of men. Dysentery, one of the leading killers of Union and Confederate soldiers, was caused by the contamination of drinking water by the feces of infected men. It could also be caused by the mishandling of food that was prepared by infected people whose hands were not properly washed. Also contributing to the life-threatening cases of diarrhea was food poisoning caused by undercooked and diseased beef, pork, and poultry. Henry Johns noted that among the Massachusetts Forty-ninth Volunteers it was difficult to find a single man who was not suffering from a gastrointestinal disorder:

> [T]his insidious disease is rarely overcome while living on camp fare. If not speedily overcome it becomes chronic and then farewell comfort, energy, life itself.[11]

Aware that dangers were posed to the military by the unclean living conditions, even if they had no real understanding of their actual causes, influential Northern citizens organized the U.S. Sanitary Commission in 1861, and it soon began its camp inspections. As nonmilitary observers, the commission volunteers may not always have been welcomed by lazy officers, but they did more for the welfare of the soldiers than the army medical staffs did. Their responsibilities included reporting on the sanitary conditions of military camps, food and hospitals and making recommendations for improvement. They also provided medical supplies, assisted with medical care, and sometimes treated patients in the absence of military doctors. In addition, commission inspectors compiled statistics on diseases, battlefield wounds, and deaths. They also assisted with the transportation of wounded men to hospitals and, when it was possible or necessary, to their home states. And, earning the commission its greatest popularity among the troops, they also dispensed supplemental rations when necessary and holiday treats when appropriate.

The success of the sanitary commission is apparent in the hostile attitude of Confederate soldiers toward its efforts, which more than likely masked envy. While the Confederacy did have local aid societies, it had nothing that could match the Union's well-funded and highly effective organization.

Dietary Diseases

Despite the exertions of well-intentioned people, many obstacles to the health of the troops remained. Although both nations' military commands were aware of the dangers of scurvy and would have liked to upgrade the diet of their soldiers, it usually was not possible to do so. While the sanitary commission tried to supplement the Union soldiers' rations and Southern farmers and townspeople attempted to do the same for their men, the lack of fresh vegetables and fruits took its toll. Some soldiers went for months without fresh vegetables or fruits, and the acute deficiency of ascorbic acid, or vitamin C, led to scurvy, the breakdown in a body's production of tissue. The manifestations of the disease were bulging gums that were prone to bleeding, tooth loss, aching joints, general anemia, and an inability of wounds to heal.

Scurvy could be easily remedied by dietary improvement, and often victims could be saved. Some soldiers, however, were unable to get the food they needed, and the disease would run its fatal course. Warren Lee Goss witnessed the destructive power of scurvy among fellow Union prisoners at the notorious Andersonville prison in Georgia:

> A common form of scurvy was in the mouth: this was the most horrible in its final results that afflicted the prisoners. The teeth would become loosened, the gums rot away, and swallowing the saliva thus tainted with the poison of scurvy, would produce scurvy in the bowels, which often took the form of chronic diarrhea. . . . [O]ften scurvy sores would gangrene and maggots would crawl from the flesh and pass from the bowels and under the tortures of a slow death the body would become in part putrid before death.[12]

Even when scurvy was not fatal, it contributed to a general weakening of the soldiers and made them susceptible to illnesses, such as pneumonia, for which there were no cures.

Deadly Medical Facilities and Lethal Attitudes

At the outset of the war, both nations discovered that they were grossly unprepared to handle the onslaught of sick and wounded. In the entire U.S. army, there were only thirty surgeons and eighty-four assistant surgeons. Almost immediately, the Union medical ranks were emptied as almost a third of the doctors defected to the Confederacy. Hospitals were rare, and a program was started to build more. Initially, the facilities were little more than field hospitals set up in tents to treat the wounded and sick and keep them separate from the general camp population. Inside, the conditions were not all that much better than normal camp life, and with the desperate shortage of doctors, the patients were often cared for by men with little, or poor, medical training. While the sick men did not have to participate in the daily camp routine, they still suffered from bad weather, insects, mud, and other discomforts. As the demand for hospital beds became more pronounced, facilities were established in hotels, warehouses, and abandoned buildings. Sometimes the conditions inside were beneficial, while at other times they were extremely detrimental. Hospitals were also organized as sprawling "tent cities" with equally mixed results.

Indeed, a combination of insufficient medical knowledge, the concentration of sick men in a small area, scarce supplies, and unsanitary conditions often contributed to the spread of diseases instead of their cure. One of the terrible ironies for the sick fighting men of the Civil War is that some of the best efforts to cure them may actually have furthered their decline. C. W. Wills described the hospitals he had visited:

> The hospitals at Hamburg make almost a city. I think there can be no more sorrowful sight, real or imaginary, than that camp of the sick. . . . I don't know the number of patients, somewhere in the thousands, all packed in tents as closely as they can lie, and with not one-tenth the care

As seen in this stereoscopic view, many wounded soldiers walked out of strange buildings like this one into lives like none they had seen or imagined when they enlisted.

a sick horse would get at home. I suppose the surgeons, stewards and nurses have feelings like men when they first enter the hospitals, but familiarity with disease and suffering seem to make them careless and indifferent to a degree that surprises me, and I can't but look upon it as criminal.[13]

Nurse Kate Cumming tried to do her job in an equally poor situation at a hospital that had been created in the Tishomingo Hotel in Corinth, Mississippi. Today, the conditions she found would exist only in nightmares:

[F]ound the men lying on the floors, the air bad, and the floor filthy with blud [sic] and mud. The patients had one meal a day consisting of bad soup and bread. . . . Much vermin, no cots, little bedding, and few blankets.[14]

The results of placing sick men in such unsatisfactory conditions were predictable. Called to the bedside of a soldier she knew from days prior to the war, Mary Chesnut was appalled by what she found:

Then we went to the St. Charles. Horrors upon horrors again—want of organization. Long rows of them dead, dying. Awful smells. Awful sights. A boy from home had sent for me. He was lying in a cot, ill of fever. Next to him a man died in convulsions while we stood there.[15]

Over a two-week period, Henry T. Johns recorded the appalling death rate among the diseased of his regiment:

R. Weberer died of fever on the 15th of March. He was a married man from New Marlboro, aged 37 years, and is spoken of as a very nice man. . . . [O]n March 20th "struck down" with the hand of fever [was] William Taylor, formerly a finisher in Taconia Mills, Pittsfield. . . . Morton Olds died here March 21st. Fever was his foe. He was a steady even tempered farmer boy of 18 years of age from Sandisfield. . . . Fever also struck low in death March 22 Eugene W. Pierce, sergeant of Windsor. . . . He was one of our reliable farmer boys, aged 21 years with bright eye denoting no ordinary intelligence. . . . Allen M Dewey corporal in Company C died at New Orleans on March 23. . . . I saw him lying on his one blanket emaciated the bones working through the skin which was

raw and marked with putrid sores gasping for breath yet seemingly resigned. . . . [O]n the same day Typhoid Fever cut down Lyman Lind-
say . . . aged 22 years and officers speak of him as a good nice boy. . . .
Nelson Steson died on the first instant of fever. He was one of Windsor's
best soldiers a farmer aged 28 years.[16]

As if the sick Civil War soldier did not have enough problems, he faced yet
another grave and astonishing obstacle to his recovery: the attitude of some
military doctors. To some of these betrayers of the Hippocratic oath, their responsibilities required them to administer exclusively to soldiers suffering from
wounds suffered in fighting. These doctors left the care of the diseased to members of the U.S. Sanitary Commission. Katherine Prescott Wormeley described
their attitude to her mother in a letter:

> The Sanitary Commission is not treated in the handsomest manner; its
> benevolence is imposed upon. Squads of civilian doctors are here, wait-
> ing for "surgical cases" . . . there must be dozens of them doing nothing,
> and their boats doing nothing,—waiting for a battle. They would not
> look at a sick man; bless you, he's not their game! It is "cases" they want;
> and their whole influence goes to getting off the sick upon the Commis-
> sion instead of taking their proper share of the work, so that they may
> when a battle occurs get a harvest of wounded.[17]

War Wounds

If it were true that some doctors were interested in treating only soldiers who
had been wounded in action, it did not necessarily follow that their care
yielded any better results. While Civil War surgeons did make progress in their
understanding of combat wounds because they treated so many, a great many
cases ended unsuccessfully. Again, the fault lay with their obliviousness to the
danger posed by germs and the resulting infection.

The basics of modern medical hygiene, such as the sterilization of instruments prior to surgery, were unknown. Accordingly, a scalpel or saw covered
with gore from one patient would often be used on another without being
washed. Doctors wore bloody uniforms, masks and gloves were nonexistent,
and bandages taken from one man might be given a cursory cleaning before
being strapped onto another. Doctors often performed invasive surgery, tying
arteries, removing bullets, and amputating limbs without even washing their

hands after working on the previous patient. If the doctors of the Civil War had tried to design a system for the breeding and spreading of disease and infection, they could not have found a more efficient method.

Another contributing factor to the disabling and death of many troops was the massive injuries caused by the kind of ammunition used during the war. While bullets used in modern warfare can cause catastrophic damage, the "minié balls" that were used in the 1860s were in some ways more dangerous. Moving at substantially slower velocities than modern ammunition and more prone to breaking apart upon impact, minié balls would not simply pass through the flesh of a body and leave a clean exit wound. Instead they would shatter, and their fragments would destroy the bone of an arm, leg, or torso, acting more like a small explosive device than a twentieth-century bullet.

Civil War surgeons often received their patients hours, even days, after a wound was suffered. This delay could be catastrophic, as the destruction caused by a minié ball created many opportunities for contamination. Often soldiers were already suffering from deadly infections by the time they received care. Even in cases where patients were treated quickly, there was still a great risk of infection because the medical staff performed their tasks without knowledge of hygienic requirements.

Once the immediate threat of battlefield death was past, the greatest danger to the wounded men was gangrene. Deep wounds often created excellent, oxygen-deprived conditions for the growth of the *Clostridium* bacterium. Within a matter of days, the infection would cause a dark, offensive-smelling discharge to erupt. As the tissue near a victim's wound died, powerful toxins were released that would kill the patient unless the source of the poison could be removed.

The doctors had few choices in the treatment of such injuries. They would wash wounds and rebandage them frequently, aware that cleanliness was advantageous, even if they had no idea why. But washing alone was often not enough to help a patient, and other, more dramatic remedies were required. The great majority of combat wounds were to the soldiers' arms and legs, and there developed a radical if effective treatment for limbs mangled beyond restoration: amputation.

Amputation was the only reliable treatment of badly wounded or infected limbs. Sometimes executed in as little as fifteen minutes with the patient tranquilized with chloroform as a general anesthetic, the removal of an arm or leg also removed the source of the gangrenous infection or acted preventively. Surgeries were commonly performed in the open air, on tables that were not sanitized, with instruments coated with the blood of other patients, by doctors

Army doctor performing an amputation in a makeshift hospital

using their bare hands. Observers of amputations that occurred after a battle remarked on the horror of the scene: the screaming, bleeding patients, the exhausted doctors and nurses covered in blood, and—worst of all—piles of feet, hands, legs, and arms lying on the ground waiting to be disposed of. Despite the horrific nature of the surgery and the general atmosphere, up to 75 percent of the amputees survived their treatment; many of them would have died without the procedure.

Proven remedy though it may have been, amputation was such a frightening prospect that it gave doctors a bad reputation and some soldiers did whatever they could to avoid it. John England of Company E, Second New York Cavalry, was one of the few fortunate soldiers who refused the surgery and survived:

> At last by much ado I succeeded in getting into the hospital for the purpose of having it [a badly mangled limb] amputated but thanks to god after burning it with nitric acid, nitrate of silver, and keeping turpentine and linseed meal to it for about six weeks I succeeded but not without infinite pain in getting the gangrene out.[18]

For those who had suffered wounds to the chest, abdomen, lower body, or head there was little the doctors could do. Attempts would be made to remove the minié ball, and the patients were provided with a nurturing environment, if at all possible, in which to heal. Despite the best efforts of doctors and nurses, the results were grim. While many more soldiers died of disease during the Civil War than of war wounds, the death rate of the injured was still atrociously high.

As a result, hospital tents and wards were perceived by the common Civil War soldier to be as threatening and deadly as any battlefield. If today, in modern warfare, an injured soldier is relieved to be brought back to a hospital unit, the Civil War soldier understood that he was exchanging one nightmarish situation for another. Confederate surgeon Spencer Welch noted in a letter to his wife that even the journey from the battlefield to the hospital was an arduous one for the wounded:

> On Sunday I was sent to Richmond to look after our sick and did not return until late yesterday afternoon. . . . Our casualties were certainly very great, for every house which could be had was being filled with the wounded. Even the depots were being filled with them and they came pouring into the hospital by wagon loads. Nearly all were covered with mud, as they had fought in a swamp most of the time and lain out all night after being wounded. Many of them were but slightly wounded, many others severely, large numbers mortally, and some would die on the road from the battlefield. In every direction the slightly wounded were seen with their arms in slings, their heads tied up, or limping about. One man appeared as if he had been entirely immersed in blood, yet he could walk.[19]

Nor was arrival at a hospital a guarantee of beneficial treatment. Conditions were often primitive, the medical staffs were overwhelmed, and some staffers were cynically inclined toward their wards as there was so little hope for their recovery. Aboard the Union hospital ship *Elizabeth*, Katherine Prescott Wormeley received word that a sister vessel, *The State of Maine*, needed assistance and was stunned by the atrocious circumstances to which the wounded were delivered:

> We went aboard and such a scene as we entered and lived in for two days I trust never to see again. Men in every condition of horror, shattered and shrieking were being brought in. . . . [Medical staff] walked

over men without compassion, men shattered in the thigh and even cases of amputation were shovelled into top berths without thought or mercy. The men had mostly been without food for three days but there was nothing on board either boat for them. . . . [I]magine a great river or sound steamer filled on every deck, every berth, and every square inch covered with wounded men; even the stairs and gangways and guards filled . . . [20]

The worst, however, was not immediately evident to Wormeley. In the panic to get the wounded men aboard the hospital ships, she did not know that the military's medical department had not supplied surgeons, medicines, or equipment. The only people available to treat the soldiers were volunteers like herself, and the outcome was chaos:

Conceive of the medical director sending down over 4,500 wounded men without—yes almost literally without—anything for them: without surgeons, no one authorized to take charge of them, nothing but empty boats to receive them. [21]

On other occasions the Union medical service was better prepared in that doctors were at least present, but even so there was a limit to what they could do. Wormeley was often reduced to serving her patients rations of brandy, water, bread, and butter in the place of real medicine. Aboard another hospital ship, the *Wilson Small,* she could offer little more than distraction and the warmth of human contact to a wounded man

shot through the knee and enduring more than mortal agony, a fair haired boy of 17 shot through the lungs every breath he draws hissing through the wound. . . . [W]e begin the day by seeing them all washed, and freshened up, and breakfasted. Then the surgeons . . . make their rounds, open the wounds, apply the remedies and replace the bandages. This is an awful hour; I sat with my fingers in my ears this morning. . . . [Later on in the day] we were remaking several of the beds, and giving clean handkerchiefs with a little cologne or baywater on them,—so prized in the sickening atmosphere of wounds. [22]

Still, the hordes of injured men kept appearing. The volunteers did what they could, but frequently their attention came too late:

The men were just as they fell in their muddy clothing saturated with blood and filth . . . one died in Mrs. Griffin's care and one in mine; there were some too far gone to know anything more in this world.[23]

For some of the patients the conditions of the hospital ships, combined with their atrocious injuries, were too much, and they went mad. Wormeley wrote home to her mother about one soldier who

jumped overboard. He rushed past me and sprang from the bulwark. I heard the splash but all that I or any one saw of him were the rings in the water widening in the moonlight.[24]

Often the Confederate wounded fared even worse than the Union soldiers. In general, the U.S. Medical Department could provide basic medical supplies, such as chloroform for an anesthetic or morphine for the most gravely wounded. The Confederacy, however, was rarely able to obtain such fundamentals, as its supply routes were cut off by the Union naval blockade of its ports. Confronted by shortages, the Confederate Medical Corps turned to natural "medicines" that it hoped would cure its patients. When quinine was unavailable for soldiers suffering from malaria, they would be given "old indig.," which was a concoction of willow, yellow poplar, and dogwood barks mixed with alcohol. "Painkillers" were brewed from jimsonweed, leaves, and seeds, and maypop roots blended with alcohol. Boneset was used to reduce fevers, and Queen's root was given to deal with "depraved blood." Although today we may recognize the helpfulness of medications taken from nature, during the Civil War there was so little knowledge regarding their use that their application was often little more than an exercise in wishful thinking.

Consequently, Confederate doctors could do little more than give injured men palliative care, often under atrocious circumstances, while the soldiers either fought off infection and survived or died. Even for those who could be helped by radical surgery, the prospect of convalescence was no less hellish. One surgeon recounted:

I then went back to the field infirmary, where I saw large numbers of wounded lying on the ground as thick as a drove of hogs in a lot. They were groaning or crying out with pain, and those shot in the bowels were crying for water. Jake Fellers had his arm amputated without chloroform. I held the artery and Dr. Huot cut it off by candle light. We continued to

Wounded soldiers found on the battlefield were lucky. Most wounds were inoperable, so many of the wounded were left where they lay—to die in agony and alone.

operate until late at night and attended to all our wounded. I was very tired and slept on the ground.[25]

For those soldiers who were strong enough—and lucky enough—to endure drastic surgeries, infection, and the deadly diseases that swept through the camps, there was one last obstacle to survival: the assault upon their spirits by the nightmare they were living. While the army provided chaplains to minister to their religious needs and nurses did their best to provide comfort, what they most needed was a connection with their families at home. It was for their wives, children, mothers, and fathers that they had gone to war and been wounded. More than anything, they needed to believe that when they recovered they would be reunited with their loved ones. If letters from home were important under normal circumstances, correspondence from family to a convalescing soldier was sometimes a matter of life and death:

[T]o the sick letters are more invigoration than all the remedies of the surgeon. . . . [The absence of letters written to the invalid] hastens him to the hospital or the grave. This is a real sickness . . . "died of homesick-ness" should be written on many a grave. The victims are not babes or cowards but the finest spirits of the army. Alone in a crowd craving sympathy and fearing the sneer they wilt and die.[26]

When the men who fought the Civil War left the cities, small towns, and rural farming communities where they had grown up, they did so with the intention of struggling with a clearly defined enemy to protect the rights of their homes, families, and loved ones. Once given the opportunity to do so, they defended the values they believed in with bravery and some success. To their dying days, the veterans of the Civil War considered its battles to be the defining moments of their lives.

But viewed from the end of the twentieth century, it is also clear that the soldiers were involved in another war without ever being aware of it, fighting an enemy they could not know in a battle that would not be won until science revealed their microscopic adversaries.

If the adage "My enemy's enemy is my friend" is true at some level that might not have been immediately apparent to the Confederate and Union soldiers, they were engaged in an alliance against a common foe. As the years passed, however, the surviving veterans were bound together by shared sympathies for the younger men they once had been, who had suffered greatly. Of all the memories of the Civil War, these remembrances offered the least controversial common ground upon which they could relate. For in their trials they had not been enemies at all but brothers in suffering.

Aftermath and Epilogue

*F*or the soldiers who were not killed or broken by the trials of the Civil War, the day finally came when the fighting was over. For those serving the Confederacy, their defeat and dismissal offered a dignity not previously extended to them by a government that could provide neither regular food nor adequate shelter:

General Order No. 9
  After four years of arduous service, marked by unsurpassed courage and fortitude, the Army of Northern Virginia has been compelled to yield to overwhelming numbers and resources.
  I need not tell the brave survivors of so many hard fought battles, who have remained steadfast to the last, that I have consented to this result from no distrust of them; but feeling that valor and devotion could accomplish nothing that would compensate for the loss that must have attended a continuance of the contest, I determined to avoid the useless sacrifice of those whose past services have endeared them to their countrymen.
  By the terms of their agreement, officers and men can return to their homes and remain until exchanged. You will take with you the satisfaction that proceeds from the consciousness of duty faithfully performed, and I earnestly pray that a merciful God will extend to you his blessing and protection.
  With an unceasing admiration for your constancy and devotion to your country, and a grateful remembrance of your kind and generous consideration for myself, I bid you all an affectionate farewell.
  R. E. Lee[1]

For the Union soldiers, there was a tremendous sense of relief combined with joy in their victory. As most of the war had been fought on Confederate territory, the Union army began the long trip north toward home and demobilization. The first men started marching in the late spring, and the sense of renewal and rebirth was strong. Elisha Rhodes traveled back to Providence, Rhode Island, in late July 1865 knowing that his efforts in the great trial had all been worth it:

> Today the Second RI was paid off and discharged. The regiment met at 9 am and without arms marched into a building on South Main street where they received their money and final discharge papers. About noon the paymaster told me that I was the only man left in the regiment and that he would be ready to pay me at 2 pm. I went home took off my uniform and put on a suit of citizen's clothes for the first time in over four years. I then went down to the office and received my pay and discharge. As I came out of the building I found the regiment, yes, my regiment, drawn up on the sidewalk and again I took each man by the hand. It was sad yet joyful for the war is over and we are at home. No more suffering. No more scenes of carnage and death. Thank God it is over and that the Union is restored. And so at last I am a simple citizen. Well, I am content but should my country call again, I am ready to respond.[2]

Four years earlier, as the soldiers of the United and Confederate States of America had set off to war, each man had had his own vision of what his experiences might be. Few could have imagined that their severest tests would take place in the hours and days when they were not fighting.

Undeniably, the battlefields of the Civil War were places of unimaginable terror and brutality. But soldiers spent a great deal more time in, and suffered a substantially higher mortality rate from, the day-to-day life in their stationary and mobile military camps. If the battlefields of the Civil War provided a concentrated trial of soldiers' ability to survive, the makeshift places they called home provided a relentless challenge to their souls. Day in, day out, month after month, year after year, the common soldiers' camp life was an uninterrupted and harsh test of their commitment to their beliefs.

Additionally, when their camps became mobile and they marched great distances, they discovered a country that they were defending but that had been only an abstract concept in their minds when they had enlisted. The Civil War soldier was challenged and educated in the days and months between fighting.

Inspired by a commitment forged in the adversity and comradeship of camp life, combined with a new knowledge of a people and their land, the men who had once been raw recruits changed. Once considering themselves Vermonters, New Yorkers, Kentuckians—Yankee soldiers all—they evolved into hardened American warriors fighting to save a nation. Georgians, Floridians, Texans—rebel soldiers all—were equally transformed by their shared experience in camp and on the march. Although they rejected and fought the U.S. armies, ultimately they could not deny their defeat by Union forces. As witnesses to the subjugation of their homeland, the rebels could no longer deny the reality of the United States of America. With bitterness, regret—and, for some, relief—the rebels became American citizens once again.

Transformed by their wartime experiences and returning home, the veterans could not help but influence the towns, farms, and cities in which and the family, friends, and neighbors with whom they spent the rest of their lives. Although it would be difficult to link "causes" in military camps to specific "effects" in civilian life, these men made the decisions that would shape American society for the next half century. As they returned to their fields, shops, universities, hospitals, newspapers, theaters, factories, state capitals, and even the White House, they brought a part of the military camp they had known during the war with them. Surviving the ordeal had proved both their physical and mental toughness, demonstrating that strangers could join together from distant points on a map to achieve great and moral goals, most importantly the creation of a unified country.

It is no coincidence that the men who starved, shivered, sang, bled, played games, fell ill—and survived—during four years of living in battlefield conditions, laid the foundations of what is known as the American Century. The men who saved the nation went on to make it great. Under their guidance, the United States became a dominant world power, economically, politically, socially, and culturally.

Today, the great men of the war—Lincoln, Lee, Grant, Jackson—and their exploits are extolled. Ordinary soldiers, however, such as C. W. Wills, E. F. Palmer, John Perry, Mortimer Legget, James Sawyer, Henry Johns, and Spencer Welch, and their years of tribulation have receded into the past and are all but forgotten. Their ordeal and the world of war they knew—the tastes, sounds, smells, fears, entertainments, sicknesses, pleasures, and discomforts—are deserving of our appreciation. We owe them for everything we have and, indeed, for no less than what we are. Without these men and their extraordinary fortitude, we would live in a very different place. The states of North America would not be united and might well exist as several lesser nations.

Many histories have already been written about the trials of the Civil War battlefield. But by taking note of the common soldiers' difficult lives while they were not fighting, we recognize a substantial, vital, and previously ignored contribution on their part toward the freedom we enjoy today. Without their sacrifices and triumphs over a period of almost fifteen hundred camp days, our world would surely be a more dangerous, less just, and poorer place.

Notes

Introduction: On the Path to War

1. Carl Bode, *The American Impression* (Carbondale: Southern Illinois University Press, 1972), p. 6.
2. Robert Gayet, *Everyday Life in the United States Before the Civil War* (New York: Frederick Unger, 1969), p. 11.
3. Salomon de Rothschild, *A Casual View of America*, ed. Sigmund Diamond (Stanford, Calif.: Stanford University Press, 1961), p. 70.
4. Thomas Nichols, *40 Years of American Life* (Harrisburg, Pa.: Telegraph, 1937), pp. 130–131 (first published 1874).
5. Ibid., p. 19.
6. Barbara Bodichon, *An American Diary*, ed. Joseph Reed (London: Routledge & Kegan Paul, 1972), p. 58.
7. George Rawick, ed., *The American Slave: A Composite Biography*, vol. 8 (Westport, Conn.: Greenwood, 1977), pp. 1080–1081.
8. Ibid., p. 1257.
9. William Howard Russell, *My Diary North and South*, ed. Eugene Berwanger (Philadelphia: Temple University Press, 1988), p. 86.
10. George Templeton Strong, *Diary*, vol. 3, ed. Nevins Thomas (New York: Macmillan, 1952), p. 21.
11. Found at Jefferson.village.virginia.edu/vshadow/letters.html
12. Found at Jefferson.village.virginia.edu/vshadow2/letters.html

Chapter One: In the Beginning

1. Fred C. Ainsworth, ed., *The War of the Rebellion: A Compilation of the Official Records of the Union and Confederate Armies*, series III, vol. 1 (n.p.: Historical Times, 1985), p. 2 (first published 1899).

2. Fred C. Ainsworth, ed., *The War of the Rebellion: A Compilation of the Official Records of the Union and Confederate Armies*, ser. IV, vol. 1 (n.p.: Historical Times, 1985), p. 1 (first published 1900).

3. Ibid., p. 38.

4. Ainsworth, *The War of the Rebellion*, ser. III, vol. 1, p. 53.

5. Ibid., p. 71.

6. Paul Steiner, *Disease in the Civil War* (Springfield, Ill.: Charles C. Thomas, 1968), p. 8.

7. Ainsworth, *The War of the Rebellion*, ser. III, vol. 1, p. 71.

8. Ibid., p. 70.

9. Ibid., p. 107.

10. William Watson, *Life in the Confederate Army* (London: Chapman & Hill, 1887).

11. Newspaper recruiting ad on www.infinet.com/~lstevens/burt/burtad.html; originally published in *The Newark* [Ohio] *True American* (Oct. 10, 1861).

12. George P. Morris, *The Picket Line & Camp Fire Stories* (publication details unavailable; however, the typesetting is clearly pre-1900 and the author is listed as a member of the GAR), p. 26.

13. Ibid., p. 44.

14. Ibid., p. 27.

15. Ibid.

16. Mills Lane, ed., *"Dear Mother: Don't Grieve About Me. If I Get Killed I'll Only Be Dead": Letters from Georgia Soldiers in the Civil War* (Savannah, Ga.: Beehive Press, 1990), p. 6. Lane found this letter at the Georgia State Department of Archives and History, Atlanta.

17. Ibid., p. 11. Lane found this letter at the Georgia State Department of Archives and History, Atlanta.

18. Morris, *The Picket Line & Camp Fire Stories*, p. 103.

19. M. D. Legget Papers, Wyles Collection, University of California, Santa Barbara.

20. Lane, *"Dear Mother,"* p. 10. Lane found this material in the William Letcher Mitchell Papers, University of North Carolina.

21. Legget Papers, Wyles Collection, University of California, Santa Barbara.

22. "Albion Martin Diary, 33rd Virginia Volunteer Infantry Company A . . . Inc," at members.aol.com/vir33edreg/p.51-198.html.

23. John D. Billings, *Hardtack and Coffee* (Boston: George M. Smith, 1888), p. 37.

24. Ibid.

25. Ibid., p. 37.

26. Ibid., p. 44.

27. Sam Watkins, *"Co. Aytch,"* Maruy Grays, *First Tennessee Regiment* (Jackson, Tenn.: McCowat-Mercer, 1952), p. 69 (first published 1882).

28. Ibid.

29. Lane, *Dear Mother*, p. 103. Lane found this letter at the Georgia State Department Historical Archives, Atlanta.

30. Ainsworth, *The War of the Rebellion*, ser. IV, vol. 3, p. 36.

31. John Perry, *Letters from a Surgeon of the Civil War*, ed. Martha Derby Perry (Boston: Little, Brown, 1906), p. 21.
32. Ainsworth, *The War of the Rebellion*, ser. IV, vol. 3, p. 660.
33. Ibid., p. 1041.

Chapter Two: The New World: Military Life and Camp Conditions

1. James Sawyer Letters, Wyles Collection, University of California, Santa Barbara.
2. Mills Lane, ed., *"Dear Mother: Don't Grieve About Me. If I Get Killed I'll Only Be Dead": Letters from Georgia Soldiers in the Civil War* (Savannah, Ga.: Beehive Press, 1990), p. 48.
3. E. F. Palmer, *The Second Brigade or Camp Life by a Volunteer* (Montpelier, Vt., 1864), p. 23.
4. Philip Cheek, *Sauk Riflemen Company A 6th Wisconsin* (n.p., 1909), p. 23.
5. Thomas Wentworth Higginson, *Army Life in a Black Regiment and Other Writings* (Boston: Fields, Osgood, 1870), p. 14.
6. C. W. Wills, *Army Life of an Illinois Soldier* (Washington, D.C.: Globe, 1906) p. 49.
7. John Perry, *Letters from a Surgeon of the Civil War*, ed. Martha Derby Perry (Boston: Little, Brown, 1906), p. 123.
8. Palmer, *The Second Brigade or Camp Life by a Volunteer*, p. 38.
9. Wills, *Army Life of an Illinois Soldier*, p. 29.
10. Carlton McCarthy, *Detailed Minutiae of Soldier Life in the Army of Northern Virginia 1861–1865* (Richmond, Va.: Carlton McCarthy, 1882), p. 25.
11. Spencer Glasgow Welch, *A Confederate Surgeon's Letters to His Wife* (New York: Neal, 1911), p. 41.
12. Jedediah Hotchkiss, *Make Me a Map of the Valley* (Dallas: Southern Methodist University Press, 1989), p. 33.
13. Perry, *Letters from a Surgeon of the Civil War*, p. 123.
14. Lydia Minturn Post, ed., *Soldiers' Letters from Camp, Battlefield, and Prison* (New York: Bunce & Huntington, 1865), p. 239.
15. Richard Lewis, *Camp Life of a Confederate Boy* (Charleston, S.C.: News & Courier Book Presses, 1883).
16. Palmer, *The Second Brigade or Camp Life by a Volunteer*, p. 73.
17. *The War of the Rebellion: A Compilation of the Official Records of the Union and Confederate Armies*, ser. I, vol. 51, pt. 2, *Confederate Correspondence* (n.p.: Historical Times, 1985), p. 171 (first published 1897).
18. Henry T. Johns, *Life with the 49th Massachusetts Volunteers* (Pittsfield, Mass., 1864), p. 80.
19. Wills, *Army Life of an Illinois Soldier*, p. 259.
20. Welch, *A Confederate Surgeon's Letters to His Wife*, p. 42.
21. Found at U.S. Civil War Center "letters" Web site, but no other copyright information was provided. Letter was originally published in *The Jewish Messenger*, Aug. 1, 1862.

22. U.S. Sanitary Commission, *Documents of the U.S. Sanitary Commission*, vol. 1 (New York, 1866).

23. Ibid.

24. Palmer, *The Second Brigade or Camp Life by a Volunteer*, p. 25.

25. John Billings, *Hardtack & Coffee* (Boston: George M. Smith, 1888).

26. James Sawyer Letters, Wyles Collection, University of California, Santa Barbara.

27. Higginson, *Army Life in a Black Regiment and Other Writings*, p. 107.

28. Johns, *Life with the 49th Massachusetts Volunteers*, p. 88.

29. James Sawyer Letters, Wyles Collection, University of California, Santa Barbara.

30. Ibid.

31. Onley Andrus, *The Civil War Letters of Sergeant Onley Andrus*, ed. Fred Albert Shannon (Urbana: University of Illinois Press, 1947), p. 53.

32. Wills, *Army Life of an Illinois Soldier*, p. 12.

33. Palmer, *The Second Brigade or Camp Life by a Volunteer*, p. 25.

34. Johns, *Life with the 49th Massachusetts Volunteers*, p. 35.

35. Perry, *Letters from a Surgeon of the Civil War*, p. 79.

36. James Sawyer Letters, Wyles Collection, University of California, Santa Barbara.

37. Johns, *Life with the 49th Massachusetts Volunteers*, p. 237.

38. Ibid., p. 222.

39. Robert Hunt Rhodes, *All for the Union* (New York: Orion, 1985), p. 112.

40. Lane, *Dear Mother*, p. 51. Lane found this material at the Georgia State Department of Archives and History, Atlanta.

41. Ibid., p. 82.

42. Roy Mathis, *In the Land of the Living* (Troy, Ala.: Troy State University Press), p. 94.

43. John F. L. Hartwell, *To My Beloved Wife and Boy at Home*, ed. Ann Hartwell Britton (Cranbury, N.J.: Fairleigh Dickinson University Press, 1997), p. 26.

44. Joshua K. Callaway, *The Civil War Letters of Joshua K. Callaway*, ed. Judith Hallock (Athens: University of Georgia Press, 1997), p. 138.

45. Marion Hall Fitzpatrick, *Letters to Amanda*, ed. Jeffrey Lowe and Sam Hodges (Macon, Ga.: Mercer University Press, 1998), p. 26.

46. Joe Kirschberger, *The Civil War and Reconstruction: An Eyewitness History* (New York: Facts on File, 1991), p. 128.

47. Ibid., p. 132.

48. Ibid., p. 134.

49. Ibid., p. 228.

50. Welch, *A Confederate Surgeon's Letters to His Wife*, p. 23.

51. Sam Watkins, *"Co. Aytch," Maruy Grays, First Tennessee Regiment* (Jackson, Tenn.: McCowat-Mercer, 1952), p. 121 (first published 1882).

52. Perry, *Letters from a Surgeon of the Civil War*, p. 119.

53. Lewis, *Camp Life of a Confederate Boy*.

54. Welch, *A Confederate Surgeon's Letters to His Wife*, p. 19.

55. Lane, *"Dear Mother,"* p. 59.

56. Watkins, *"Co. Aytch,"* p. 57.

57. Fred C. Ainsworth, ed., *The War of the Rebellion: A Compilation of the Official Records of the Union and Confederate Armies*, ser. III, vol. 1 (n.p.: Historical Times, 1985), p. 324 (first published 1899).

58. Johns, *Life with the 49th Massachusetts Volunteers*, p. 221.

59. McCarthy, *Detailed Minutiae*, p. 43.

60. Francis Miller, *The Photographic History of the Civil War in Ten Volumes*, vols. 7 and 8 (New York: Review of Reviews, 1911), p. 204.

61. Welch, *A Confederate Surgeon's Letters to His Wife*, p. 31.

62. W. Miller Owen, *In Camp and Battle with the Washington Artillery of New Orleans (Confederate)* (Boston: Ticknor, 1885), p. 171.

63. Geoffrey Ward, *The Civil War* (New York: Borzoi Books, 1991), p. 216.

64. Watkins, *"Co. Aytch,"* p. 225.

Chapter Three: Fun, Games, and Other Matters of Life and Death

1. Carlton McCarthy, *Detailed Minutiae of Soldier Life in the Army of Northern Virginia 1861–1865* (Richmond, Va.: Carlton McCarthy, 1882), p. 31.

2. C. W. Wills, *Army Life of an Illinois Soldier* (Washington, D.C.: Globe, 1906), p. 27.

3. Adam Gurowski, *Diary from March 4, 1861, to November 12, 1862* (Boston: Lee & Shepard, 1862), p. 121.

4. Spencer Glasgow Welch, *A Confederate Surgeon's Letters to His Wife* (New York: Neal, 1911), p. 121.

5. Wills, *Army Life of an Illinois Soldier*, p. 11.

6. Thomas Lowry, *The Stories Soldiers Wouldn't Tell: Sex in the Civil War* (Mechanicsburg, Pa.: Stackpole, 1994), p. 54.

7. John Perry, *Letters from a Surgeon of the Civil War*, ed. Martha Derby Perry (Boston: Little, Brown, 1906), p. 154.

8. Ibid., p. 11.

9. Hurst, *The Picket Line & Camp Fire Stories* (New York), p. 50.

10. Lowry, *The Stories Soldiers Wouldn't Tell*, p. 51.

11. Ibid.

12. Wyles Collection, University of California, Santa Barbara.

13. Thomas Wentworth Higginson, *Army Life in a Black Regiment and Other Writings* (Boston: Fields, Osgood, 1870), p. 13.

14. W. Miller Owen, *In Camp and Battle with the Washington Artillery of New Orleans (Confederate)* (Boston: Ticknor, 1885), p. 171.

15. Found at www.access.digex.net/~bdboyle/cohen.txt

16. Owen, *In Camp and Battle with the Washington Artillery*, p. 205.

17. Ibid.

18. Ibid.

19. Richard Lewis, *Camp Life of a Confederate Boy* (Charleston, S.C.: News & Courier Presses, 1883), p. 38.

20. Philip Cheek, *Sauk Riflemen Company A 6th Wisconsin* (n.p., 1909), pp. 21–22.

21. St. Clair Mulholland, *The Story of the 116th Regiment Pennsylvania Volunteers* (Philadelphia: F. McManus Jr., 1903), p. 81.

22. Listed in U.S. Civil War Center index with no other information. This was probably written in the spring of 1863 by J. Cohen for publication in *The Jewish Messenger*.

23. Owen, *In Camp and Battle with the Washington Artillery*, p. 71.

24. Mrs. Thomas Taylor, *South Carolina Women in the Confederacy* (Columbia, S.C.: South Carolina Daughters of the Confederacy, 1903), p. 200.

25. U.S. Sanitary Commission, *Documents of the U.S. Sanitary Commission*, vol. 1 (New York, 1866).

26. Lewis, *Camp Life of a Confederate Boy*, p. 40.

27. E. F. Palmer, *The Second Brigade or Camp Life by a Volunteer* (Montpelier, Vt., 1864), p. 156.

28. Irwin Bell Wiley, *The Life of Johnny Rebel* (New York: Bobbs-Merrill, 1943).

29. D. P. Hopkins, "Diary of D. P. Hopkins" (unpublished manuscript, University of Texas), pp. 19–20.

30. J. G. B. Adams, *Reminiscences of the 19th Massachusetts Regiment* (Boston: Wright and Potter, 1899).

31. The details of the wartime baseball came in part from the *Civil War Times Illustrated Magazine*, May 1998, as stated in an article by George B. Kirsch entitled "Bats, Balls, and Bullets," p. 36.

32. T. M. Aldrich, *The History of Battery A, First Regiment, Rhode Island Light Artillery in the War to Preserve the Union, 1861–1865* (Providence, R.I.: Snow & Farnham, 1904).

33. George B. Kirsch, "Bats, Balls, and Bullets," *Civil War Times Illustrated* (May 1998), p. 36.

34. William H. Sallada, *Silver Sheaves: Gathered Through Clouds and Sunshine* (Des Moines, Iowa, 1879), p. 76.

35. G. G. Benedict, *Vermont in the Civil War* (Burlington, Vt.: Free Press Association, 1886–1888), p. 80.

36. From an unpublished manuscript by A. F. Hill, who was a member of the 8th Pennsylvania.

37. Ibid.

38. E. R. Brown, *The 27th Indiana Volunteer Infantry in the War of the Rebellion* (Monticello, Ind.: n.p., 1899), p. 87.

39. A. Buell, *The Cannoneer: Recollections of Service in the Army of the Potomac* (Washington, D.C.: National Tribune, 1890), p. 274.

40. Mulholland, *The Story of the 116th Regiment Pennsylvania Volunteers*, p. 77.

41. D. D. Coyingham, *The Irish Brigade and Its Campaigns* (Boston: P. Donahoe, 1869), p. 144.

42. J. C. Robert, "A Ring Tournament in 1864," *Journal of Mississippi History* 3 (October 1941), p. 293.

43. F. L. Hitchcock, *War from Inside: Or Personal Experiences, Impressions, and Reminiscences of One of "the Boys" in the War of the Rebellion* (Philadelphia: J. B. Lippincott, 1904), pp. 149–151.

44. F. McGrath, ed., *The History of the 127th New York Volunteers "Monitors" in the War for the Preservation of the Union. Sept. 8th 1862–June 30th, 1865* (N.P., N.D. 1898?), p. 28.

45. Ibid.

46. Aldrich, *The History of Battery A, First Regiment*, p. 234.

47. E. H. Locke, *Three Years in Camp and Hospital* (Boston: G. D. Russell, 1870), p. 190.

48. Cheek, *Sauk Riflemen Company A 6th Wisconsin*, p. 21.

49. John Casler, *Four Years in the Stonewall Jackson Brigade* (Dayton, Ohio: Morningside Bookshop, 1906), p. 202.

50. Mulholland, *The Story of the 116th Regiment Pennsylvania Volunteers*, p. 140.

51. Wiley, *The Life of Johnny Rebel*.

52. Sallada, *Silver Sheaves*, p. 77.

53. Names of papers from Wiley, *The Life of Johnny Rebel*, p. 171.

54. Palmer, *The Second Brigade or Camp Life by a Volunteer*, p. 27.

55. J. Cohen, *The Jewish Messenger*, 1862. Listed in U.S. Civil War Center index.

56. Mills Lane, ed., *"Dear Mother: Don't Grieve About Me. If I Get Killed I'll Only Be Dead": Letters from Georgia Soldiers in the Civil War* (Savannah, Ga.: Beehive Press, 1990), p. 220. Lane found this letter at the Georgia State Department of Archives and History, Atlanta.

57. Letters of Private James Sawyer, Wyles Collection, University of California, Santa Barbara.

58. Sam Watkins, *"Co. Aytch," Maruy Grays, First Tennessee Regiment* (Jackson, Tenn.: McCowat-Mercer, 1952), p. 107 (first published 1882).

59. Cheek, *Sauk Riflemen Company A 6th Wisconsin*, p. 22.

60. Lewis, *Camp Life of a Confederate Boy*, p. 38.

61. Wills, *Army Life of an Illinois Soldier*, p. 193.

62. Watkins, *"Co. Aytch,"* p. 76.

63. Lydia Minturn Post, ed., *Soldiers' Letters from Camp, Battlefield, and Prison* (New York: Bunce & Huntington, 1865), p. 220.

64. Ibid., p. 211.

65. Letters of Edward Boots, found at members.aol.com/vir33rdreg/P51-98.html

66. Jedediah Hotchkiss, *Make Me a Map of the Valley* (Dallas: Southern Methodist University Press, 1989), p. 64.

67. Perry, *Letters from a Surgeon of the Civil War*.

68. Robert Hunt Rhodes, *All for the Union* (New York: Orion, 1985), p. 123.

69. Hotchkiss, *Make Me a Map of the Valley*, p. 123.

70. Found at www.iwaynet.net/~1sci/DCletters.htm

71. Cheek, *Sauk Riflemen Company A 6th Wisconsin*, p. 29.

72. Mulholland, *The Story of the 116th Regiment Pennsylvania Volunteers*, p. 72.

73. Fred C. Ainsworth, ed., *The War of the Rebellion: A Compilation of the Official Records of the Union and Confederate Armies*, ser. IV, vol. 3 (n.p.: Historical Times, 1985), p. 395 (first published 1900).

74. Ibid.

75. Perry, *Letters from a Surgeon of the Civil War*, p. 191.

Chapter Four: Rations, Recipes, and the Ravenous

1. Robert Hunt Rhodes, *All for the Union* (New York: Orion, 1985), p. 21.

2. C. W. Wills, *Army Life of an Illinois Soldier* (Washington, D.C.: Globe, 1906), p. 59.

3. Fred C. Ainsworth, ed., *The War of the Rebellion: A Compilation of the Official Records of the Union and Confederate Armies*, ser. III, vol. 1 (n.p.: Historical Times, 1985), p. 197 (first published 1899).

4. "Camp Fires & Camp Cooking" (Washington, D.C.: U.S. Government Printing Office, 1862.

5. Ibid.

6. Ibid.

7. Irwin Bell Wiley, *The Life of Johnny Rebel* (New York: Bobbs-Merrill, 1943), p. 104. Wiley found the letter at the Alabama Archives, Richmond, Va.

8. Carlton McCarthy, *Detailed Minutiae of Soldier Life in the Army of Northern Virginia 1861–1865* (Richmond, Va.: Carlton McCarthy, 1882), p. 59.

9. John D. Billings, *Hardtack and Coffee* (Boston: George M. Smith, 1888).

10. Thomas P. Lowry, *The Stories Soldiers Wouldn't Tell: Sex in the Civil War* (Mechanicsburg, Pa.: Stackpole, 1994), p. 51.

11. Billings, *Hardtack and Coffee*.

12. Wiley, *The Life of Johnny Rebel*, p. 105. Wiley found this information in "The History of Company K, 27th Mississippi Infantry," unpublished manuscript in private possession.

13. Billings, *Hardtack and Coffee*.

14. Dr. W. J. Worsham, *The Old Nineteenth Tennessee Regiment, CSA* (Knoxville, Tenn.: Press of Paragon Printing Co., 1902), p. 97.

15. Wiley, *The Life of Johnny Rebel*, p. 103. Wiley found this letter written by Saltus on January 13, 1962, in the Heartman Collection, Indianapolis.

16. Lydia Minturn Post, ed., *Soldiers' Letters from Camp, Battlefield, and Prison* (New York: Bunce & Huntington, 1865), p. 140.

17. Henry T. Johns, *Life with the 49th Massachusetts Volunteers* (Pittsfield, Mass., 1864), p. 173.

18. Thomas Wentworth Higginson, *Army Life in a Black Regiment and Other Writings* (Boston: Fields, Osgood, 1870), p. 105.

19. Washington Davis, *Campfire Chats of the Civil War* (Chicago: Coburn, 1884), p. 34.

20. Wiley, *The Life of Johnny Rebel*, p. 43.

21. Wills, *Army Life of an Illinois Soldier*, p. 13.

22. These stories appear in a number of sources, including *Tenting Tonight*, by James Robertson, Jr., and the editors of Time-Life Books (New York: Time-Life Books, 1984).

23. E. F. Palmer, *The Second Brigade or Camp Life by a Volunteer* (Montpelier, Vt., 1864), p. 116.

24. Wiley, *The Life of Johnny Rebel*.

25. Post, *Soldiers' Letters from Camp, Battlefield, and Prison*, p. 220.

26. Wiley, *The Life of Johnny Rebel*, p. 43. Wiley cites Eppa Hunton's autobiography, published in 1933, as the source. The same story is told in *Tenting Tonight* (Time-Life Books, 1984).

27. Ibid. Wiley lists "clipping from newspaper, scrapbook, Alabama Archives" as his source. The story also appears in *Tenting Tonight*.

28. U.S. Sanitary Commission, *Documents of the U.S. Sanitary Commission*, vol. 1 (New York, 1866).

29. Robert Hunt Rhodes, *All for the Union*, p. 83.

30. McCarthy, *Detailed Minutiae of Soldier Life*, p. 27.

31. Ibid., p. 57.

32. Wiley, *The Life of Johnny Rebel*, p. 91. Wiley cites as his source *Official Records of the Union and Confederate Armies*, vol. XXI, p. 1110.

33. Ibid., p. 93. Wiley cites as his source an unpublished manuscript at the University of Texas.

34. Paul Steiner, *Disease in the Civil War* (Springfield, Ill: Charles C. Thomas, 1968), p. 140.

35. Sam Watkins, *"Co. Aytch," Maruy Grays, First Tennessee Regiment* (Jackson, Tenn.: McCowat-Mercer, 1952), p. 52 (first published 1882).

36. Wiley, *The Life of Johnny Rebel*, p. 105.

37. Watkins, *"Co. Aytch,"* p. 53.

38. Wiley, *The Life of Johnny Rebel*, p. 105. Wiley cites several sources for this information.

39. Watkins, *"Co. Aytch,"* p. 98.

40. Higginson, *Army Life in a Black Regiment and Other Writings*, p. 105.

41. Rhodes, *All for the Union*, p. 83.

42. Higginson, *Army Life in a Black Regiment and Other Writings*, p. 16.

43. Johns, *Life with the 49th Massachusetts Volunteers*, p. 280.

44. Wills, *Army Life of an Illinois Soldier*, p. 109.

45. M. D. Legget Papers, Wyles Collection, University of California, Santa Barbara.

46. Onley Andrus, *The Civil War Letters of Sergeant Onley Andrus*, ed. Fred Albert Shannon (Urbana: University of Illinois Press, 1947), p. 31.

47. Wills, *Army Life of an Illinois Soldier*, p. 74.

48. Ibid., p. 108.

49. Palmer, *The Second Brigade or Camp Life by a Volunteer*, p. 115.

50. Watkins, "*Co. Aytch*," p. 137.

51. Wiley, *The Life of Johnny Rebel*, p. 44. Wiley found this letter at the University of Texas, Austin.

52. John Perry, *Letters from a Surgeon of the Civil War*, ed. Martha Derby Perry (Boston: Little, Brown, 1906), p. 20.

53. Fred C. Ainsworth, ed., *The War of the Rebellion: A Compilation of the Official Records of the Union and Confederate Armies*, ser. IV, vol. 3 (n.p.: Historical Times, 1985), p. 47 (first published 1900).

54. Wiley, *The Life of Johnny Rebel*, p. 93. Wiley cites as his source *Official Records of the Union and Confederate Armies*, ser. 1, vol. XXIV, pt. 3, p. 983.

55. Ibid., p. 93.

56. Ainsworth, *The War of the Rebellion*, ser. IV, vol. 3, p. 115.

57. McCarthy, *Detailed Minutiae of Soldier Life*, p. 129.

58. Watkins, "*Co. Aytch*," p. 108.

59. McCarthy, *Detailed Minutiae of Soldier Life*, p. 67.

Chapter Five: Socializing with the Enemy

1. E. F. Palmer, *The Second Brigade or Camp Life by a Volunteer* (Montpelier, Vt., 1864), p. 63.

2. Mills Lane, ed., "*Dear Mother: Don't Grieve About Me. If I Get Killed I'll Only Be Dead*": *Letters from Georgia Soldiers in the Civil War* (Savannah, Ga.: Beehive Press, 1990), p. 67. Lane found this letter in the Tomlinson Fort Papers, Emory University, Atlanta.

3. Henry T. Johns, *Life with the 49th Massachusetts Volunteers* (Pittsfield, Mass., 1864), p. 135.

4. Sam Watkins, "*Co. Aytch*," *Maruy Grays, First Tennessee Regiment* (Jackson, Tenn.: McCowat-Mercer, 1952), p. 61 (first published 1882).

5. Robert Hunt Rhodes, *All for the Union* (New York: Orion, 1985), p. 99.

6. Ibid., p. 103.

7. Spencer Glasgow Welch, *A Confederate Surgeon's Letters to His Wife* (New York: Neal, 1911), p. 39.

8. Ibid., p. 52.

9. Rhodes, *All for the Union*, p. 103.

10. Welch, *A Confederate Surgeon's Letters to His Wife*, p. 52.

11. Irwin Bell Wiley, *The Life of Johnny Rebel* (New York: Bobbs-Merrill, 1943), p. 318.

12. Lane, "*Dear Mother*," p. 67. Lane found this letter in the Tomlinson Fort Papers, Emory University, Atlanta.

13. Wiley, *The Life of Johnny Rebel*, p. 320.

14. John Robert Taylor Journal, Wyles Collection, University of California, Santa Barbara.

15. Rhodes, *All for the Union*, p. 187.

16. Welch, *A Confederate Surgeon's Letters to His Wife*, p. 62.

17. John Perry, *Letters from a Surgeon of the Civil War*, ed. Martha Derby Perry (Boston: Little, Brown, 1906), p. 8.

18. Johns, *Life with the 49th Massachusetts Volunteers*, p. 137.

19. C. W. Wills, *Army Life of an Illinois Soldier* (Washington, D.C.: Globe, 1906), p. 29.

20. Ibid., p. 123.

21. M. D. Legget Papers, Wyles Collection, University of California, Santa Barbara.

22. Rhodes, *All for the Union*, p. 189.

23. Wills, *Army Life of an Illinois Soldier*, p. 124.

24. James Sawyer Letters, Wyles Collection, University of California, Santa Barbara.

25. Welch, *A Confederate Surgeon's Letters to His Wife*, p. 93.

26. Lane, "*Dear Mother*," p. 67. Lane found this letter at the Georgia State Department of Archives and History, Atlanta.

Chapter Six: Their Brothers' Jailers

1. Alfred Ely, *The Journal of Alfred Ely, A Prisoner of War in Richmond*, ed. Charles Lanham (New York: D. Appleton, 1862), p. 12.

2. Ibid., p. 15.

3. Ibid., p. 26.

4. Washington Davis, *Campfire Chats of the Civil War* (Chicago: Coburn, 1884), p. 100.

5. Ibid., p. 101.

6. Ely, *The Journal of Alfred Ely*, p. 101.

7. Warren Lee Goss, *The Soldier's Story of His Captivity at Andersonville, Belle Isle, and Other Rebel Prisons* (Boston: Lee & Shepard, 1866), p. 38.

8. F. F. Cavada, *Libby Life* (n.p.: J. B. Lippincott, 1865), p. 30.

9. Ibid., p. 33.

10. Ibid., p. 158.

11. Ely, *The Journal of Alfred Ely*, p. 102.

12. Cavada, *Libby Life*, p. 98.

13. Ibid., p. 101.

14. Ibid., p. 126.

15. Ely, *The Journal of Alfred Ely*, p. 63.

16. Fred C. Ainsworth, ed., *The War of the Rebellion: A Compilation of the Official*

Records of the Union and Confederate Armies, ser. II, vol. 3 (n.p.: Historical Times, 1985), p. 35 (first published 1898).

17. James Sawyer Letters, Wyles Collection, University of California, Santa Barbara.

18. Ainsworth, *The War of the Rebellion*, ser. II, vol. 3, p. 50.

19. Ibid., p. 196.

20. M. D. Legget Papers, Wyles Collection, University of California, Santa Barbara.

21. Ibid.

22. Ainsworth, *The War of the Rebellion*, ser. II, vol. 3, p. 227.

23. James Sawyer Letters, Wyles Collection, University of California, Santa Barbara.

24. Ainsworth, *The War of the Rebellion*, ser. II, vol. 3, p. 152.

25. Ibid., p. 155.

26. Ibid., p. 312.

27. Ibid., p. 367.

28. Goss, *The Soldier's Story*, p. 36.

29. Ibid., p. 35.

30. Ibid., p. 36.

31. Ainsworth, *The War of the Rebellion*, ser. II, vol. 3, p. 35.

32. John Perry, *Letters from a Surgeon of the Civil War*, ed. Martha Derby Perry (Boston: Little, Brown, 1906), p. 14.

33. Ainsworth, *The War of the Rebellion*, ser. II, vol. 3, p. 579.

34. Goss, *The Soldier's Story*, p. 66.

35. Ibid., p. 76.

36. Francis Miller, *The Photographic History of the Civil War in Ten Volumes*, vols. 7, 8 (New York: Review of Reviews, 1911), p. 81.

37. Goss, *The Soldier's Story*, p. 75.

38. Lydia Minturn Post, ed., *Soldiers' Letters from Camp, Battlefield, and Prison* (New York: Bunce & Huntington, 1865), p. 453.

39. Miller, *The Photographic History of the Civil War in Ten Volumes*, vols. 7, 8, p. 84.

40. Goss, *The Soldier's Story*, p. 89.

41. This estimate was found in, among other sources, *Tenting Tonight*, by James Robertson, Jr., and the editors of Time-Life Books (New York: Time-Life Books, 1984).

42. Goss, *The Soldier's Story*, p. 89.

43. Davis, *Campfire Chats of the Civil War*, p. 106.

44. Ibid.

45. Ibid., p. 115.

46. Ainsworth, *The War of the Rebellion*, ser. II, vol. 3, p. 50.

47. Mrs. Thomas Taylor, *South Carolina Women in the Confederacy* (Columbia, S.C.: South Carolina Daughters of the Confederacy, 1903), p. 282.

Chapter Seven: Military Crimes and Punishments

1. William H. Sallada, *Silver Sheaves: Gathered Through Clouds and Sunshine* (Des Moines, Iowa, 1879), p. 64.

2. Sam Watkins, "Co. Aytch," *Maruy Grays, First Tennessee Regiment* (Jackson, Tenn.: McCowat-Mercer, 1952), p. 71 (first published 1882).

3. John Perry, *Letters from a Surgeon of the Civil War*, ed. Martha Derby Perry (Boston: Little, Brown, 1906), p. 77.

4. Spencer Glasgow Welch, *A Confederate Surgeon's Letters to His Wife* (New York: Neal, 1911), p. 45.

5. Ibid., p. 79.

6. Watkins, "Co. Aytch," p. 69.

7. Mills, Lane, ed., *"Dear Mother: Don't Grieve About Me. If I Get Killed I'll Only Be Dead": Letters from Georgia Soldiers in the Civil War* (Savannah, Ga.: Beehive Press, 1990), p. 90. Lane found this letter at the Georgia State Department of Archives and History, Atlanta.

8. Fred C. Ainsworth, ed., *The War of the Rebellion: A Compilation of the Official Records of the Union and Confederate Armies*, ser. II, vol. 3 (n.p.: Historical Times, 1985), p. 645 (first published 1898).

9. Ibid.

10. Esther Hill Hawks, *A Woman Doctor's Civil War: Esther Hill Hawks Diary*, ed. Gerald Schwartz (Columbia: University of South Carolina Press, 1984), p. 61.

Chapter Eight: Letters, Lovers, and Lifelines

1. John D. Billings, *Hardtack and Coffee* (Boston: George M. Smith, 1888).

2. C. W. Wills, *Army Life of an Illinois Soldier* (Washington, D.C.: Globe, 1906), p. 27.

3. Billings, *Hardtack and Coffee*.

4. Mills Lane, ed., *"Dear Mother: Don't Grieve About Me. If I Get Killed I'll Only Be Dead": Letters from Georgia Soldiers in the Civil War* (Savannah, Ga.: Beehive Press, 1990), p. 177. Lane found this letter at the Georgia State Department of Archives and History, Atlanta.

5. Ibid.

6. Spencer Glasgow Welch, *A Confederate Surgeon's Letters to His Wife* (New York: Neal, 1911), p. 43.

7. Lane, *"Dear Mother,"* p. 81.

8. Onley Andrus, *The Civil War Letters of Sergeant Onley Andrus*, ed. Fred Albert Shannon (Urbana: University of Illinois Press, 1947), p. 42.

9. Ibid.

10. M. D. Legget Papers, Wyles Collection, University of California, Santa Barbara.

11. Found at members.aol.com/vir33reg/~33rd Virginia Volunteers Regiment.

12. Ibid.

13. Welch, *A Confederate Surgeon's Letters to His Wife*, pp. 44, 48, 54, 59, 61.

14. Jedediah Hotchkiss, *Make Me a Map of the Valley* (Dallas: Southern Methodist University Press, 1989).

15. John Perry, *Letters from a Surgeon of the Civil War*, ed. Martha Derby Perry (Boston: Little, Brown, 1906), p. 148.

16. Hotchkiss, *Make Me a Map of the Valley*, p. 19.

17. Welch, *A Confederate Surgeon's Letters to His Wife*, p. 83.

18. Ibid.

19. U.S. Civil War Center link: Shadow Project/Valley Project Team Copyright © 1998. Edward Ayers, director of the University of Virginia project.

20. M. D. Legget Papers, Wyles Collection, University of California, Santa Barbara.

21. Ibid.

22. Ibid.

23. *The Picket Line & Camp Fire Stories* (New York: Hurst, n.d.).

24. Robert Hunt Rhodes, *All for the Union* (New York: Orion, 1985), p. 218.

25. Flora Adams Darling, *Mrs. Darling's Letters* (New York: John W. Lovell, 1883), p. 62.

26. Carlton McCarthy, *Detailed Minutiae of Soldier Life in the Army of Northern Virginia, 1861–1865* (Richmond, Va.: Carlton McCarthy, 1882), p. 90.

27. Irwin Bell Wiley, *The Life of Johnny Rebel* (New York: Bobbs-Merrill, 1943), pp. 277–278. Wiley found this material in the manuscript collection at the University of North Carolina.

28. Lane, "*Dear Mother*," p. 13. Lane found this material in Confederate Miscellany IA, Emory University, Atlanta.

29. W. Miller Owen, *In Camp and Battle with the Washington Artillery of New Orleans (Confederate)* (Boston: Ticknor, 1885), p. 302.

30. Sam Watkins, "*Co. Aytch*," *Maruy Grays, First Tennessee Regiment* (Jackson, Tenn.: McCowat-Mercer, 1952), p. 111 (first published 1882).

31. Ibid., p. 103.

32. Wiley, *The Life of Johnny Rebel*, p. 52. Wiley found this article in *The New Orleans Daily Crescent*, January 8, 1862.

33. Thomas P. Lowry, *The Stories Soldiers Wouldn't Tell: Sex in the Civil War* (Mechanicsburg, Pa.: Stackpole, 1994).

34. *The Picket Line & Camp Fire Stories*.

35. Lowry, *The Stories Soldiers Wouldn't Tell*, p. 29.

36. Ibid., p. 28.

37. Ibid., p. 31.

38. Lane, "*Dear Mother*," p. 177. Lane found this letter at Georgia State Department of Archives and History, Atlanta.

39. John Casler, *Four Years in the Stonewall Jackson Brigade* (Dayton, Ohio: Morningside Bookshop, 1906), p. 200.

40. Joe Kirschberger, *The Civil War and Reconstruction: An Eyewitness History* (New York: Facts on File, 1991), p. 135.

41. Wills, *Army Life of an Illinois Soldier*, p. 192.

42. Lane, *"Dear Mother,"* p. 99. Lane found this letter at Georgia State Department of Archives and History, Atlanta.

Chapter Nine: The Invisible Enemy

1. W. O. Gulick, *Journal and Letters of W. O. Gulick*, ed. Max Guyer (State Historical Society of Iowa, 1942), p. 224.

2. *The War of the Rebellion: A Compilation of the Official Records of the Union and Confederate Armies*, ser. I, vol. 51, pt. 2, *Confederate Correspondence* (n.p.: Historical Times, 1985) (first published 1897).

3. Paul Steiner, *Disease in the Civil War* (Springfield, Ill.: Charles C. Thomas, 1968), p. 13.

4. Spencer Glasgow Welch, *A Confederate Surgeon's Letters to His Wife* (New York: Neal, 1911), p. 45.

5. C. Vann Woodward, *Mary Chesnut's Civil War* (New Haven, Conn.: Yale University Press, 1981), p. 99.

6. Katherine Prescott Wormeley, *The Cruel Side of the War with the Army of the Potomac* (Cambridge, Mass.: John Wilson and Sons, University Press, 1888), p. 148.

7. Steiner, *Disease in the Civil War*, p. 17.

8. Henry T. Johns, *Life with the 49th Massachusetts Volunteers* (Pittsfield, Mass., 1864), p. 49.

9. James Robertson, Jr., *Tenting Tonight* (New York: Time-Life Books, 1984), p. 85.

10. James Katchner, *Civil War Sourcebook* (Alexandria, Va.: Time-Life Books, 1992), p. 121.

11. Johns, *Life with the 49th Massachusetts Volunteers*, p. 182.

12. Warren Lee Goss, *The Soldier's Story of His Captivity at Andersonville, Belle Isle, and Other Rebel Prisons* (Boston: Lee & Shepard, 1866), p. 88.

13. C. W. Wills, *Army Life of an Illinois Soldier* (Washington, D.C.: Globe, 1906), p. 92.

14. Steiner, *Disease in the Civil War*, p. 167.

15. Woodward, *Mary Chesnut's Civil War*, p. 158.

16. Johns, *Life with the 49th Massachusetts Volunteers*, p. 188.

17. Wormeley, *The Cruel Side of the War with the Army of the Potomac*, p. 89.

18. Lydia Minturn Post, ed., *Soldiers' Letters from Camp, Battlefield, and Prison* (New York: Bunce & Huntington, 1865), p. 458.

19. Welch, *A Confederate Surgeon's Letters to His Wife*, p. 12.

20. Wormeley, *The Cruel Side of the War with the Army of the Potomac*, p. 103.

21. Ibid., p. 101.

22. Ibid., p. 25.
23. Ibid.
24. Ibid., p. 45.
25. Welch, *A Confederate Surgeon's Letters to His Wife*, p. 27.
26. Johns, *Life with the 49th Massachusetts Volunteers*, p. 185.

Aftermath and Epilogue

1. Fred C. Ainsworth, ed., *The War of the Rebellion: A Compilation of the Official Records of the Union and Confederate Armies*, ser. IV, vol. 3, (n.p.: Historical Times 1985, p. 1171) (first published 1900).
2. Robert Hunt Rhodes, *All for the Union* (New York: Orion, 1985), p. 249.

Selected Bibliography

Adams, J. G. B. *Reminiscences of the 19th Massachusetts Regiment*. Boston: Wright & Potter, 1899.

Ainsworth, Fred C., ed. *The War of the Rebellion: A Compilation of the Official Records of the Union and Confederate Armies*, ser. II, vol. 3. N.p.: Historical Times, 1985 (first published 1898).

————. *The War of the Rebellion: A Compilation of the Official Records of the Union and Confederate Armies*, ser. III, vol. 1. N.p.: Historical Times, 1985 (first published 1899).

————. *The War of the Rebellion: A Compilation of the Official Records of the Union and Confederate Armies*, ser. IV, vol. 1. N.p.: Historical Times, 1985 (first published 1900).

————. *The War of the Rebellion: A Compilation of the Official Records of the Union and Confederate Armies*, ser. IV, vol. 3. N.p.: Historical Times, 1985 (first published 1900).

Aldrich, T. M. *The History of Battery A, First Regiment, Rhode Island Light Artillery in the War to Preserve the Union, 1861–1865*. Providence, R.I.: Snow & Farnham, 1904.

Andrews, J. Cutler. *The South Reports the Civil War*. Pittsburgh, Pa.: University of Pittsburgh Press, 1985.

Andrus, Onley. *The Civil War Letters of Sergeant Onley Andrus*. Ed. Fred Albert Shannon. Urbana: University of Illinois Press, 1947.

Bagby, Milton, ed., *Private Soldiers and Public Heroes: An American Album of the Common Man's Civil War*. Nashville, Tenn.: Rutledge Hill Press, 1998.

Benedict, G. G. *Vermont in the Civil War* (2. vols.). Burlington, Vt.: Free Press Association, 1886–88.

Billings, John D. *Hardtack and Coffee*. Boston: George M. Smith, 1888.

Black, Robert C., III. *Railroads of the Confederacy*. Chapel Hill: University of North Carolina Press, 1998.

Bodichon, Barbara. *An American Diary*. Ed. Joseph Reed. London: Routledge & Kegan Paul, 1972.

Brown, E. R. *The 27th Indiana Volunteer Infantry in the War of the Rebellion.* Monticello, Ind.: n.p., 1899.

Buell, A. *The Cannoneer: Recollections of Service in the Army of the Potomac.* Washington, D.C.: National Tribune, 1890.

Callaway, Joshua K. *The Civil War Letters of Joshua K. Callaway.* Ed. Judith Lee Hallock. Athens, Ga.: University of Georgia Press, 1997.

Casler, John. *Four Years in the Stonewall Jackson Brigade.* Dayton, Ohio: Morningside Bookshop, 1906.

Cavada, F. F. *Libby Life.* N.p.: Philadelphia: J. B. Lippincott, 1865. Reprinted by University Press of America, Lanham, Md., 1985.

Cheek, Philip. *Sauk Riflemen Company A 6th Wisconsin.* N.p., 1909.

Connelly, Thomas L. *Army of the Heartland: The Army of Tennessee 1861–1862.* Baton Rouge: Louisiana State University Press, 1967.

———. *Autumn of Glory: The Army of Tennessee 1862–1865.* Baton Rouge: Louisiana State University Press, 1971.

Cooke, John Esten. *Wearing of the Gray: Being Personal Portraits, Scenes, and Adventures of the War.* Baton Rouge: Louisiana State University Press, 1997.

Coyingham, D. D. *The Irish Brigade and Its Campaigns.* Boston: P. Donahoe, 1869.

Darling, Flora Adams. *Mrs. Darling's Letters.* New York: John W. Lovell, 1883.

Davis, C. E. *3 Years in the Army: The Story of the 13th Massachusetts Volunteers.* Boston: Esters & Lauriat, 1894.

Davis, Washington. *Campfire Chats of the Civil War.* Chicago: Coburn, 1884.

Douglas, Henry Kyd. *I Rode with Stonewall.* Chapel Hill: University of North Carolina Press, 1940.

Dyja, Thomas. *Play for a Kingdom.* New York: Harcourt Brace, 1998.

Eaton, Clement. *History of the Southern Confederacy.* New York: Free Press, 1965.

Ely, Alfred. *Journal of Alfred Ely, A Prisoner of War in Richmond.* Ed. Charles Lanham. New York: D. Appleton, 1862.

Fitzpatrick, Marion Hall. *Letters to Amanda.* Ed. Jeffrey Lowe and Sam Hodges. Macon, Ga.: Mercer University Press, 1998.

Freeman, Douglas Southall. *Lee's Lieutenants, A Study in Command.* New York: Scribner, 1997.

Furnas, J. C. The Americans: *A Social History of the United States, 1587–1914.* New York: Putnam, 1969.

Gayet, Robert. *Everyday Life in the U.S. Before the Civil War.* New York: Frederick Unger, 1969.

Goss, Warren Lee. *The Soldier's Story of His Captivity at Andersonville, Belle Isle, and Other Rebel Prisons.* Boston: Lee & Shepard, 1866.

Gulick, W. O. *Journal and Letters of W. O. Gulick.* Ed. Max Guyer. State Historical Society of Iowa, 1942.

Gurowski, Adam. *Diary from March 4, 1861, to November 12, 1862.* Boston: Lee & Shepard, 1862.

Hartwell, John F. L. *To My Beloved Wife and Boy at Home*. Ed. Ann Hartwell Britton. Cranbury, N.J.: Fairleigh Dickinson University Press, 1997.

Hawks, Esther Hill. *A Woman Doctor's Civil War: Esther Hill Hawks Diary*. Ed. Gerald Schwartz. Columbia: University of South Carolina Press, 1984.

Hesseltine, William B., ed. *Civil War Prisons*. Kent, Ohio: Kent State University Press, 1997.

Higginson, Thomas Wentworth. *Army Life in a Black Regiment and Other Writings*. Boston: Fields, Osgood, 1870.

Hill, A. F. Unpublished letters and correspondence by a member of the 8th Pennsylvania.

Hitchcock, F. L. *War from the Inside: Or Personal Experiences, Impressions, and Reminiscences of One of "the Boys" in the War of the Rebellion*. Philadelphia: J. B. Lippincott, 1904.

Hotchkiss, Jedediah. *Make Me a Map of the Valley*. Dallas: Southern Methodist University Press, 1989.

Johns, Henry T. *Life with the 49th Massachusetts Volunteers*. Pittsfield, Mass., 1864.

Jones, J. B. *A Rebel War Clerk's Diary at the Confederate States Capital*, vol. 1. Philadelphia: J. B. Lippincott, 1866.

Kean, R. G. H. *Inside the Confederate Government: The Diary of Robert Garlick Hill Kean*. Ed. Edward Younger. Baton Rouge: Louisiana State University Press, 1993.

Kirschberger, Joe. *The Civil War and Reconstruction: An Eyewitness History*. New York: Facts on File, 1991.

Lane, Mills, ed. *"Dear Mother: Don't Grieve About Me. If I Get Killed, I'll Only Be Dead": Letters from Georgia Soldiers in the Civil War*. Savannah, Ga.: Beehive Press, 1990.

Lewis, Richard. *Camp Life of a Confederate Boy*. Charleston, S.C.: News & Courier Book Presses, 1883.

Locke, E. H. *Three Years in Camp & Hospital*. Boston: G. D. Russell, 1870.

Lowry, Thomas P. *The Stories Soldiers Wouldn't Tell: Sex in the Civil War*. Mechanicsburg, Pa.: Stackpole, 1994.

Mathis, Roy. *In the Land of the Living*. Troy, Ala.: Troy State University Press, n.d.

McCarthy, Carlton. *Detailed Minutiae of Soldier Life in the Army of Northern Virginia 1861–1865*. Richmond, Va.: Carlton McCarthy, 1882.

McClellan, Henry B. *I Rode with Jeb Stuart: The Life and Campaigns of Major General J. E. B. Stuart*. New York: Da Capo Press, 1994.

McDonald, Cornelia Peake. *A Woman's Civil War: A Diary with Reminiscences of the War, from March 1862*. Ed. Minrose C. Gwin. Madison: University of Wisconsin Press, 1992.

McGrath, F., ed. *The History of the 127th New York Volunteers "Monitors" in the War for the Preservation of the Union, Sept. 8th 1862–June 30th, 1865*. N.p., n.d. (1898?).

Miller, Francis. *The Photographic History of the Civil War in Ten Volumes*, vols. 7, 8. New York: Review of Reviews, 1911.

Moore, Albert Burton. *Conscription and Conflict in the Confederacy.* Columbia: University of South Carolina Press, 1996.

Moore, Jerrold Northrop. *Confederate Commissary General Jerrold Northrop Moore.* Shippensburg, Pa.: White Mane Publishing Co., Inc.

Mulholland, St. Clair. *The Story of the 116th Regiment Pennsylvania Volunteers.* Philadelphia: F. McManus, Jr., 1903.

Myers, Robert Manson. *Children of Pride: A True Story of Georgia and the Civil War.* New Haven, Conn.: Yale University Press, 1987.

Newberry, Dr. J. S. *Documents of the U.S. Sanitary Commission,* vol. 1. Cleveland: Fairbanks, Benedict & Company, 1871.

Nichols, Thomas. *40 Years of American Life.* Harrisburg, Pa.: Telegraph, 1937 (first published 1874).

Owen, W. Miller. *In Camp and Battle with the Washington Artillery of New Orleans (Confederate).* Boston: Ticknor, 1885.

Palmer, E. F. *The Second Brigade or Camp Life by a Volunteer.* Montpelier, Vt., 1864.

Pearson, Elizabeth Ware. *Letters from Port Royal.* Boston: W. B. Clarke, 1906.

Perry, John. *Letters from a Surgeon of the Civil War.* Ed. Martha Derby Perry. Boston: Little, Brown, 1906.

The Picket Line & Camp Fire Stories. New York: Hurst, n.d.

Post, Lydia Minturn, ed. *Soldiers' Letters from Camp, Battlefield, and Prison.* New York: Bunce & Huntington, 1865.

Reid-Green, Marcia. *Letters Home.* Lincoln: University of Nebraska Press, 1993.

Rhodes, Robert Hunt. *All for the Union.* New York: Orion, 1985.

Robert, J. C. "A Ring Tournament in 1864." *Journal of Mississippi History* 3 (October 1941).

Robertson, James I. *Stonewall Brigade.* Baton Rouge: Louisiana State University Press, 1978.

Rothschild, Salomon de. *A Casual View of America.* Ed. Sigmund Diamond. Stanford, Calif.: Stanford University Press, 1961.

Russell, William Howard. *My Diary North and South.* Ed. Eugene Berwanger. Philadelphia: Temple University Press, 1988.

Sallada, William H. *Silver Sheaves: Gathered Through Clouds and Sunshine.* Des Moines, Iowa, 1879.

Steiner, Paul. *Disease in the Civil War.* Springfield, Ill.: Charles C. Thomas, 1968.

Strong, George Templeton. *Diary of the Civil War.* New York: Macmillan, 1962.

Taylor, Mrs. Thomas. *South Carolina Women in the Confederacy.* Columbia, S.C.: South Carolina Daughters of the Confederacy, 1903.

Thomas, Emory M. *The Confederate Nation: 1861–1865.* New York: HarperCollins, 1979.

U.S. Sanitary Commission. *Documents of the U.S. Sanitary Commission,* vol. 1. New York, 1866.

Vandiver, Frank E. *Their Tattered Flags: The Epic of the Confederacy.* College Station: Texas A&M University Press, 1987.

The War of the Rebellion: A Compilation of the Official Records of the Union and Confederate Armies, ser. I, vol. 51, pt. 2: *Confederate Correspondence*. N.p.: Historical Times, 1985 (first published 1897).

Watkins, Sam. *"Co. Aytch," Maruy Grays, First Tennessee Regiment*. Jackson, Tenn.: McCowat-Mercer, 1952 (first published 1882).

Watson, William. *Life in the Confederate Army*. London: Chapman & Hill, 1887.

Welch, Spencer Glasgow. *A Confederate Surgeon's Letters to His Wife*. New York: Neal, 1911.

Wheeler, Richard. *Voices of the Civil War*. New York: Thomas Y. Crowell, 1976.

Wiley, Irwin Bell. *The Life of Johnny Rebel*. New York: Bobbs-Merrill, 1943.

Wills, C. W. *Army Life of an Illinois Soldier*. Washington, D.C.: Globe, 1906.

Woodward, C. Vann. *Mary Chesnut's Civil War*. New Haven, Conn.: Yale University Press, 1981.

Wormeley, Katherine Prescott. *The Cruel Side of the War with the Army of the Potomac*. Cambridge, Mass.: John Wilson and Sons, University Press, 1888.

Worsham, W. J. *The Old Nineteenth Tennessee Regiment, C.S.A.* Knoxville, Tenn.: Press of Paragon Printing Co., 1902.

Index

Photo Credits